THE END OF THE AGE

OTHER BOOKS BY JOHN HAGEE

THE
END
OF THE
AGE

THE COUNTDOWN
HAS BEGUN

JOHN HAGEE

W PUBLISHING GROUP

AN IMPRINT OF THOMAS NELSON

Portions of this book adapted from *From Daniel to Doomsday: The Countdown Has Begun* (ISBN 9780785269663, © 1999).

Published in Nashville, Tennessee, by W Publishing, an imprint of Thomas Nelson.

Thomas Nelson titles may be purchased in bulk for educational, business, fundraising, or sales promotional use. For information, please email SpecialMarkets@ThomasNelson.com.

Unless otherwise noted, Scripture quotations are taken from the New King James Version®. Copyright © 1982 by Thomas Nelson. Used by permission. All rights reserved.

Scripture quotations marked KJV are taken from The Authorized (King James) Version. Rights in the Authorized Version in the United Kingdom are vested in the Crown. Reproduced by permission of the Crown's patentee, Cambridge University Press.

Scripture quotations marked NASB are taken from the (NASB®) New American Standard Bible®. Copyright © 1960, 1971, 1977, 1995, 2020 by The Lockman Foundation. Used by permission. All rights reserved. www.lockman.org

Scripture quotations marked NIV are taken from the Holy Bible, New International Version®, NIV®. Copyright © 1973, 1978, 1984, 2011 by Biblica, Inc.® Used by permission of Zondervan. All rights reserved worldwide. www.zondervan.com. The "NIV" and "New International Version" are trademarks registered in the United States Patent and Trademark Office by Biblica, Inc.®

Scripture quotations marked NLT are taken from the Holy Bible, New Living Translation. Copyright © 1996, 2004, 2015 by Tyndale House Foundation. Used by permission of Tyndale House Ministries, Carol Stream, Illinois 60188. All rights reserved.

Scripture quotations marked NRSV are taken from the New Revised Standard Version Bible. Copyright © 1989 National Council of the Churches of Christ in the United States of America. Used by permission. All rights reserved worldwide.

Scripture quotations marked RSV are taken from the Revised Standard Version of the Bible. Copyright © 1946, 1952, and 1971 National Council of the Churches of Christ in the United States of America. Used by permission. All rights reserved worldwide.

Editorial note: Explanatory clarifications for certain Scripture passages and quoted material are the author's additions and are indicated by brackets.

ISBN 978-0-7852-3766-2 (Jacketed Hardcover)
ISBN 978-0-7852-3767-9 (eBook)
ISBN 978-0-7852-6453-8 (ITPE)

Library of Congress Cataloging-in-Publication Data

Names: Hagee, John, author.
Title: The end of the age: the countdown has begun / John Hagee.
Description: Nashville, Tennessee: W Publishing Group, an imprint of Thomas Nelson, [2021] | Includes bibliographical references. | Summary: ""The end of the world is coming, but there's not a thing anyone can do to stop it. . . . There's no turning back with God."—John Hagee The world as we know it will end, neither with a bang nor a whimper, but in stages clearly set forth in God's word"—Provided by publisher.
Identifiers: LCCN 2021019068 | ISBN 9780785237662 (jacketed hardcover) | ISBN 9780785237679 (ebook)
Subjects: LCSH: End of the world—Biblical teaching. | Bible—Prophecies—End of the world. | BISAC: RELIGION / Christian Living / Spiritual Warfare | RELIGION / Christian Theology / Eschatology
Classification: LCC BS649.E63 H325 2021 | DDC 236/.9—dc23 LC record available at https://lccn.loc.gov/2021019068

Printed in the United States of America

21 22 23 24 25 LSC 10 9 8 7 6 5 4 3 2 1

*Lovingly dedicated to The Hagee Ministry
Legacy Partners who make it possible for me
to preach the gospel of hope, love, and peace
to America and the nations of the world.*

CONTENTS

CHAPTER ONE

11:50 PM

The End of the Age

And lo, I am with you always, even to the end of the age.
Matthew 28:20

The common proverb "Everything comes to an end" assumes that what has a beginning must logically have a conclusion. From the earliest recorded time, man has intuitively believed that the world will end. The Assyrians foretold the end of the world in 2800 BCE. French physician Nostradamus predicted a coming doomsday in his book *Prophecies* published in 1555. The belief that the world would be destroyed by flood or fire has been found among the writings of the ancient Persians, the natives of the Pacific islands, and past Nordic cultures. Even the Hopi Indians of the Americas prophesied that ashes would fall from the sky at the world's death.

Modern man is not immune from speculating about the end of the world. Movies like *Independence Day, Outbreak, Deep Impact,* and *War of the Worlds* entertain us with rollercoaster thrills and impressive computer graphics, all the while forcing us to think of the end of days. I ask you—If you knew sudden destruction would fall upon the earth in the next twenty-four hours, how would you spend your last moments?

The characters in *Independence Day* fought fire with fire— they blasted the threatening aliens out of the sky. The lethal virus in *Outbreak* was countered with a vaccine, and the people threatened by the asteroid in *Deep Impact* succeeded in shattering the huge stone with a nuclear device. Sure, people died—but the world was saved. In the 2005 remake of the classic 1953 *War of the Worlds*, Martians succumb to Earth's bacteria for which humans have built an immunity.

What else would you expect from Hollywood? Lots of drama, piles of dead bodies, but ultimate victory in the end. In the movies, mankind always wins. But what happens when the entertainment ends? When the rise of weapon-grade plutonium disappears into the world community without a trace? When known enemy-nations begin to test nuclear weapons? When the war with radical Islam expands into global battlegrounds? When China, Russia, and Iran begin to flex their economic and nuclear power? When the COVID-19 pandemic gives rise to worldwide speculation of continued biological warfare?

Who wins then?

My friend, in many ways, the end of the world as we know it is here. It arrived neither with a bang nor a whimper but is occurring in stages clearly set forth in God's Word. In 1 Thessalonians 5:3, the apostle Paul used the analogy of giving birth to describe the beginning of the end: "For when they say, 'Peace and safety!' then sudden destruction comes upon them, as labor pains upon a pregnant woman. And they shall not escape."

I've never given birth to a child, but my wife has, and from her experience I know that certain signs indicate an impending birth. First, even before labor begins, the mother becomes increasingly uncomfortable as the baby grows larger within her body. There is a feeling of increased pressure as the baby drops lower into the birth canal, preparing itself for birth. Next, the mother experiences twinges and sharp contractions, and finally, after days of false starts and unsettling sensations, labor officially begins. The bag of water surrounding the child breaks, and the mother's contractions intensify, growing sharper and steadier until the baby passes through the birth canal, leaving his or her safe place of quiet darkness for a world of light and sound.

The analogy of childbirth is a good one, for our world and

everyone in it is undergoing a similar experience. Paul, writing in the eighth chapter of Romans, explained that the earth itself waits for the new world to come: "Because the creation itself also will be delivered from the bondage of corruption into the glorious liberty of the children of God. For we know that the whole creation groans and labors with birth pangs together until now" (vv. 21–22).

Two features of birth pains are universally true: First, when they begin, there is no stopping them. Second, the pain becomes more intense and more frequent as time passes until the child—in this case, the new era—is born. As the Dispensation of Grace races toward its conclusion, there is no denying that the birth pains have begun.

Notice the pattern of increasing "groans and labors" since the early twentieth century:

- 1914–1918: World War I
- 1929–1939: The stock market crashed causing worldwide economic havoc.
- 1939–1945: World War II
- 1950–1953: The Korean Conflict
- 1953–1962: The Cold War
- 1960–1972: The Vietnam Conflict
- 1990–1991: The Gulf War
- 2000–present: Natural disasters such as earthquakes, hurricanes, and tsunamis have exponentially increased in both number and intensity.
- 2001–present: Radical Islamic jihadists crashed planes into the World Trade Center Towers and the Pentagon, creating a worldwide war on terror that has no end.
- 2020–present: A global pandemic begins to sweep the

world, taking the lives of more than 4.4 million souls by August 2021.[1]

From the beginning of the last century until today, there is no doubt that rumors of wars, earthquakes, pestilence, and signs in the heavens have increased. The new age is about to be born, but the most severe contractions are just before us.

As of this writing, we are almost a quarter of the way through the twenty-first century, and doomsday scenarios are as abundant as dandelions in an overgrown pasture. Some scientists believe a Yellowstone volcano eruption that will shroud the sun and destroy crops worldwide is long overdue. NASA offers continued reports of devastating asteroids in deep space, potentially headed toward Earth. Seismologists have long predicted the inevitable recurrence of the San Francisco earthquake. Politicians keep the media debates heated with warnings that climate change will render our planet uninhabitable within a few years. These and other doomsday predictions are nothing new.

In the 1890s, one prognosticator predicted that New York City would be abandoned as unfit for human habitation by the 1930s. He correctly projected that the city's population would grow from four to seven million but then stated that the number of horses necessary to provide transportation for so many people would result in a public health hazard—manure would pile up to the third floor of every window in Manhattan![2] A *Newsweek* editorial written a century later addressed the same subject:

Long before Bill Gates, John D. Rockefeller made the word "monopoly" a household term with the bullying tactics of Standard Oil. A series of financial and industrial mergers in the last years of the century . . . only fueled the public's fears about the power of big business. [Can anyone say Amazon, Google, Facebook, and Twitter?] The depletion of the Western frontier had Americans concerned about environmental preservation, while the telegraph and automobile were seen as exciting—but ominous—new technologies. Meanwhile, tuberculosis, the 19th-century equivalent of AIDS, continued to baffle physicians and ravage entire towns.[3]

The article went on to say that doomsayers were in full battle dress, predicting disaster on midnight of December 31, 1899. The New York and Chicago newspapers featured full-page ads announcing the Second Coming of Jesus Christ. A story in the *New York Times* quoted scientists' predictions that the sun would eventually go out, leaving the solar system in darkness and the earth an uninhabited ball of ice.

Sound familiar? We're hearing the same types of stories today. I found a story online by David Nicholson-Lord of London's *Independent* newspaper. Nicholson-Lord asked an oddsmaker, William Hill, to formulate odds for various end-of-the-world scenarios. The bookie's report was fascinating:

Odds that the world will end by natural causes like a "big bang": 50 million to 1.

Odds that humanity will be wiped out due to over-population: 25 million to 1.

Odds that the human race will be wiped out by pollution: 1 million to 1.

Odds that the world will be conquered by aliens: 500,000 to 1.

Odds that life as we know it will be destroyed by climate change: 250,000 to 1.

Odds that humanity will be wiped out by drought: 100,000 to 1.

Odds that the human race will be starved out by famine: 75,000 to 1.

Odds that life as we know it will be snuffed out by anarchy: 50,000 to 1.

Odds that the world will be wiped out by an asteroid: 10,000 to 1.

Odds that humanity will be wiped out by disease: 5,000 to 1.

Odds that humanity will be annihilated by war: 500 to 1.[4]

As I look over William Hill's list of possible doomsday scenarios, I am struck by the realization that many of the situations on this list will come to pass. The earth will shudder through several calamities before it is reborn. The Word of God describes famines, disease, war, climate changes, earthquakes, drought, and fire from heaven. Who but God could have predicted the coronavirus pandemic of 2020, which brought the world to its knees in less than sixty days—shutting down universal economic engines and taking the lives of millions?

Mark it down: the End of the Age is approaching, but it won't be ushered in by the advent of space aliens or catastrophic asteroids. It will come like a woman in travail, and each intensifying contraction will signal the earth's imminent destiny. These birth pains are only the beginning of a series of events unlike anything the world has ever seen. They will precede the final judgment day—when the ungodly must stand before the terrifying Great White Throne and give an account for their lives. The staggering significance of that moment makes all catastrophes seem like insignificant footnotes in the scroll of life.

THE DOOMSDAY CLOCK

Faced with the threatening possibility that mankind's bent toward evil just might result in total annihilation, the *Bulletin of the Atomic Scientists* created the Doomsday Clock to remind the world how close we could come to destruction. Eugene Rabinowitch, an American biophysicist and cofounder of the *Bulletin* said:

> The *Bulletin*'s clock is not a gauge to register the ups and downs of the international power struggle; it is intended to reflect basic changes in the level of continuous danger in which mankind lives in the nuclear age.[5]

In 1947, when the clock first appeared, the hands were set at seven minutes to midnight, with midnight being the moment of ultimate doom. As mankind alternated between hostility and peace in the succeeding years, the hands of the Doomsday Clock have moved back and forth, constantly reminding us that, if left unchecked, nuclear annihilation is only a few moments away.

God has a similar clock; however, its hands never move backward. In designing the layout of this book, I've taken a cue from the inventors of the Doomsday Clock. The hands on the clock pictured at the beginning of each chapter do not represent an actual moment, of course, but rather the order in which a predetermined event will come to pass. God's prophetic timepiece is currently approaching the stroke of midnight when the world as we know it will end.

Even before the creation of man, the Almighty devised a plan that allows free choice, accounts for man's natural disposition for sin, and provides a means for a loving, compassionate Father to draw wayward men and women back into fellowship with Him. This plan began in the Garden of Eden and will end with the creation of a new heaven and a new earth. The crimson thread of God's redemptive plan is woven into Holy Scripture from Genesis to Revelation and at times comes together to create prophetic images of astounding clarity and beauty.

Nowhere is God's prophetic plan more fully illustrated than in the book of Daniel. Here we see, with startling accuracy, how God allows each individual to choose their eternal destiny while future events unfold.

THE PANORAMA OF PROPHECY

During the 1990s, there was much speculation of what the beginning of a new millennium would bring. Was it the end of an age or the dawn of a new one? Prognosticators of all stripes, from Edgar Cayce, Ruth Montgomery, Sun Myung Moon, and even various Christian leaders predicted that the year 2000 would either reveal the Antichrist, initiate the Tribulation, ignite Armageddon, bring about Christ's Second Coming, or usher in the New Millennium of Revelation.

One such theory involved members of a millennial cult based in Denver called Concerned Christians. Several sect members flew to Israel because their leader, Kim Miller, taught that the way to salvation was based on dying in the city of Jerusalem on the eve of the year 2000. Miller, a former Procter & Gamble executive with no formal religious training,[6] declared that he would die in Jerusalem in December 1999 and be resurrected three days later.[7] Rightfully concerned that Miller's followers might actually provoke the violence necessary to achieve their aims, a special

Israeli task force detained the group in Jerusalem before sending them home.

The fact that all these millennial-related predictions failed has not deterred subsequent self-appointed prophets from misleading gullible people. The late Harold Camping was a preacher who raised money from his followers to purchase several radio stations. Over these stations he preached his prophetic message and end-time predictions. Using his own devised system of numerology, Camping announced in 2008 that the Rapture would occur on May 21, 2011, accompanied by massive earthquakes.

Camping then predicted that the world would end months later on October 21, 2011. According to the *New York Times*, "No one knows how many people rushed into marriages, scrambled to repent, ran up credit-card debts, threw their last parties, quit their jobs or gave away their possessions. But the reaction was widespread and in some cases tragic, especially among people who feared being left behind to face an agonizing end."[8] Camping conned his followers out of more than $100 million to publicize his predictions, and after his prophecies proved false, when asked if he would return the money, he declined to do so.

If you attend a Bible-preaching church, you may find it difficult to understand how professing Christians could sell all their earthly belongings and follow a cult leader like Kim Miller or a deluded preacher like Harold Camping. The reason, however, is simple: people succumb to false doctrine when they don't know the truth of God's Word. Many of our nation's churches, both mainline and nondenominational, dismiss prophecy as irrelevant or something that cannot be humanly understood and therefore should be avoided. They forget the biblical mandate of 2 Peter 1:19, "And so we have the prophetic word confirmed, which you do well to heed as a light that shines in a dark place." Believers

11

can fall into deep deception if they are without knowledge and understanding of what the Bible says.

Imagine for a moment that you have set your precious two-year-old daughter on the kitchen table. "Come on, Honey, jump!" you say to her as you hold out your arms. Your baby girl jumps because she knows you'll be there to catch her. She trusts you to keep her safe, and she is confident in what you'll do when she takes that literal leap of faith. The same thing holds true for us.

We need to know what God has planned for the End of the Age. Through the study of biblical prophecy, we attain wisdom and understanding and come to accept God's perfect plans (Proverbs 19:8). It is in this knowing that we gain confidence, strength, peace, and hope.

However, too many people have turned away from the study of Bible prophecy to place their confidence in false teachers and counterfeit prophets. Our trust should be in God Almighty—the Creator of heaven and Earth. I urge you not to be carried away on the winds of false doctrine. God, our loving Father, wants His children to understand His Word, and a large portion of that Word is prophecy. The Almighty's plan existed from the foundations of the earth—and just as God Himself does not change—His plans for the world will not change either.

Can you trust the Bible? Absolutely! All Scripture, to include prophecy, attests to the divine inspiration of the Architect of the Ages. The Bible is different from all other books that form the foundation for other major religions. Those writings only interpret the present or deal with the past. In contrast, the Bible is 25 percent prophecy. From Genesis to Revelation, countless prophecies were given, and most have been exactly fulfilled. This confirms the revelation, validity, and authority of Scripture. The apostle Peter wrote that Bible prophecy would be of benefit to the Church until the End of the Age, "Until the day dawns and the morning star rises in your hearts" (2 Peter 1:19). The "morning star" is none other than Jesus Christ: "I, Jesus, have sent My angel to testify to you these things in the churches. I am the Root and the Offspring of David, the Bright and Morning Star" (Revelation 22:16).

As we contemplate the future, we will discover that prophecy produces peace and hope in the heart of every believer. Jesus said, "Let not your heart be troubled; you believe in God, believe also in Me" (John 14:1). The Savior comforted His disciples' hearts—and our own—with a prophetic promise: "In My Father's house are many mansions; if it were not so, I would have told you. I go to prepare a place for you. And if I go and prepare a place for you, I will come again and receive you to Myself; that where I am, there you may be also" (John 14:2–3).

As we witness daily news reports predicting a global economic collapse, the dangerous increase of Iran's nuclear power capabilities, China's quest for world dominance, the skyrocketing rate of suicide, the rising threat of socialism, the anarchy spilling into the streets, the attack on our nation's capital, and the mounting death toll due to the coronavirus, we can *still* be comforted in the prophetic Scriptures, which confirm that God is still on His throne and will reign in power and glory in the age to come.

I have often heard the statement, "This didn't take God by surprise!" This is very true, but we, too, have been given insight to what the future holds through biblical prophecy. Therefore, what is happening in our world today should not take believers by surprise either. The prophetic Scriptures shout from every book in the Bible, "Lift up your heads and rejoice; God is in charge!"

DANIEL'S VISION OF THE
END OF THE AGE

No other prophet's writing is as significant as Daniel's. His book portrays several visions in which the future of the world is revealed, and many of these insights have been fulfilled with 100 percent accuracy.

Daniel's prophecies have impacted world events for centuries. The ancient historian Josephus told a story about Daniel's writings and Alexander the Great. Nearly 270 years after Daniel chronicled his visions and their interpretations, Alexander the Great and his army marched on Jerusalem. As he neared the Holy City, Jaddua, the high priest at the time, went out to meet the Greek emperor and showed him the passage where Alexander and his empire were described by Daniel centuries before their existence. Alexander was so impressed by Daniel's visions that "instead of destroying Jerusalem, he entered the city [in peace] and worshiped at the temple."[9]

Daniel was a great influencer. Jesus quoted from the book of Daniel in His Mount Olivet Discourse (Matthew 24:15; Mark 13:14). The book of Revelation becomes clearer when studied alongside the book of Daniel, and Paul's "man of sin" (2 Thessalonians 2:3), the Antichrist, becomes a flesh-and-blood being when viewed in the light of Daniel's insight.

God gave the prophet Daniel a glimpse into the future, and one of those prophetic visions shook Daniel so profoundly that he fainted and took to his bed for several days (Daniel 8:27). He saw what was coming, he accepted it as the work of a sovereign and just God, yet still he was taken aback by the sight of future events.

Daniel's story began in the third year of the reign of Jehoiakim, king of Judah. Because of Jehoiakim's extreme ungodliness,

"Nebuchadnezzar king of Babylon came to Jerusalem and besieged it" in 605 BCE (Daniel 1:1).

Nebuchadnezzar was an eccentric king, but he was no fool. He sifted through his spoils and took the choice golden vessels from the temple, placing them in the house of his own god. Rather than simply dragging his prisoners of war into slavery, the king instructed the master of his eunuchs to evaluate the captives and select the "young men in whom there was no blemish, but good-looking, gifted in all wisdom, possessing knowledge and quick to understand, who had ability to serve in the king's palace" (1:4). Among those chosen for royal service were Daniel, Hananiah, Mishael, and Azariah—the latter three better known as Shadrach, Meshach, and Abed-Nego.

Daniel and the other "sons of Israel" had a legitimate right to think the inevitable—perhaps their own end was at hand. However, these young men had been taught by their fathers about God's eternal covenant with Abraham for the title deed to the Promised Land (Genesis 15:9–21). They knew that God promised King David that his seed would sit upon the throne of Israel forever (Psalm 89:4). God had made unconditional and unbreakable covenants with the nation of Israel, but now it appeared He had deserted His Chosen people. What happened? Where was Jehovah when they needed Him?

Daniel looked around and saw foreign faces, heard unfamiliar voices, and witnessed hordes of people worshiping pagan gods. The holy vessels from the sacred temple were now used to hold oil and incense offered to idols of man's own creation. How could God have allowed this desecration?

Daniel and his companions were strangers in a strange land, captives living under a pagan king. Had God forgotten His promises? Had He broken His covenant? I'm certain Daniel and his

15

friends were shaken and confused, but they had to choose to either focus on their dire circumstances or stand with the God of their fathers, Abraham, Isaac, and Jacob, and His Word.

The prophecies of the Old Testament made God's reasons for allowing the exile very clear. God always judges sin. Israel had sinned repeatedly, without acknowledgment or repentance, and subsequently, God permitted the siege of Jerusalem and the Israelite captivity into Babylon.

The prophet Ezekiel painted Israel's past sins and well-deserved fate in a series of visions of the abominations in the temple (Ezekiel 8), the slaying of the wicked (3:18–19), and the departing glory of God. Israel had been a fruitless vine and an adulterous wife (16:32), said the prophet, and Babylon would swoop down like an eagle and pluck them up. But Israel's warranted judgment would be followed by glorious restoration (43:9). The prophet Hosea depicted Israel as a harlot who went whoring after idols. As a portrait of God's amazing grace and the redemption of Israel, Hosea went to the slave market and redeemed his adulterous wife (Hosea 1:1–11).

God wants us to understand why He does what He does. The Jewish people of Daniel's day had been warned, just as men and women are warned today. God's nature and character are unchanging; there is no shadow of turning in Him (James 1:17). Paul wrote, "Yet indeed I also count all things loss for the excellence of the knowledge of Christ Jesus my Lord, for whom I have suffered the loss of all things, and count them as rubbish, that I may gain Christ . . . that I may know Him" (Philippians 3:8, 10). There is a vast difference between knowing about God and actually knowing who God is. When you personally know God and have a close relationship with Him, you can better understand what He does and why He does it.

America knows about God, but she has no comprehension of His character. The Supreme Being of the Bible is a God of majesty, wisdom, truth, love, and grace, and He is jealous over His children. He is also a God of judgment and wrath, and He *does not change*. He is just as ready to judge sin today as He was in Daniel's day.

The man or nation that breaks the Ultimate Judge's law without repentance will discover His severity. Remember this very important truth: You don't break God's laws—God's laws break you. You either fall on the Cornerstone, Jesus Christ, and are broken, or the Cornerstone will fall on you, grinding you to powder. The choice is yours.

To know God is to recognize that He cannot change and will not lie. He is "from everlasting" (Psalm 93:2), He is "the incorruptible God" (Romans 1:23), and He "alone has immortality" (1 Timothy 6:16). King David wrote, "But You are the same, and Your years will have no end" (Psalm 102:27).

When my children were young, they often asked me, "Daddy, who made God?" I would explain that God did not need to be made, for He is eternal; He has always been and will always be. He does not grow older. He does not gain or lose power. He does not evolve or regress; He does not improve or deteriorate, for He was perfect from the beginning and will be so forevermore.

Many circumstances can alter the character of a man—strain, shock, illness, loss—but nothing can alter the character of God. "The counsel of the LORD stands forever, the plans of His heart to all generations" (Psalm 33:11). He "is the same yesterday, today, and forever" (Hebrews 13:8). What God does in time, He planned from eternity—and what He planned in eternity, He carries out in time.

God judged Sodom and Gomorrah because of their citizens'

17

immoral conduct. God judged Noah's generation because "every intent of the thoughts of [man's] heart was only evil continually" (Genesis 6:5).

If God judged Israel because of their moral and spiritual corruption, God will judge America or any nation of the world for the same reasons—if not, as Ruth Bell Graham said, "He will have to apologize to Sodom and Gomorrah."[10]

Every day we hear of another abomination entering the cultural mainstream. Pro-abortion advocates want not merely to conduct "safe, rare, and legal" medical procedures, they insist on the right to abort a child up to the time of delivery and even murder the baby after it is born. Not only is homosexuality tolerated and accepted as an alternative lifestyle, it is now institutionalized in gay marriage, and Christians are being sued or forced out of business for refusing to cater to gay demands. The fallacious notion of transgenderism has arisen, and now the United States is once again allowing transgendered soldiers to serve in the military.

However, we can't blame America's moral corruption on gay or transgendered persons or abortionists. They have chosen to use their unalienable rights to promote their agenda, and they have been successful. They are united, passionate, patient, and prudent in achieving their goals. They invest their resources and their time. They are informed and are satisfied to initially get their nose under the tent—because eventually they intend to own the tent.

Where are the Christians? We are cowering in our homes, believing we don't have a voice in government. Many of us are not registered to vote, or if we are, we don't vote because we are not excited about a candidate. Know this: your nonvote is a vote! Still other Christians demand "all or nothing," and consequently, we get *nothing*! We are not passionate, patient, prudent, or united! We are viewed as unorganized, uninformed, unproductive, and unnecessary! And as a result of our apathy, we are giving away our Judeo-Christian rights—one election cycle at a time.

At the start of the COVID-19 pandemic, certain governors, mayors, and city councils across America prohibited gatherings of worship under the guise of curbing the spread of the virus— people of faith were seemingly deemed unessential. Law-abiding citizens were threatened with legal action, exorbitant fines, and even prison if they attempted to gather in houses of worship. Yet these same civil leaders allowed anarchists to riot in the streets, destroying property and innocent people's livelihoods, while calling it an expression of social justice and freedom of speech. Most Christians stood silent and allowed this insanity to thrive— shame on us.

Sadly, this apathy should come as no surprise. A survey released in August 2020 "by George Barna's Cultural Research Center shows that professing Christians are developing more and more decidedly unchristian beliefs, demonstrating that many of these professing Christians are in fact un-professing pagans. According to the *American Worldview Inventory 2020*, syncretism rules the day, with the majority of Christians having fundamental, troubling, primary belief problems."[11]

What is "syncretism"? It is "combining or bringing together different philosophical, religious, or cultural principles and practices."[12] Bottom line—the cancel culture, which condemns and ostracizes anyone considered to be politically incorrect, has overtaken our basic fundamental beliefs and replaced them with the "whomsoever will" god of this age.

Researcher George Barna commented:

People are in an "anything goes" mindset when it comes to faith, morals, values, and lifestyle. . . . Americans appear to be creating unique, highly customized worldviews based on feelings, experiences, and opportunities. . . . We find that most people say that the objective of life is feeling good about yourself; that all faiths are of equal value; that entry into God's eternal presence is determined by one's personal means of choice; and that there are no absolutes to guide or grow us morally.[13]

America is no longer "one nation under God." We have ridiculed the truth of God's Word and called it pluralism. We have worshiped other gods and called it multiculturalism. We have rewarded laziness and called it welfare and entitlement. We have neglected to discipline our children and called it the building of self-esteem. We have polluted the air with profanity and pornography and called it freedom of expression. We have institutionalized perjury and deception in government and called it politically correct.[14]

Sadly, Christians are assimilating themselves into extinction. D. L. Moody warned believers:

> Christians should live in the world, but not be filled with it. A ship lives in the water; but if the water gets into the ship, she goes to the bottom. So Christians may be in the world; but if the world gets into them, they sink.[15]

NEBUCHADNEZZAR'S DREAM

If ever a man was in the right place at the right time—it was Daniel. God took him from Jerusalem and planted him in Babylon, the wonder city of the ancient world. The kingdom of

Babylon was the first great world empire. The monarchy rose to its zenith during Daniel's lifetime, with Daniel serving Babylon's most influential and powerful king.

The city of Babylon itself was a marvel. Ancient historians have reported that its wall was sixty miles in circumference, three hundred feet high, eighty feet thick, and extended thirty-five feet underground so enemies could not tunnel beneath it. Two hundred fifty towers were built into the wall, along with guard rooms for the king's astute watchman and vigilant soldiers.

Inside the city, the great temple of Marduk contained a golden image of Bel and a golden table, which together weighed at least fifty thousand pounds. At the top of the temple were golden images of Bel and Ishtar, two golden lions, and a human figure of solid gold eighteen feet tall. Isaiah wasn't exaggerating when he described Babylon as a golden city (Isaiah 14:4).[16]

The monarch and absolute ruler of this gilded city was Nebuchadnezzar. The Bible tells us in Daniel 2 that one night King Nebuchadnezzar—king over the Assyrians, the Syrians, and the Egyptians—was troubled by a dream. In Babylonian society, dreams were considered messages from the gods. When the king awoke, however, he retained nothing of his nightmare except a profound sense of doom. He had forgotten the dream, but he remembered enough of the disturbing event to know that it was important. The dream left a deep, permanent, and powerful impression on his mind.

How could a mere dream, especially a forgotten one, trouble the most powerful king on the face of the earth? Why couldn't he remember it? The dream—and the concealing of it—were engineered by God. Through Daniel, a captive Jewish boy, Nebuchadnezzar's world would learn that the God of Abraham, Isaac, and Jacob was the omnipotent and One True Living God of all gods.

21

When Nebuchadnezzar could not remember his dream, he sent for his magicians, astrologers, sorcerers, and the Chaldeans. The magicians were masters of fortune-telling; the astrologers predicted events based on the position of the stars. Sorcerers communicated with the dead with the assistance of evil spirits, and the Chaldeans were philosophers who had mastered every field of science. They were part of the king's cabinet and Babylon's think tank.

These men were not fools—the mere fact that they had access to the royal court speaks volumes about their skill and diplomacy. For years they had been listening to the king's recitations of dreams, watching his expressions, judging his moods. Then they performed their specialty acts and structured their answers in such an ambiguous manner that their words would prove true, no matter which way future events developed—in essence, they were skilled politicians!

When this cast of characters assembled before the king, Nebuchadnezzar looked out and demanded: "Tell me the contents of my dream and the meaning" (Daniel 2:3).

I wish I'd been there to see their startled faces! With one ultimatum, Nebuchadnezzar turned the tables on these sycophantic masters of the occult and guaranteed he'd receive a true answer. For if a man had the power to correctly interpret the dream, he certainly ought to have power enough to know what the dream was.

The princes of the occult who stood before Nebuchadnezzar claimed they could communicate directly with the gods, but they were completely powerless when Nebuchadnezzar hurled his demand at them. Some protested that the king's question was unfair, but the king's reply was simple: "My decision is firm: if you do not make known the dream to me, and its interpretation, you shall be cut in pieces, and your houses shall be made an ash heap" (Daniel 2:5).

Faced with the ax and the flame, the terrified charlatans did the only thing they could do: they tried to buy time; they bargained and begged. But Nebuchadnezzar had enough. He said:

I know for certain that you would gain time, because you see that my decision is firm: if you do not make known the dream to me, there is only one decree for you! For you have agreed to speak lying and corrupt words before me till the time has changed. Therefore tell me the dream, and I shall know that you can give me its interpretation.

(Daniel 2:8–9)

For once, the Chaldeans answered with the truth:

There is not a man on earth who can tell the king's matter; therefore no king, lord, or ruler has ever asked such things of any magician, astrologer, or Chaldean. It is a difficult thing that the king requests, and there is no other who can tell it to the king except the gods, whose dwelling is not with flesh.

(vv. 10–11)

The overwrought king was ready to clean house. Straight away, Nebuchadnezzar sentenced the entire lot of "wise" men to death. This condemnation included Daniel and his companions, who knew nothing of the events that had transpired in the royal throne room. When Arioch, the king's captain, came to arrest Daniel, the Jewish captive pled his case. Daniel "went in and asked the king to give him time, that he might tell the king the interpretation" (Daniel 2:16). By then young Daniel—probably between seventeen and twenty years old at the time—was known and respected enough that the king granted him one night's stay.

THE PRAYER MEETING

After hearing of Nebuchadnezzar's edict, Daniel went out and told Hananiah, Mishael, and Azariah that he was holding a prayer meeting at his house. They might not be living in Jerusalem, the Holy City, but God was still on His throne, listening to their prayers and available to meet their needs.

As they gathered to petition the Lord, every man was aware that his life depended on the outcome of this prayer meeting. If God did not send an answer and deliver them, they would die the next morning. The Bible tells us that Daniel and his friends sought "mercies from the God of heaven concerning this secret, so that Daniel and his companions might not perish with the rest of the wise men of Babylon. Then the secret was revealed to Daniel in a night vision" (2:18–19).

And what a secret it was! Locked within Nebuchadnezzar's dream was the most important prophetic revelation God had yet given to mankind. This dream described events of the future with such graphic and dramatic detail that it would be known as the portrait of prophecy.

We are not told how long the prayer meeting lasted, but we know they didn't stop praying until they heard from heaven. Because they had to have an answer for the king the next morning, it is logical to assume they prayed into the night and Daniel fell asleep while an angel, perhaps Gabriel, revealed the meaning of the king's dream.

The next morning, Daniel awoke. With a spirit of gratitude, he blessed the Lord for His supernatural revelation:

> *Blessed be the name of God forever and ever,*
> *For wisdom and might are His.*
> *And He changes the times and the seasons;*
> *He removes kings and raises up kings;*
> *He gives wisdom to the wise*
> *And knowledge to those who have understanding.*
> *He reveals deep and secret things;*
> *He knows what is in the darkness,*
> *And light dwells with Him.*
>
> *I thank You and praise You,*
> *O God of my fathers;*
> *You have given me wisdom and might,*
> *And have now made known to me what we asked of You,*
> *For You have made known to us the king's demand.*
>
> (Daniel 2:20–23)

After profoundly expressing thanksgiving, Daniel went to Arioch, the king's man, and immediately requested that the death sentence be lifted for all involved.

Daniel exhibited unexpected mercy. As the princes of the occult were being led out to be executed, Daniel interceded for their lives. Imagine it—Daniel was the greatest of the prophets, a righteous man submitted in every way to the God of Abraham, Isaac, and Jacob; yet he interceded to spare the lives of the most spiritually corrupt people in a very corrupt kingdom. What a prime example of love, grace, and mercy. If Christians would show the same even to other Christians, we would experience a mighty revival of repentance, restoration, and renewal.

THE SCENE CHANGES

As a result of Nebuchadnezzar's dream, God's prophetic A-Team—Daniel and his three friends—were instantly thrust into the national spotlight. This wasn't the first time an unknown Jewish captive had risen to national prominence—remember Joseph? Joseph was literally taken from the pit of his jail cell and sent to the pinnacle of the palace to explain Pharaoh's dream. Now another Jewish captive, Daniel, stood waiting in the wings with God's supernatural power of revelation. Daniel 2:25–47 records the story:

It was still early morning; perhaps the evening torches still smoldered on the walls of the king's throne room as Arioch ushered Daniel into the royal chamber. Servants scurried out of the way as Arioch shouldered his way past, but the captain's eyes were filled with expectation as he lifted his gaze to meet the king's thunderous expression.

"I have found a man," he said, his voice echoing in the cavernlike stillness of the vast chamber. "I have found a man of the captives of Judah, who will make known to the king the interpretation." Notice that Arioch didn't mention the dream itself—though he had every trust in Daniel, he didn't have faith enough to remind the king that he was seeking the dream *and* the interpretation. Perhaps Arioch was thinking that a night's sleep had softened the king's heart and expunged his memory. Perhaps the hotheaded ruler had reconsidered his decision to execute every wise man. If this young Hebrew could satisfy the royal curiosity with some sort of innocent babble about the future and the gods . . .

The king, however, had not forgotten. Nebuchadnezzar transferred his gaze from his captain to the young man standing in the shadows. He remembered Daniel and that he had granted him a few additional hours to explain the mysterious dream. The handsome youth's face stirred a vague memory, then another recollection surfaced. This captive was one of four Hebrew children who had caused a bit of a stir when they were first assimilated into palace life. They had wanted only vegetables and water, and to everyone's surprise, their diet made them healthier in appearance than the others who had eaten meat killed in a sacrificial rite to honor the king's gods. This one, the apparent leader, had been given the esteemed name of Belteshazzar, meaning "Bel protects his life."

"Belteshazzar," the king said, his steely gaze meeting his captive's. "Are you able to make known to me the dream which I have seen, and its interpretation?"

A silence, thick as a dense fog, wrapped itself around the occupants of the throne room as Daniel stepped forward. He did not begin with the ceremonial greetings and wishes for long life, health, and prosperity; instead he met the king's gaze with determination. "The secret which the king has demanded," Daniel began, his voice ringing with authority, "the wise men, the astrologers, the magicians, and the soothsayers cannot declare to the king." He paused, and Arioch caught his breath, wondering if he would be called upon to execute this wise young man on the spot. So far Daniel had displayed nothing but a gift for stating the obvious.

Daniel took another step forward, and his voice softened with something akin to insightful compassion as he held the king's gaze. "But there is a God in heaven who reveals secrets," he continued, "and He has made known to King Nebuchadnezzar what will be in the latter days. Your dream, and the visions of your head upon your bed, were these . . ."

Ignoring royal protocol, Arioch gaped, openmouthed, as Daniel painted a verbal portrait of kingdoms and rulers and the world to come. The Hebrew prophet spoke of Nebuchadnezzar, the Babylonian empire, and of a coming Kingdom that would never end. Daniel foretold of glorious power, terrible destruction, and coming doom.

When he finished, King Nebuchadnezzar stumbled from his throne and fell on his face, prostrate before Daniel. "Bring incense," he called, his voice hoarse. "We will present an offering to Belteshazzar."

Daniel reached out, daring to touch the king's shoulder, and urged Nebuchadnezzar to a standing position, inaudibly refusing his worship. The king's eyes flashed with understanding, then he lifted his hands and closed his eyes, overcome with the realization that today he had honestly heard from the One True God.

Nebuchadnezzar's rough whisper echoed in the vast room as he declared, "Truly your God is the God of gods, the Lord of kings, and a revealer of secrets," and all who heard it marveled at the power of Daniel's God.

NEBUCHADNEZZAR'S DREAM REVEALED

Remarkably, Daniel's interpretation of Nebuchadnezzar's dream described future events. We are currently living in the dream's timeline; we can see the fulfilled events of the first part of the dream, and we can look expectantly toward the future for its conclusion.

Let's examine the dream as Daniel described it:

You, O king, were watching; and behold, a great image! This great image, whose splendor was excellent, stood before you; and its form was awesome. This image's head was of fine gold, its chest and arms of silver, its belly and thighs of bronze, its legs of iron, its feet partly of iron and partly of clay. You watched while a stone was cut out without hands, which struck the image on its feet of iron and clay, and broke them in pieces. Then the iron, the clay, the bronze, the silver, and the gold were crushed together, and became like chaff from the summer threshing floors; the wind carried them away so that no trace of them was found. And the stone that struck the image became a great mountain and filled the whole earth.

This is the dream. Now we will tell the interpretation of it before the king. You, O king, are a king of kings. For the God of heaven has given you a kingdom, power, strength, and glory; and wherever the children of men dwell, or the beasts of the field and the birds of the heaven, He has given them into your hand, and has made you ruler over them all—you are this head of gold. But after you shall arise another kingdom inferior to yours; then another, a third kingdom of bronze, which shall rule over all the earth. And the fourth kingdom shall be as strong as iron, inasmuch as iron breaks in pieces and shatters everything; and like iron that crushes, that kingdom will break in pieces and crush all the others. Whereas you saw the feet and toes, partly of potter's clay and partly of iron, the kingdom shall be divided; yet the strength of the iron shall be in it, just as you saw the iron mixed with ceramic clay. And as the toes of the feet were partly of iron and partly of clay, so the kingdom shall be partly strong and partly fragile. As you saw iron mixed with ceramic clay, they will mingle with the seed of men; but they will not adhere to one another, just as iron does not mix with clay. And in the days of these kings the God of heaven will set up a kingdom which shall never be destroyed; and the kingdom shall not be left to other people; it shall break in pieces and consume all these kingdoms, and it shall stand forever. Inasmuch as you saw that the stone was cut out of the mountain without hands, and that it broke in pieces the iron, the bronze, the clay, the silver, and the gold—the great God has made known to the king what will come to pass after this. The dream is certain, and its interpretation is sure.

(Daniel 2:31–45)

History has proven Daniel's interpretation of the king's dream to be fully accurate. As he had prophesied, the empire that replaced Nebuchadnezzar's head of gold was Medo-Persia, the breastplate of silver. The Medo-Persians were displaced by Alexander the Great of Greece, the loins of brass. Alexander's empire fell to the Romans, the strong and mighty domain that eventually divided into eastern and western empires.

Notice that as Daniel's eye traveled down the image, the strength of the metals progressed from soft (gold) to very hard (iron). This corresponds to the military strength of nations that would develop in centuries to come. Mankind has progressed from relatively weak and primitive weapons such as sticks, spears, and swords to strong and sophisticated weapons like smart bombs, long-range missiles, and thermonuclear devices.

It is important to note that the strength of the iron kingdom seemed to dilute in time. The lower the eye descended, the weaker the material became, until the feet were composed of iron and clay—two materials that simply do not merge with each other. The "partly strong and partly broken" kingdom of Rome weakened as it aged, until it finally divided into ten toes, or ten kingdoms.

What are the two substances that will not mix? Scholar William Kelly suggests that the final form of power of the old Roman Empire will be a federation composed of autocracies and democracies, represented by iron and clay. In his view, iron represents nations ruled by a monarch; clay represents nations that adhere to a democratic or representative form of government.[17] Just as iron and clay don't integrate, neither do autocracies and democracies.

These ten nations—some ruled by monarchs, some by democratic governments—representing the most powerful kingdoms of the world, will be ground to powder by the Stone cut without hands: the Lord Jesus Christ. The King of kings will conquer all dominions and rule a final empire—a Kingdom that will last forever.

Nebuchadnezzar was satisfied by Daniel's interpretation of his dream—so much so that the king of Babylon gave glory to the God of Israel. But Daniel wasn't done with unraveling dreams . . . nor was God finished painting a portrait of prophecy.

THE DREAM OF FOUR BEASTS

Daniel continued to faithfully serve Nebuchadnezzar's successors, and it was during the first year of Belshazzar's reign over Babylon that Daniel awoke from a deep sleep and wrote down the aspects of another disturbing dream:

31

I saw in my vision by night, and behold, the four winds of heaven were stirring up the Great Sea. And four great beasts came up from the sea, each different from the other. The first was like a lion, and had eagle's wings. I watched till its wings were plucked off; and it was lifted up from the earth and made to stand on two feet like a man, and a man's heart was given to it.

(Daniel 7:2–4)

In this dream we see the same parade of nations described in Nebuchadnezzar's vision, but with a different and disturbing twist. Daniel saw four beasts rise up from the sea. The first beast was like a lion with the wings of an eagle, the exact representation of the Babylonian national symbol. Daniel had already seen the fulfillment of the first part of this vision. Nebuchadnezzar, who had risen to staggering heights of accomplishment, took pride in his success, but God struck him to the ground in a supernatural display of divine power. Nebuchadnezzar lost his mind and actually ate grass like an ox for seven years, after which God restored his sanity. He returned to his kingdom with the heart "of a man" and a new appreciation for the power of Daniel's God (Daniel 4).

But Babylon was doomed to failure. On the night of October 13, 539 BCE, Cyrus the Great of Persia defeated Babylon's army on the Tigris River just south of modern-day Baghdad. He entered the city and had Belshazzar executed. (Please note that Daniel also foretold the city's fall to the Persians—the story is told in Daniel 5.)

The second beast, a lopsided bear (because the Medes were more prominent than the Persians), represents the Medo-Persian Empire:

And suddenly another beast, a second, like a bear. It was raised up on one side, and had three ribs in its mouth between its teeth. And they said thus to it: "Arise, devour much flesh!"

(Daniel 7:5)

The three ribs in the bear's mouth graphically illustrate the three prominent conquests of the empire: Lydia in 546 BCE, Babylon in 539 BCE, and Egypt in 525 BCE. A succession of kings ruled this empire, including King Ahasuerus (Xerxes) of the book of Esther. The Persian king Artaxerxes was king during Nehemiah's royal service.

The third beast, the leopard with four wings and four heads, represents Greece under Alexander the Great:

After this I looked, and there was another, like a leopard, which had on its back four wings of a bird. The beast also had four heads, and dominion was given to it.

(Daniel 7:6)

The leopard is a swift animal, symbolizing the blinding speed with which Alexander's military juggernaut attacked its enemies. Noteworthy, Greece's Golden Age also produced some of the most prominent personalities of the ancient world, including Hippocrates, the father of modern medicine, and Socrates, Plato, and Aristotle—all renowned philosophers.

Through the telescope of history, the significance of the four heads becomes clear. In 323 BCE, at age thirty-two, Alexander died in Babylon. At his death, his four leading generals divided his kingdom: Ptolemy I took Israel and Egypt; Seleucus I reigned over Syria and Mesopotamia; Lysimachus ruled Thrace and Asia Minor; and Cassander took charge of Macedonia and Greece.

The frightening fourth beast, more terrifying than its predecessors, represents the Roman Empire and the final form of Gentile power on Earth:

> *After this I saw in the night visions, and behold, a fourth beast, dreadful and terrible, exceedingly strong. It had huge iron teeth; it was devouring, breaking in pieces, and trampling the residue with its feet. It was different from all the beasts that were before it, and it had ten horns.*
>
> (Daniel 7:7)

Rome controlled central Italy by 338 BCE, and the Empire gradually expanded. Pompey, the famous Roman general, conquered the Holy Land in 63 BCE. Rome ruled Judea with an iron fist during the time of Christ and afterward. In 70 CE, the Roman general Vespasian ordered his son, Titus, to destroy Jerusalem. The temple was demolished, just as Jesus predicted it would be (Matthew 24:1–2).

In 284 CE, Diocletian separated the Eastern Empire from the West and appointed Maximian to rule the eastern realm. A succession of rulers struggled for control over the years, and in 476 CE the last Roman emperor, Romulus Augustus, was dethroned. The Roman Empire was not conquered—it collapsed through internal and moral corruption; however, the dominating spirit of Rome is alive and well today.

The most important thing to note about this last horrifying beast is not its strength, its ferocity, or the fact that it destroyed all the other beasts. What is most significant is what will arise from the beast's ten horns.

The ten horns of Daniel's dream correspond to the ten toes in Nebuchadnezzar's dream. The horns represent ten kings or leaders who will lead nations (a European federation) that will rise from the fourth great world kingdom—the Roman Empire:

> *I was considering the horns, and there was another horn, a little one, coming up among them, before whom three of the first horns were plucked out by the roots. And there, in this horn, were eyes like the eyes of a man, and a mouth speaking pompous words.*
>
> (Daniel 7:8)

From among the ten kingdoms (ten horns) will arise one individual (little horn) who will control the entire federation of nations. Who is this little horn, and what is his purpose?

Before we consider the answer to these questions, which will be discussed in a later chapter, let's look at the end of Daniel's dream:

> *I watched till thrones were put in place,*
> *And the Ancient of Days was seated;*
> *His garment was white as snow,*
> *And the hair of His head was like pure wool.*
> *His throne was a fiery flame,*
> *Its wheels a burning fire;*
> *A fiery stream issued*
> *And came forth from before Him.*
> *A thousand thousands ministered to Him;*
> *Ten thousand times ten thousand stood before Him.*
> *The court was seated,*
> *And the books were opened.*

I watched then because of the sound of the pompous words
which the horn was speaking; I watched till the beast was slain,
and its body destroyed and given to the burning flame. As for
the rest of the beasts, they had their dominion taken away, yet
their lives were prolonged for a season and a time.

> *I was watching in the night visions,*
> *And behold, One like the Son of Man,*
> *Coming with the clouds of heaven!*
> *He came to the Ancient of Days,*
> *And they brought Him near before Him.*
> *Then to Him was given dominion and glory and a kingdom,*
> *That all peoples, nations, and languages should serve Him.*
> *His dominion is an everlasting dominion,*
> *Which shall not pass away,*
> *And His kingdom the one*
> *Which shall not be destroyed.*

(Daniel 7:9–14)

Though Daniel's dream ended with the good news of the eternal reign of the Ancient of Days (Jesus Christ), still he was troubled. Four great empires would arise in the timeline allotted to the world's kingdoms, and from a final confederation would come a pompous destroyer (little horn). Yes, the victory would ultimately be God's, but not before the world suffered greatly at the hand of the Antichrist, Satan's messiah.

We will learn more from Daniel in the chapters ahead, and we will see how his dreams, visions, and prophecies fit into the entire canon of Scripture. But before we move on, let's consider an important truth about Bible prophecy.

Remember Peter's comment that prophecy would be useful

"until . . . the morning star rises in your hearts" (2 Peter 1:19)? The apostle went on to add, "knowing this first, that no prophecy of Scripture is of any private interpretation, for prophecy never came by the will of man, but holy men of God spoke as they were moved by the Holy Spirit" (vv. 20–21).

Prophecy is not "private interpretation"—that is, the prophets didn't create it from their own imaginations, but their words were inspired by the Holy Spirit. Since all biblical prophecy comes from the same source, shouldn't one prophecy reinforce another? We must study the entire panorama of prophecy and not be like those who take one or two verses and create a cult around them.

In the pages ahead, we will see how other biblical writers reinforce Daniel's revelations and, more importantly, we will see that the End of the Age, following the intense pains of a dying world, cannot be avoided.

CHAPTER TWO

11:51 PM

Messiah the Prince Enters Jerusalem

And when He had come into Jerusalem, all the city was moved, saying, "Who is this?"
Matthew 21:10

The next event on God's Prophetic Clock was forecast in 575–538 BCE and partially fulfilled when Jesus entered Jerusalem for the Passover Feast celebration in 32 CE (John 12:12–15). To better understand the significance of Christ's Triumphal Entry into the City of David we must look again to Daniel's prophecies.

In the first year of Darius's reign, Daniel was in his private chamber, reading the following words of the prophet Jeremiah:

> *"And this whole land shall be a desolation and an astonishment, and these nations shall serve the king of Babylon seventy years.*
>
> *Then it will come to pass, when seventy years are completed, that I will punish the king of Babylon and that nation, the land of the Chaldeans, for their iniquity," says the* LORD; *"and I will make it a perpetual desolation."*
>
> (Jeremiah 25:11–12)

Jeremiah had prophesied that God would send the children of Israel into Babylonian exile for seventy years and then promised deliverance. Those seventy years were nearly complete. Struck by the realization that God could have delayed the Jewish captives' liberation due to their continued disobedience, Daniel began to pray that he and his people would walk rightly before God:

> *Then I set my face toward the Lord God to make request by prayer and supplications, with fasting, sackcloth, and ashes. And I prayed to the* LORD *my God, and made confession, and*

said, "O Lord, great and awesome God, who keeps His cove-
nant and mercy with those who love Him, and with those who
keep His commandments, we have sinned and committed iniq-
uity, we have done wickedly and rebelled, even by departing
from Your precepts and Your judgments."

(Daniel 9:3–5)

Daniel closed his eyes and continued to pray, willingly acknowledging Israel's sin. Though Scripture does not record a single iniquity committed by Daniel, he still humbly identified himself as a sinner and pled for forgiveness, mercy, and compassion. He extolled God's righteousness and contrasted it to Israel's sustained sinfulness. Caught up in a wave of emotion, Daniel prayed, "O Lord, hear! O Lord, forgive! O Lord, listen and act! Do not delay for Your own sake, my God, for Your city and Your people are called by Your name" (9:19).

The prophet slowly opened his eyes and suddenly realized he was not alone. Though the door had not creaked, and the windows remained closed, a man had entered the room and stood before Daniel. Rendered speechless, the prophet lifted his gaze, and remembered the man's face. It was the angel Gabriel, whom Daniel had seen before (9:21).

The archangel broke the silence and said to the prophet, "I was sent to you from the throne of God the moment you began to pray. Because you are greatly beloved, I have come to tell you something important and give you the skill to understand the vision" (9:22–23, paraphrased).

I want you to take a moment and appreciate that Daniel was greatly loved, but, my friend, so are you and I. Paul declared that every believer in Christ has been "accepted in the Beloved" (Ephesians 1:6). We are all loved by God, just like Daniel. Our prayers are heard, just as Daniel's was; the angels are charged to aid us, just as Gabriel was charged to rush to Daniel's side. I encourage you to pray as Daniel did—with a repentant heart, with praise and thanksgiving, and then open your eyes and watch God work on your behalf.

Daniel gave Gabriel his full attention as the angel of the Lord began to explain yet another vision God wanted the prophet to receive and record:

> *Seventy weeks are determined*
> *For your people and for your holy city,*
> *To finish the transgression,*
> *To make an end of sins,*
> *To make reconciliation for iniquity,*
> *To bring in everlasting righteousness,*
> *To seal up vision and prophecy,*
> *And to anoint the Most Holy.*
>
> *Know therefore and understand,*
> *That from the going forth of the command*
> *To restore and build Jerusalem*
> *Until Messiah the Prince,*
> *There shall be seven weeks and sixty-two weeks;*
> *The street shall be built again, and the wall,*
> *Even in troublesome times.*
>
> *And after the sixty-two weeks*
> *Messiah shall be cut off, but not for Himself;*
> *And the people of the prince who is to come*
> *Shall destroy the city and the sanctuary.*
> *The end of it shall be with a flood,*

And till the end of the war desolations are determined.
Then he shall confirm a covenant with many for one week;
But in the middle of the week
He shall bring an end to sacrifice and offering.
And on the wing of abominations shall be one who makes
  desolate,
Even until the consummation, which is determined,
Is poured out on the desolate.

(Daniel 9:24–27)

The key to understanding the whole of Daniel's vision lies in the meaning of the Seventy Weeks. The explanation of this unique concept never fails to send a surge of divine joy through my soul. The Word is so precise that when properly studied, God reveals to the believer His authority, wisdom, power, promises, and purpose.

Just as the minutes on the Prophetic Clock do not stand for actual minutes, the phrase *seventy weeks* does not mean "seventy weeks of seven days each." The Hebrew word for *seven* is *shabua*, meaning "a unit of measure."[1] It is similar to our word *dozen*, which we could use to signify a dozen grouping of anything— people, eggs, doughnuts, and in this case, years.

Daniel had been reading about the seventy years of exile in the writings of Jeremiah, and he thought of them as literal years; however, the Lord revealed through Gabriel that the Seventy Weeks is a specific period of time totaling "seventy sets of seven." Again, seven could refer to seven days, weeks, months, or years, and in this case the Seventy Weeks translates to seven times seventy years, for a total of 490 years. God's angelic messenger further subdivided the Seventy Weeks into intervals, each week representing seven years on man's calendar. The first segment totaled seven weeks (7 x 7 or

49 years), the second period equated to sixty-two weeks (62 x 7 or 434 years), and the final interval was one week (7 years).

Why 490 years? According to 2 Chronicles 36:21, the Babylonian exile lasted for seventy years, seventy sets of seven. This was the exact span required for the Israelites to atone for the previous 490 years in the Promised Land, in which they failed to observe the Sabbath year of rest for the land. In Leviticus 25:3–5, God mandated His people to do the following:

> *Six years you shall sow your field, and six years you shall prune your vineyard, and gather its fruit; but in the seventh year there shall be a sabbath of solemn rest for the land, a sabbath to the* LORD. *You shall neither sow your field nor prune your vineyard. What grows of its own accord of your harvest you shall not reap, nor gather the grapes of your untended vine, for it is a year of rest for the land.*

For 490 years the Jewish people violated this commandment—as well as others. As a consequence of their disobedience, they were sent by God to toil in Babylonian captivity while His covenant land experienced the full "seventy years" of rest it was owed.

THE TIMELINE OF THINGS TO COME

The decree to rebuild Jerusalem—issued during the time of Nehemiah—was given in 445 BCE. For forty-nine years (the first unit of seven "weeks" of years), Nehemiah and his men labored to rebuild the wall, even during "troublesome times" (Daniel 9:25) until the work was completed in 396 BCE. Nehemiah and his fellow laborers courageously battled through discouragement, fear, internal and external strife, ridicule, lying prophets, pure laziness, and Satanic opposition as they struggled to rebuild the wall used to protect and defend Jerusalem.

Daniel prophesied that following an additional sixty-two-week period (creating a total of sixty-nine "weeks" of years), the Messiah would be "cut off" (Daniel 9:26). The brilliant scholar Sir Robert Anderson calculated the beginning and end of this group of sevens:

> What then was the length of the period intervening between the issuing of the decree to rebuild Jerusalem and the public advent of "Messiah the Prince"—between the 14th March BC 445, and the 6th April AD 32? *The interval contained exactly and to the very day [173,880] days, or seven times sixty-nine prophetic years of 360 days, the first sixty-nine weeks of Gabriel's prophecy.*[2]

On the tenth day of Nisan, Jesus rode into Jerusalem, publicly offering Himself as Israel's suffering Messiah, not the conquering messiah the people longed for. In ancient times, the way a king entered a city symbolized his intent. If the king rode in on a horse—his purpose was war. If he came into the city on a donkey—he came in peace. Jesus rode into Jerusalem as a man of peace on a humble donkey. Christ came to Earth the first time as a sacrificial lamb to redeem the world from sin, not to free Israel from the brutal grip of Rome.

The people of Jerusalem were looking for earthly peace, which they believed could only come after overthrowing Rome's corrupt regime. This time, however, Jesus came into the world to bring a lasting spiritual peace between God and man. And to accomplish this divine assignment, Jesus had to suffer and die (John 12:27). The Jews were looking for a messiah who would be a powerful political leader, one who would deliver Israel from oppression and provide for their physical needs. *Why not Jesus?*

Jesus' followers had seen Him feed the multitudes from a boy's sack lunch, heal the blind and paralyzed, and perform other wondrous miracles—surely, He could lead a successful revolt. But God the Father had another plan—a divine plan. Jesus would first come as the Suffering Servant before He comes a second time as the Reigning King.

The day Jesus entered Jerusalem, millions gathered there from all of Judea to celebrate the Passover Feast. As was required, the Jewish people brought unblemished male lambs for their sacrificial sin offering (Exodus 12:1–28, 43–49; Deuteronomy 16:1–8). The Passover lambs were chosen on the tenth day of Nisan (Exodus 12:3) and sacrificed at twilight on the fourteenth day (v. 6). Jesus was received into Jerusalem (Triumphal Entry) on the tenth day of Nisan and sacrificed on Calvary on the eve of Passover—four days later. Just as the pascal lamb atoned for Israel's sin, Jesus— the Lamb of God—would take away the sins of the world.

NOT YET TIME

Jesus didn't speak to His followers about a political revolt; instead, He foretold them of His betrayal, suffering, death, and resurrection (Matthew 16:21–23; 17:22–23; 20:18–19; Mark 9:31; 14:18; Luke 24:46; John 3:14; 12:20–36). When the mother of James and John pressed Jesus to appoint her sons to prominent positions in His future government, Jesus replied, "You do not know what you ask. . . . I didn't come to rule; I came to die" (Matthew 20:20, 28, paraphrased).

After Jesus was asked by His disciples to promote His miracles, He responded:

"No one who wants to become a public figure acts in secret. Since you are doing these things, show yourself to the world." For even his own brothers did not believe in him.

Therefore, Jesus told them, "My time is not yet here; for you any time will do. The world cannot hate you, but it hates me because I testify that its works are evil. You go to the festival. I am not going up to this festival, because my time has not yet fully come."

(John 7:4–8 NIV)

Time and time again, the Gospels record various occasions when Jesus discouraged the recognition of His miracle-working power so as not to mislead the people that He was their future political king. Jesus instructed the healed leper of Matthew 8:1–4 to "see that you tell no one." As soon as Jesus healed the deaf man, He "commanded them that they should tell no one" (Mark 7:36). Jesus said the same to the man who was healed of blindness (Mark 8:26). On another occasion, Jesus rebuked and silenced the demons that came out of those He delivered from bondage, "for they knew that He was the Christ" (Luke 4:41). And again, Jesus told Jairus and his wife to "tell no one what had happened" when he raised their daughter from the dead (Luke 8:56).

Jesus also instructed His disciples not to reveal His identity after they acknowledged that He was the Christ (Matthew 16:20; Mark 8:29). Even after Peter, James, and John witnessed Jesus' transfiguration and saw Elijah and Moses speak with Him and heard the voice of God declare, "This is my Son, whom I love. Listen to him!" (Mark 9:7 NIV), the Scripture records, "Now as they came down from the mountain, He commanded them that they should tell no one the things they had seen, till the Son of Man had risen from the dead" (v. 9).

My friend, archaeologist and Bible scholar Vendyl Jones, was often rumored to be the inspiration for Indiana Jones. Vendyl spent more than four decades studying Torah, Jewish history, and Middle Eastern customs as they related to the New Testament while in search of the Ark through the Judean desert. "Vendy," as he was known, stated that when Jesus rode into Jerusalem, "he certainly presented Himself in a very strange manner as king—no white horse, no consort, no cavalry, and no color guard. Not even the official herald to proclaim His entry."

Jones further concluded the following:

> Jesus not only avoided publicity, he acted aggressively to minimize his popularity among the people of Israel. . . . The followers of Jesus—not only the twelve but the multitudes, as well—followed him under the illusion that he would be the Messianic king of Israel. . . . On the contrary, he made repeated statements and allusions in which he states his purpose as the anointed one of G-d to be the savior of the Gentile world.[3]

Jesus did all He could to dissuade His followers from believing He was the conquering messiah who would deliver them from Rome's oppression.

Even so, the crowds that followed Jesus were impressed with His miracles—surely this man could deliver them from Rome's bondage. Jesus knew that the multitudes followed Him for what He could provide (John 6:26). But He also accepted that He had a purpose to fulfill: "Now My soul is troubled, and what shall I say? 'Father, save Me from this hour'? But for this purpose I came to this hour" (John 12:27).

Jones continued, "[Jesus] never performed a miracle to prove to the Sanhedrin or to the people that he was their national deliverer." Instead, the miracles were done to meet the needs of the people—He ministered to the need of the individual not the nation: "From the beginning, as well as throughout his entire ministry, he repeatedly emphasized that his purpose in coming into the world [the first time] was a cross and not a crown—an altar, not a throne."[4]

After Jesus entered Jerusalem, Luke 19:47 states that Jesus taught daily in the temple. He was a recognized rabbi—He was at home in the temple—it was His place. Jesus worshiped there and offered sacrifices as commanded by the law of Moses. But the chief priests were threatened by this popular rabbi's presence, and believed the rumors that Jesus was in Jerusalem to establish the throne of David. That claim appeared to become fact when Jesus drove the moneychangers and vendors out of the temple. Could Herod the "fox" (Luke 13:32) and his personally appointed Sanhedrin, Pilate, and the apostate priests (Matthew 26:59) be the next to be driven from the temple? Fearing that their own well-established dynasty, although corrupt, was in jeopardy, they sought to destroy Jesus.

Four days after Christ's entry into Jerusalem, the Messiah was "cut off," just as Daniel's prophecy predicted.

And the Prophetic Clock ticks on.

MESSIAH THE PRINCE

Gabriel told Daniel of two princes: "Messiah the Prince," who would appear after sixty-nine weeks, and "the prince who is to come." We'll discuss this latter prince in another chapter, but make no mistake, Jesus Christ is "Messiah the Prince" of Daniel's prophecy.

When Diocletian abdicated as emperor of Rome, a war of succession between Maxentius and Constantine became inevitable. Maxentius held possession of Rome, but Constantine invaded from Gaul in 312 CE. In preparation for battle on the Tiber River, Maxentius consulted the *Sibylline* books, a collection of oracular utterances given by Sibyl of Cumae, for prophetic insight.

The oracle declared, "On that day the enemy of Rome will perish." Confident that Constantine's doom was at hand, Maxentius stalked into battle and perished there, inadvertently identifying himself as the "enemy of Rome."[5] However, the deliberate vagueness of the oracle's prediction guaranteed its fulfilment one way or the other.

Are the Old Testament prophecies about the Messiah equally vague? Could any number of Jewish males claim to fulfill them after rising to prominence as spiritual leaders? While that may be true about some messianic prophecies taken in isolation or out of context, there are more than three hundred separate Scriptures that point to the Messiah in the pages of the Old Testament. Examined together, they form an imposing barrier to any accidental or after-the-fact fulfillment.

Think of each of the Messianic prophecies as a filter that strains out individuals who don't meet its requirements, and you will realize how unlikely it is that anyone but Jesus of Nazareth could pass through the rigorous standards. If you try to calculate the odds of someone accidentally satisfying more than three hundred separate, personal attributes, you end up with one out of a number with 125 zeroes after it—a virtual impossibility.

The following chart contains just fifty of the Old Testament Scriptures pointing to Jesus as Messiah the Prince and their New Testament fulfillment:

	Old Testament Prophecy	Description	New Testament Fulfillment
1	Isaiah 7:14	"Behold, the virgin shall conceive and bear a Son."	Luke 1:34; Matthew 1:20
2	Genesis 3:15	He shall bruise Satan's head. [paraphrase]	1 John 3:8
3	Genesis 12:3	"All the nations shall be blessed."	Galatians 3:8
4	Genesis 14:18	"High Priest forever according to the order of Melchizedek"	Hebrews 6:20
5	Genesis 22:18	In Isaac's seed, all nations will be blessed. [summary]	Galatians 3:16
6	Exodus 12:5	"A lamb without blemish"	1 Peter 1:19
7	Exodus 12:21–27	"Christ, our Passsover, was sacrificed for us."	1 Corinthians 5:7
8	Leviticus 23:36–37	"If anyone thirsts, let him come to Me and drink."	John 7:37
9	Psalm 34:20	Not a bone of Him broken [paraphrase]	John 19:33, 36
10	Deuteronomy 18:15	"This is truly the Prophet who is to come into the world."	John 6:14
11	Joshua 5:14–15	The Captain of salvation [paraphrase]	Hebrews 2:10
12	Ruth 4:4–10	"He made us accepted in the Beloved. In Him we have redemption through His blood."	Ephesians 1:3–7
13	1 Samuel 2:35	"A faithful priest"	Hebrews 3:1–3

	Old Testament Prophecy	Description	New Testament Fulfillment
14	2 Samuel 7:13	"Everlasting Kingdom of our Lord and Savior"	2 Peter 1:11
15	2 Samuel 7:16	David's house established forever [summary]	Luke 3:31; Revelation 22:16
16	2 Kings 2:11	Ascension into heaven: Elijah and Christ [summary]	Luke 24:51
17	1 Chronicles 17:11	"Son of David"	Matthew 1:1
18	Job 19:25–27	Christ's Second Coming [summary]	John 5:24–29
19	Psalm 22:1	"My God, my God, why have You forsaken Me?"	Matthew 27:46
20	Psalm 22:8	"He trusted in God; let Him deliver Him."	Matthew 27:43
21	Isaiah 53:5	He was pierced because of our transgressions. [paraphrase]	John 19:34
22	Psalm 22:16	They pierced His hands and His feet. [paraphrase]	John 20:25
23	Psalm 22:18	"They divided His garments and cast lots."	Luke 23:34–35
24	Psalm 35:11	False witnesses rose up against Him. [summary]	Matthew 26:59
25	Psalm 41:9	Betrayed by a familiar friend [summary]	John 13:18, 26
26	Psalm 69:21	Given vinegar in thirst [summary]	Matthew 27:34

	Old Testament Prophecy	Description	New Testament Fulfillment
27	Psalm 118:22–23	"The stone which the buiders rejected has become the chief cornerstone."	Acts 4:11–12
28	Proverbs 8:23	"Established from everlasting"	1 Peter 1:19–20; Revelation 13:8
29	Isaiah 7:14	Called Immanuel [summary]	Matthew 1:23
30	Isaiah 25:8	"Swallow up death forever"	1 Corinthians 15:54
31	Isaiah 28:16	The Messiah is the precious cornerstone, a sure foundation. [paraphrase]	1 Peter 2:6–7
32	Isaiah 35:5–6	Miracles predicted [summary]	Matthew 11:2–6
33	Isaiah 45:23	"Every knee shall bow"	Romans 14:11
34	Isaiah 49:6	"Restore the preserved ones of Israel."	Acts 15:16–17
35	Isaiah 53:3	Despised; rejected; a man of sorrow and grief [paraphrase]	Philippians 2:6–8
36	Isaiah 53:7	"Led as a lamb to the slaughter"	Acts 8:32
37	Isaiah 59:20	"The Redeemer will come to Zion."	Luke 2:38
38	Jeremiah 23:5–6	"God was manifested in the flesh"	John 13:13; 1 Timothy 3:16
39	Ezekiel 37:24–25	Jesus will be given the throne of David. [summary]	Luke 1:31–33

	Old Testament Prophecy	Description	New Testament Fulfillment
40	Daniel 2:44–45	All kingdoms shall be consumed by the Stone. [summary]	Revelation 21:19
41	Daniel 9:24–26	Predicted the destruction of the Second Temple [summary]	Mark 13:1–3
42	Hosea 11:1	He would be called out of Egypt. [summary]	Matthew 2:15
43	Joel 2:32	"Whoever calls on the name of the Lord shall be saved."	Romans 10:9–13
44	Jonah 1:17	Death and resurrection of Christ. [summary]	Matthew 12:40
45	Micah 5:2	Born in Bethlehem; from everlasting [paraphrase]	Matthew 2:1–6; John 8:58
46	Haggai 2:6–9	He will fill the temple with glory. [paraphrase]	Luke 2:27–32
47	Zechariah 6:12–13	Priest and King [paraphrase]	Hebrews 8:1
48	Zechariah 9:9	Presented to Jerusalem riding on a donkey [paraphrase]	Matthew 21:4–10
49	Zechariah 11:12–13	Betrayed for thirty pieces of silver [summary]	Matthew 26:15
50	Malachi 4:5	Prediction of John the Baptist—the spirit of Elijah the prophet [summary]	Matthew 3:1–3; 11:10–14; 17:11–13

Indeed, Jesus was the foretold and forthcoming Messiah the Prince!

But prophecies do so much more than merely identify Him. They tell us that as God's Son, He shared the divine nature (Psalm 2:7) and as the Son of Man, He shared human nature (Genesis 3:15). As God's Suffering Servant, He fulfilled Israel's destiny by keeping the righteous standards of the law of Moses (Isaiah 49:1–3). He established God's new covenant with humanity (Jeremiah 31:31–34; Matthew 26:28). He is the focal point of history (Colossians 1:16). We wait for His return at the End of the Age to establish justice and righteousness in the Millennial Kingdom (Malachi 4:1–3; Revelation 19:11–20:4).

THE PURPOSE OF THE
SEVENTY WEEKS

The last four verses of Daniel 9 contain one of the most important prophecies in all of Scripture. They provide an outline for the whole of Daniel's prophecy. As Gabriel gave Daniel "the skill to understand" God's timetable of human history, he referred specifically to Daniel's people (the Jews) and to his city (Jerusalem).

Whether they walk in obedience or in defiance of God's mandates, the Jews will always be set apart as His covenant people. And whether draped in majesty during the golden era of King David or cloaked in ruins after Nebuchadnezzar's conquest, Jerusalem was and will always be God's holy mountain—the city that holds His heart (Daniel 9:20). Nebuchadnezzar's dream (Daniel 2) and Daniel's visions of the four beasts (Daniel 7) and of a ram and a goat (Daniel 8) principally concern the Gentiles. However, Daniel 9 refers to God's plan for the Jewish people,

Jerusalem, and His promises of Israel's restoration and reposses-
sion of the Promised Land.

In Daniel 9:24, the angel of the Lord outlined six promised
blessings that must be accomplished through Christ's death and
forthcoming reign. The first three reference Christ's redemptive
work on the cross, leading to the removal of sin from the nation.
The second three refer to the sovereignty of the Messiah and the
establishment of His Millennial Reign. Leon Wood in his commentary on Daniel said, "The first three are negative in force,
speaking of undesirable matters to be removed; and the last three
are positive, giving desirable factors to be effected."[6]

The first three accomplishments concern the sins of Israel.
Jesus' death and resurrection atoned for the sins of all mankind,
Jew and Gentile alike; however, the fulfillment of this amazing provision for Daniel's people will happen at the end of the
Seventy Weeks with the Second Coming of Christ. The second
three accomplishments relate to God's righteousness. None of
the six blessings have been entirely fulfilled but are a forecast of
the establishment of the glorious Kingdom of God on earth. The
following are the future unparalleled six blessings for the nation
of Israel.[7]

1. "To finish the transgression." To bring an end to man's rebellion
against God, a new order on earth must be established. Christ
conquered sin at the cross, but there were those who did not
receive His redeeming work. However, the prophet Zechariah
spoke of a change in Israel's attitude toward the Lord, which will
occur at the End of the Age (Zechariah 12:10). This change of
heart will result in an end to idolatry, widespread repentance, and
reconciliation of God's Chosen people: "In that day a fountain
shall be opened for the house of David and for the inhabitants of
Jerusalem, for sin and for uncleanness" (Zechariah 13:1).

2. "To make an end of sins." Sin will continue throughout the Tribulation but will be destroyed when Jesus returns to earth to establish His earthly Kingdom: "They shall not defile themselves anymore with their idols, nor with their detestable things, nor with any of their transgressions; but I will deliver them from all their dwelling places in which they have sinned and will cleanse them. Then they shall be My people, and I will be their God" (Ezekiel 37:23).

3. "To make reconciliation for iniquity." During the Seventy Weeks, God will atone for the transgressions of Jew and Gentile alike, having already provided redemption through the death and resurrection of Christ: "In Him we have redemption through His blood, the forgiveness of sins, according to the riches of His grace" (Ephesians 1:7).

4. "To bring in everlasting righteousness." Sin will be eliminated, all of Israel will be saved, and Christ's everlasting righteousness will rule and reign on the earth: "And so all Israel will be saved, as it is written: 'The Deliverer will come out of Zion, And He will turn away ungodliness from Jacob'" (Romans 11:26).

5. "To seal up vision and prophecy." All prophetic visions in Scripture will be confirmed—true prophets and their prophecies will be vindicated: "No more shall every man teach his neighbor, and every man his brother, saying, 'Know the LORD,' for they all shall know Me, from the least of them to the greatest of them, says the LORD. For I will forgive their iniquity, and their sin I will remember no more" (Jeremiah 31:34).

6. "To anoint the Most Holy." "The Most Holy" describes the Holy of Holies, the utmost sacred place within the temple. Christ's Kingdom will be established when the holy place in the Millennial temple (detailed in Ezekiel 41–46) is completed and dedicated for service: "And He said to me, 'Son of man, this is the place of My throne and the place of the soles of My feet, where I will dwell in the midst of the children of Israel forever'" (Ezekiel 43:7).

Once again, the fulfillment of these six promised blessings will coincide with the End of the Age, the completion of the Seventy Weeks, and the establishment of the Millennial Age of Christ.

THE DIVINE INTERMISSION

Most biblical scholars agree that there is a pause, an intermission so to say, between the sixty-ninth and seventieth weeks. Matthew 23:37–39 teaches that Israel will be set aside—"You shall see Me no more" (v. 39)—until the End of the Age or when the consummation of the six blessings stated in Daniel 9:24 is accomplished. *Since* none of the six blessings have yet been experienced by Israel and *since* the Church is not Israel and *since* God is bound to what He promised— one can conclude that there must be a gap or a break in proceedings between the sixty-ninth and seventieth weeks of Daniel's vision.

Daniel 9:26 states, "Then after the sixty-two weeks, the Messiah will be cut off and have nothing" (NASB). What do the words *have nothing* mean? Christ atoned for the sins of the world through His death ("cut off") on the cross—how could that be *nothing*? Dr. Thomas Ice, in his work *The Seventy Weeks of Daniel*, asked and answered the question:

> What was it that He [Christ] came for but did not receive, espe-
> cially in relationship to Israel and Jerusalem, which is the larger
> context of this overall passage? It was His Messianic Kingdom!
> Indeed, it will come, but not at the time in which He was cut
> off. . . . The coming of the Kingdom requires acceptance of
> Jesus as Messiah in order for it to be established in Jerusalem.

The Kingdom will arrive by the time the final week is brought to fruition. Since Israel's [eternal] kingdom has not yet arrived, this means it is future to our day.[8]

We have established that there is a gap, but *why*?

You could say that God called an intermission—a time-out—in His Divine timeline and it was at Calvary that He stopped His Prophetic Clock.

Gaps are not unique to the prophetic Scriptures. For instance, in Zechariah 9:9–10 we read:

> *Rejoice greatly, O daughter of Zion!*
> *Shout, O daughter of Jerusalem!*
> *Behold, your King is coming to you;*
> *He is just and having salvation,*
> *Lowly and riding on a donkey,*
> *A colt, the foal of a donkey.*
> *I will cut off the chariot from Ephraim*
> *And the horse from Jerusalem;*
> *The battle bow shall be cut off.*
> *He shall speak peace to the nations;*
> *His dominion shall be "from sea to sea,*
> *And from the River to the ends of the earth."*

Verse nine of this chapter obviously refers to Christ's Triumphal Entry into Jerusalem. The tenth verse, however, directly applies to Christ's Second Coming and the establishment of the Millennial Kingdom. Between these two verses, uttered in one prophetic breath, lies a span of at least two thousand years.

We see the same thing in Isaiah 9:6–7. These two verses, read so often at Christmas, actually pertain to two widely separated events in history. In verse six we read, "For unto us a Child is born, unto us a Son is given," an obvious reference to Christ's birth; but then, separated only by a semicolon, we read of His Millennial Kingdom:

> And the government will be upon His shoulder.
> And His name will be called Wonderful, Counselor,
>   Mighty God,
> Everlasting Father, Prince of Peace.
> Of the increase of His government and peace
> there will be no end,
> Upon the throne of David and over His kingdom.

We find another illustration of a gap in the schedule of Israel's divinely instituted feasts. Before the advent of calendars and clocks, the people of Israel lived by the unchanging seasons. The spring celebrated the first four festivals—the Feast of Passover, the Feast of Unleavened Bread, the Feast of Firstfruits, and the Feast of Pentecost. These observances are portraits of Christ's death, burial, resurrection, and the advent of the Holy Spirit.

The three fall festivals—the Feast of Trumpets, the Feast of Atonement, and the Feast of Tabernacles—depict future events. There is a wide separation—a time gap—between the spring feasts, which serve as a type of Christ's first appearing, and the fall feasts, which speak of Israel's rebirth and Christ's Second Coming.

The two sets of feasts also coincide with the two annual seasons of rain. Spring brings the former rain; the latter rain comes in the fall. The prophet Hosea knew the seasons and rain cycles were a clear picture of things to come. Inspired by the Holy Spirit, he wrote of the Messiah, saying, "He will come to us like the rain, Like the latter and former rain to the earth" (Hosea 6:3).

Hosea meant that Jesus Christ, the Messiah, would come twice—once in the former rain, and again in the latter. The four feasts of the former rain—Passover, Unleavened Bread, Firstfruits, and Pentecost—are acts I, II, III, and IV of the divine drama in God's preparation for the final act of the latter rain—Christ's Second Coming.

In my recent book, *Earth's Last Empire: The Final Game of Thrones,* I discuss the gap, or intermission, between the sixty-ninth and seventieth years:

> It is important to restate that the seventy weeks are not consecutive—there is a distinct gap of time between the sixty-ninth and seventieth weeks. Daniel 9:26 refers to two prophetic milestones: the death of Christ (33 CE) and the destruction of the temple (70 CE)—then God's prophetic clock stops.
>
> Why did the clock stop ticking, and when will it begin again?
>
> Remember, the seventy weeks relate solely to God's dealings with the Jewish people—the church of Jesus Christ is nowhere mentioned. However, the New Testament church occupies that gap from the day of Pentecost [Acts 2:1] until the Rapture of the church [1 Corinthians 15:52].
>
> What marked the beginning of the Church Age, when will it end, and when will the seventieth week begin?
>
> The Church was birthed at Pentecost, and its age will last until Christ raptures His bride into the third heaven—it is the Dispensation of Grace. Bible scholar Myer Pearlman quotes Louis C. Talbot's writing, which presents a perfect word picture

of the time space [the gap between Pentecost and the Rapture] we are referring to:

> Some years ago, I was on a train . . . and for a while we ran on schedule, to the very minute. Then my train was sidetracked for two and a half hours. Finally, I asked the conductor why we were sidetracked all that while. He answered: "We are waiting for the express to go through." After a while, I heard the shrill whistle and saw the fast train whizz by. Then my own train was put back on the mainline, and on we went, according to schedule.
>
> I thought of God's train for Israel. For sixty-nine sevens of years His people ran according to schedule. Then their train was switched to a sidetrack, as it were, in order that the heavenly express might go through. From Pentecost to the Rapture, the gospel train of this age is on the main line.
>
> One of these days, the journey will be over, and we shall be ushered into the presence of the Lord. Then the Jewish train will be put back on the main track.[9]

Think of the Jewish nation as being placed on the sidetrack by God Himself, awaiting the arrival and fulfillment of the "Gentile Express" (see Romans 11:25). The temporary sidetracking of the Jewish nation has made space for the fast-tracking of the Gentile nation. This pause on the path to the ultimate redemption we all long for is God's grace in action and in no way violates His promise to the Jewish people.[10]

THE SIDETRACK

The "sidetracking" of the Jewish people has remained a mystery to many twenty-first-century Christians. To help reveal the purpose of this event it is important to go to the book of Romans.

The apostle Paul wrote the book of Romans to resolve any conflict between Jewish and Gentile believers, thereby promoting unity within the newly established Church. When you review the doctrinal themes of this Holy Spirit–inspired work you find that chapters 1–8 deal with justification and sanctification leading to the assurances that accompany salvation. Chapters 12–16 relate to believers' relationship to God and His righteousness through selfless love and unconditional service.

However, Romans 9–11 does not connect to either theme. It is an insert that reveals God's wisdom and examines His plan for the nation of Israel and the Jewish people from Paul's day until the End of the Age. Like a court reporter, Paul detailed God's position paper on the Jewish people. This "inclusion" is often referred to as a theological codicil.

When a lawyer adds to a document to further explain or modify it, he inserts a "codicil," which is as equally binding as the original text. Some scholars have tried to set aside Romans 9–11 as a simple postscript but ignore the fact that "all Scripture is given by inspiration of God" (2 Timothy 3:16). In this line of thought, the whole of the book of Romans is equally binding, and chapters 9, 10, and 11 are the important linkage between justification, sanctification, and our relationship to God. As J. Vernon McGee so aptly described, there is a great difference between interpreting Scripture and ignoring it. The whole of Romans is like a "flowing stream" that cannot have chapters 9–11 taken from it just as the Mississippi River cannot have its middle section taken from it "without causing havoc."[11]

Romans 9 records God's past dealings with Israel:

Who are Israelites, to whom pertain the adoption, the glory, the covenants, the giving of the law, the service of God, and the promises; of whom are the fathers and from whom, according to the flesh, Christ came, who is over all, the eternally blessed God. Amen.

(Romans 9:4–5)

Paul declared that the Jewish people are the children of God (Deuteronomy 9:3; Hosea 11:1); that the shekinah glory of God rests on them (Exodus 24:16; Ezekiel 1:28; Hebrews 9:5); that God made an unconditional covenant with Abraham and his seed for the land of Israel (Genesis 15:17–21; 17:7–8); that the Law of God was given to the Jewish people (Exodus 24:12; Romans 3:1–2); that the Jewish people have served God through His distinct guidelines for temple worship (1 Kings 5–8), the sacrificial procedures of atonement (Ezekiel 46), and the keeping of the Feasts (Leviticus 23; Numbers 10:10; 1 Chronicles 23:31); that God will send a Deliverer out of Zion (Romans 9:27; 11:26); and that God's Chosen people are loved by Him now and forevermore (Psalm 102; Isaiah 44:1–5) because He made irrevocable promises to Abraham, Isaac, and Jacob concerning the future of the nation of Israel and the Jewish people (Genesis 12 and 15).

Whereas Paul makes a case for national Israel in Romans 9, Romans 10 states God's present purpose with Israel. It has a threefold theme: the present state of Israel (Romans 10:1), the present standing of Israel (Romans 10:5), and the salvation of Jew and Gentile (Romans 10:13).

And now we come to Romans 11, which is one of the most profound chapters in all of Scripture—it foretells God's future purpose with Israel. J. Vernon McGee stated that "Paul makes it quite evident here that as soon as God consummates His plan for the church, of calling out of both Jew and Gentile a people to His name and takes the church out of the earth, He will return again to the nation Israel and begin to deal with them."[12]

Therefore, in a nutshell:

- if Israel had not been reborn in a day (Isaiah 66:8), and
- if the Jewish people had not been ingathered to their covenant land (Isaiah 35:10; 43:5–6; 44:24, 26; 61:4; Ezekiel 11:17, 19; 28:25–26; 34:28–30; 37:21–28; Jeremiah 30:3, 10, 18; 31:7–8, 10–12; Zechariah 1:15–17), and
- if the cities of Israel had not been rebuilt (Psalms 147:2; Isaiah 61:4), and
- if Judea and Samaria had not been settled (Jeremiah 30:3), and
- if Israel's forests had not been replanted (Psalms 104:14–16), and
- if Israel's desert had not bloomed like a rose (Isaiah 35:1), and
- if God were to lie (Numbers 23:19) and break covenant (Psalm 89:34) . . .

Then maybe—just maybe—you could assume that God was finished with the Jewish people.

We must remember that Jesus was a teacher of prophecy. In Matthew 24, Mark 13, and Luke 21, Jesus spoke of the Jews from their deliverance from Egypt's bondage to their future at the End of the Age. Jesus' prophecy seminar of Matthew 24 places the

Jewish people in Jerusalem during the Tribulation (vv. 16–18). Jesus further promised that for the "elect's sake" these terrible days will be shortened (v. 22).

We also must never forget that the Jewish people are God's elect—they are not now nor will they ever be forgotten, replaced, or forsaken!

Returning to Romans, it would be difficult to fully discuss the importance of Romans 11 in an entire book much less within a few paragraphs; therefore I will limit my discussion to two subjects: replacement theology and judicial blindness.

REPLACEMENT THEOLOGY

Replacement theology, or Supersessionism, teaches that the Church has replaced Israel and the Jewish people. This false doctrine advocates that the first covenant (Old Testament) was supplanted by the new covenant (New Testament).

There is one Bible, and every word in the Holy Scriptures, beginning with Genesis 1:1 and ending with the "amen" of Revelation 22:21, was inspired by the Holy Spirit:

All Scripture is given by inspiration of God, and is profitable for doctrine, for reproof, for correction, for instruction in righteousness, that the man of God may be complete, thoroughly equipped for every good work.

(2 Timothy 3:16–17)

Remember this truth: The Old Testament is God's will concealed, and the New Testament is God's will revealed—every word is equally anointed, relevant, and eternally true.

The scourge of anti-Semitism severely lashed Jewish backs through Pharaoh's slavery, Haman's gallows, Spain's inquisitions, the Crusades, and Hitler's Final Solution. As generations of God's Chosen still struggle to recover from these evils, it is tragic that they must now confront the rising tide of global anti-Semitism and, even more heartbreaking, the continued false teachings within some Christian churches.

Replacement theology is "the view that the church is the new or true Israel that has permanently replaced or superseded Israel as the people of God."[13] However, I fully agree with Thomas Ice who stated, "Replacement theology has been the fuel that has energized Medieval anti-Semitism, Eastern European pogroms, the Holocaust, and contemporary disdain for the modern state of Israel."[14]

Israel and the Jewish people are weaved throughout the magnificent tapestry of God's Word. As a whole, the historical Church has miscalculated the importance of Israel in Scripture, and consequently its interpretation of the Bible's foundational message has been distorted. And this tragic misrepresentation has caused indescribable pain, suffering, and death for God's Chosen people. I write more fully about the history of the Church, replacement theology, and Christian anti-Semitism in *Earth's Last Empire: The Final Game of Thrones*.

Paul said in Romans 11:17–18, "But if some of the branches were broken off [Jewish people], and you, being a wild olive [Gentiles], were grafted in among them and became partaker with them of the rich root of the olive tree, do not be arrogant toward the branches; but if you are arrogant, *remember that* it is not you who supports the root, but the root *supports* you" (NASB).

Know this, fellow Christian—we are "partakers" not "replacers."

JUDICIAL BLINDNESS

Aside from warning believers not to be "arrogant," Paul even used himself as a way to answer the doctrinal question, Has God cast away His people?

> I say then, has God cast away His people? Certainly not! For I also am an Israelite, of the seed of Abraham, of the tribe of Benjamin. God has not cast away His people whom He foreknew.
>
> (Romans 11:1–2)

I can hear Paul pleading his case now: "I'm a Jew, here are my credentials and God has not cast me away—surely He would not cast away my people?" Yet another question arises: What then? Enter the concept of judicial blindness referred to in Romans 11:7–12:

> What then? Israel has not obtained what it seeks; but the elect has obtained it, and the rest were blinded. Just as it is written:
>
> > "God has given them a spirit of stupor,
> > Eyes that they should not see [judicially blinded]
> > And ears that they should not hear,
> > To this very day." [Isaiah 29:10; Deuteronomy 29:3–4]
>
> And David says:
>
> > "Let their table become a snare and a trap,
> > A stumbling block and a recompense to them.

69

> *Let their eyes be darkened, so that they do not see,*
> *[judicial blindness]*
> *And bow down their back always."* [Psalms 69:22–23]

> *I say then, have they stumbled that they should fall?*
> *Certainly not! But through their fall, to provoke them to jeal-*
> *ousy, salvation has come to the Gentiles. Now if their fall is*
> *riches for the world, and their failure riches for the Gentiles,*
> *how much more their fullness!*

Why is it that we ignore Paul's emphatic answer—*"Certainly not!"*? Could it be for arrogance, which exactly describes the Church's belief that God has, in fact, "cast away His people"? British commentator C. E. B. Cranfield addressed the Church's misconception that has replaced Israel and the Jewish people:

> It is only where the Church persists in refusing to learn this message [the Church has not replaced Israel], where it secretly—perhaps quite unconsciously—believes that its own existence is based on human achievement, and so fails to understand God's mercy to itself, that it is unable to believe in God's mercy for still unbelieving Israel, and so entertains the ugly and unscriptural notion that God has cast off His people Israel and simply replaced it by the Christian Church. These three chapters [Romans 9—11] emphatically forbid us to speak of the Church as having once and for all taken the place of the Jewish people. . . . But the assumption that the Church has simply replaced Israel as the people of God is extremely common.[15]

Simply stated, the sovereign God that we serve has chosen to "judicially blind" His Chosen people until the Gentiles—you and me—have had the opportunity to accept Christ as Savior and Lord. This is the amazing reason—the merciful reason and the unbelievably loving reason for the "intermission" or the "gap" between the sixty-ninth and seventieth weeks.

The sidetracking of Israel has been a source of "riches for the Gentiles"—providing us the opportunity to obtain our eternal salvation (Hosea 2:23; Romans 11:12). My friends, Israel has not been forgotten, replaced, or forsaken at the End of the Age; the fulfillment of the six blessings will occur, and the "natural branches" will again be grafted into the tree.

In conclusion, Daniel's prophecy is portrayed within Seventy Weeks, which are divided into three intervals of seven weeks, sixty-two weeks, and one final week. The whole of the prophecy has to do with the Jewish people and the city of Jerusalem. Within this period, two princes are mentioned—Messiah the Prince and the Antichrist. The start of the Seventy Weeks concerns "the going forth of the command to restore and build Jerusalem" under the leadership of Nehemiah (Daniel 9:25).

At sixty-nine weeks Jesus makes His Triumphal Entry into Jerusalem. After the sixty-nine weeks, the Messiah Prince will be "cut off" (crucified), and Jerusalem will be destroyed. At this point in time, God's Prophetic Clock stops, creating an intermission between the sixty-ninth and seventieth weeks. Once the "times of the Gentiles are fulfilled" (Luke 21:24), the Church will be raptured from the earth and the Prophetic Clock will begin again.

The last interval of seven years coincides with the forthcoming events recorded in Revelation chapters 6–19 and begins with the Antichrist making a peace treaty with Israel. In the middle of the Seventieth Week, or three and a half years later, the Antichrist will break his treaty. Scripture describes this time as the Great

71

Tribulation, which will bring with it unparalleled suffering for the Jewish people (Matthew 24:15–26).

However, the close of the Seventieth Week will usher in the grand finale of Daniel's Seventy Weeks—the Second Coming of the reigning Messiah—Jesus Christ. The establishment of His eternal Kingdom also closes Daniel's prophecies of the four great world empires: the Babylonian, the Medo-Persian, the Greek, and the Roman. It is a time when "oppressed Israel is delivered and the oppressor, the Gentile, is judged,"[16] leading to the realization of God's entire plan for His people.

CHAPTER THREE

11:52 PM

And Knowledge Shall Increase

But you, Daniel, shut up the words, and seal the book until the time of the end; many shall run to and fro, and knowledge shall increase.

Daniel 12:4

The Bible scholar Harold Willmington said that some- time around 1680, the great scientist Sir Isaac Newton read Daniel 12:4 and remarked, "Personally, I cannot help but believe that these words refer to the end of the times. Men will travel from country to country in an unprecedented manner. There may be some inventions which will enable people to travel much more quickly than they do now."

Newton later speculated that the speed of such inventions might surpass fifty miles per hour! The French atheist Voltaire read Newton's words eighty years later and stated, "See what a fool Christianity makes of an otherwise brilliant man! Here a scientist like Newton actually writes that men may travel at the rate of 30 or 40 m.p.h. Has he forgotten that if man would travel at this rate he would be suffocated? His heart would stand still!"[1]

"One wonders," Willmington added, "what Voltaire would have said had he known that some two centuries after he wrote this, an American astronaut, Edward H. White . . . would climb out of a space craft a hundred miles in the sky and casually walk across the continental United States in less than fifteen minutes, strolling along at 17,500 m.p.h.? Or that during the moon landings, man exceeded a speed some twelve times faster than a twenty-two-caliber rifle bullet travels?"[2]

The literal translation of Daniel 12:4 indicates that at the End of the Age, an explosion of knowledge will occur. We are living in that generation.

From the Garden of Eden until the beginning of the twentieth century, men walked or rode horses just as King David and Julius Caesar did. In the span of a few generations, however, mankind invented the automobile, the jet plane, and the space shuttle. Today you can fly from New York to Paris in six or seven hours. Before the supersonic transport was grounded, it made the trip in three hours.

Because of the rapid acceleration of the knowledge explosion, students graduating from high school in 2021 live in a world far different from that of their parents and grandparents. I remember going to the airport gate to pick up an arriving passenger. Now those born after the 9–11 disaster consider extensive airport security and TSA body scanning the norm. This same generation has never rolled up a car window; they don't know what it means to hang up or dial a telephone. Most children today have never used a conventional camera but take an infinite number of photos on their smartphone. With Google maps and GPS, they have never used a road atlas—nor have they ever looked up a number in a printed telephone directory or seen a phone booth, much less used one. With movies and music easily streamed or downloadable, the post-2000 generation thinks of typewriters, VHS tapes, and CD players as museum pieces.

In the first two decades of the twenty-first century, we witnessed the advent of flat-screen, high-definition TVs, smart TVs, and live online streaming of every program imaginable. I remember some of the first twelve-inch television sets. Then gradually screens as large as eighty-six inches were produced. Now my grandchildren choose from a vast list of movies or YouTube DIY videos on their three-inch-wide smartphones—go figure! We use handheld reading devices that store thousands of books. Electric and hybrid automobiles drive themselves. Robots accomplish everyday chores like vacuuming the floors and mowing lawns.

Testing on advances such as collision-proof cars, 3D TVs, and airborne drones for parcel delivery is happening now, while flying cars are on the drawing board and may fill our skies in the near future. Soon we will catch up with the Jetsons!

Today's technology has increased exponentially. While we are not necessarily advancing our personal knowledge, technology has made fathomless depths of data available to us at the click of a button. With just a single device that fits easily in the palm of our hand, we can explore endless resources of information. This deceptively small device can make international phone calls, take photos or shoot videos, send texts, write and send emails, play and record music, offer full-length movies and games, do computations, and plot routes across town or across the nation. Basically, there is an app for anything you can think of in this technologically advanced era. Alarmingly, they do all the thinking for us.

In the last three generations, we have put men on the moon, robotically explored the surface of Mars, and made major advances in the medical field. Doctors use digital guidance and robotic devices for endoscopic and laparoscopic surgery, which reduces recovery time dramatically. Tiny babies weighing less than one pound can survive outside the womb, and unborn babies can undergo surgery while in their mother's womb. We can repair DNA and clone sheep, mice, and cattle. We also have the technology to clone humans, and before too long, I'm sure we will.

All this knowledge ought to be a good thing, but still, we're heading to a day of reckoning. Our knowledge has not produced utopia; instead, it has created a generation of people who know more about rock stars than history. Our "enlightened" society seeks freedom, self-expression, and safe places, but it is actually enslaved by perversion, narcissism, addictions, and hedonism.

Our society is upside down. We favor the death sentence for the innocent and clemency for the guilty. Founding father Thomas Jefferson is now regarded by some as a bigoted racist, while some Americans consider Iranian terrorist General Qasem Soleimani a hero. We tout the benefits of secular humanism, the worship of human intellect, yet our enlightened, religion-free government finds itself impotent in the face of growing crime. Why? Because knowledge without God can only produce intellectual barbarians. Hitler surrounded himself with elite thinkers, yet these brilliant men had no conscience. They were educated monsters who had no compunction ordering innocent Jewish men, women, and children to the gas chambers and ovens of the death camps. "We have grasped the mystery of the atom," General Omar Bradley told a Boston audience in November 1948, "and rejected the Sermon on the Mount. . . . With the monstrous weapons man already has, humanity is in danger of being trapped in this world by its moral adolescents. Our knowledge of science has clearly outstripped our capacity to control it. We have many men of science; too few men of God."[3]

Seventy-one years later, a speech delivered by former Attorney General William Barr at the University of Notre Dame showed that societal conditions have only grown worse since General Bradley's time. Barr reflected on the continuing degeneration of our values in the wake of the modern secular attack on Christianity:

> By any honest assessment, the consequences of this moral upheaval have been grim. Virtually every measure of social pathology continues to gain ground. In 1965, the illegitimacy rate was eight percent. . . . Today it is over 40 percent. In many of our large urban areas, it is around 70 percent.
>
> Along with the wreckage of the family, we are seeing

record levels of depression and mental illness, dispirited young people, soaring suicide rates, increasing numbers of angry and alienated young males, an increase in senseless violence, and a deadly drug epidemic. . . . Over 70,000 people die each year from drug overdoses. That is more casualties in a year than we experienced during the entire Vietnam War. . . .

The campaign to destroy the traditional moral order has brought with it immense suffering, wreckage, and misery. And yet, the forces of secularism, ignoring these tragic results, press on with even greater militancy.[4]

We have built a society upon the pillars of technology, a capitalistic economy, and human government. Just like in the times of Babel, we have conveniently forgotten or deliberately ignored God's precepts and warnings in order to go our own way. But as the clock nears midnight, my friend, the birth pangs of the coming End of the Age are sending shock waves throughout civilization. The pillars of our society are teetering, and soon they will fall.

TECHNOLOGY: BLESSING OR BURDEN?

I'll be one of the first to admit that computers have made life easier. The simple act of typing a manuscript used to be a major trial—one little mistake, and the page went into the trash. Then came correcting typewriters, followed by word processors, then computers with word processing programs. Now, instead of actually typing out a book four or five times, authors can input the information once by dictating the text directly into the word

79

processor, and then spend the rest of the time editing the manuscript before it's printed.

The internet, while it does collect a disgraceful amount of propaganda and pornography, is also an ocean of facts and up-to-the-minute news. Used wisely, it can be a godsend when researching almost any topic.

Computers are used in virtually every aspect of life today. There are computer chips in our cars, kitchen appliances, TVs, smartphones, credit cards, and even our dogs. We now can have a "smart" home; Alexa and Siri provide the latest weather forecast, inform us when a package has been delivered, keep inventory of our pantries, and provide the score of our favorite team's latest game.

Technology has brought us to the place where the phrase "the internet is down" is the most feared expression in society. Without access to information, we are perplexed and paralyzed. Without smartphones, we're incommunicado. Without technology, we may as well take the day off and curl up with a good book—that is, if all our books are not on a Kindle, Nook, or iPad. But we can't afford to relax for long. COVID-19 showed the world that meeting in person could soon be a thing of the past with the advent and widespread use of Zoom conferences. Our society hums along efficiently only as long as our virtual world is operational.

VIRTUAL TERRORISM IS REAL

Personal comfort, increased knowledge, and technological efficiency have also resulted in an escalating threat of cyberterrorism. According to information warfare specialists, the last two decades have introduced the "cyberterrorism" age. George Orwell predicted that "Big Brother"[5] was always watching. Have you noticed that ads come onto your Instagram shortly after you have discussed a specific topic or product with someone while your smartphone is nearby? "Big Brother" is watching and listening! But this is only the beginning.

In March 1998, a host of computer professionals met in Israel to discuss threats of the technological age. Conference organizer Yonah Alexander believed that the globalization of cultures, economies, and securities opened us up to a "new world disorder." Technology has connected the world, but this connection carries a great risk, leaving us vulnerable to cyberattacks.

"We are moving toward a new age of Internet or 'click' terrorism," said Alexander. "This is the new face of terrorism in the future."[6] My friends, the future is in the here and now.

The internet not only enables groups from around the world to communicate, but web pages are also used for propaganda, psychological warfare, and recruitment. The internet has replaced military training camps. If you want to know how to build a bomb or learn the latest terrorism techniques, you can easily find it online.

The American Security Project (ASP) continues to affirm the seriousness of a potential cyberterrorism attack. As tensions escalate worldwide, it seems unrealistic to think America's enemies would not use all means available to do us harm. In fact, the ASP sees this happening now, an ominous shadow of darker things to come. For example:

On Thursday [June 20, 2019], the city council of Riviera Beach, Florida, paid a $600,000 ransom in Bitcoin to hackers after its computer systems were targeted in a cyberattack. This event, the most recent of several so far this year, shows

81

how detrimental a cyberattack can be on a city. Furthermore, it enhances apprehension over the possibility of a cyberterrorist attack, a phenomenon we have largely avoided thus far.[7]

According to the ASP report, "As of 2018, 81% of Americans viewed cyberterrorism as a critical threat."[8] Additionally, the ASP cites the 2019 Worldwide Threat Assessment by the US intelligence community, which raises the following concerns:

"financially motivated cyber criminals" may target the U.S. within the next few years. They warn that this could "disrupt U.S. critical infrastructure in the health care, financial, government, and emergency service sectors." Officials are also concerned that terrorists may hack into databases and obtain personal information that could be used to inspire and enable physical attacks.[9]

We are seeing a growing number of cyber incidents that expose how vulnerable we are, on both a corporate and an individual level. We've witnessed large corporations' computers hacked and private files invaded, leaving millions of their customers vulnerable to identity theft.

In 2015, the ISIS Cyber Caliphate hacked into the Twitter and YouTube accounts of the US Central Command, where they posted threats and ominous messages.[10] In 2017, hackers broke into the computer system of Equifax, one of the nation's largest credit bureaus, and "stole the personal data of 145 million people."[11] In July 2019, a hacker broke into the computer system of Capital One bank, creating a data breach that exposed more than 100 million customers.[12]

Identity theft is the fastest-growing crime in America. The FBI reported that "every three seconds, an identity is stolen. That's 35,000 every day and more than 15 million every year."[13] For millions of Americans this has become their living nightmare. One's complete identity can be virtually erased through computer hacking. Using the stolen information, evildoers can demolish a person's credit rating, insert a police record, or alter medical records. The person or organizations whose records have been altered might not even realize they have been invaded by hackers, and when they do learn of it, many find that it becomes a grueling ordeal to try to set things right again. No one is immune—it can happen to anyone. Back in 2010, LifeLock CEO Todd Davis had his identity stolen thirteen times![14] Billions of people are being affected worldwide by data breaches.

With every computer system connected to all others via the internet—cybercriminals, national enemies, and terrorist extremists are using the web as a sophisticated and advanced weapon. It is only a matter of time before they will attempt to bring down the critical infrastructures on which our economy and security rest. All it takes is one successful attack on a central bank, an electrical grid, a metropolitan utility, or a city's emergency services.

We have indisputable evidence that terrorists are gearing up to attempt such disruptions. In 2015, Ardit Ferizi hacked into a government computer and stole "the data of 1,300 military personnel and federal employees." He turned the information over to ISIS to aid them in targeting attacks. In 2017, British teenager Kane Gamble stole confidential information from CIA, FBI, and Department of Justice databases—including specific information on twenty thousand FBI employees—which he leaked to terrorist organizations via the internet. It is no wonder that Al-Qaeda has been recruiting new members possessing "strong computer and hacking skills."[15]

Security experts are increasingly concerned about cyberterrorism. In fact, some of their worst fears were realized in late 2020 as a massive global data security breach commonly known as the SolarWinds hack came to light. In it, a group likely backed by the Russian government penetrated thousands of organizations globally including multiple parts of the United States federal government. The cyberattack and data breach, which had gone undetected for months, are believed to be the worst in US history. Thousands of organizations around the world are believed to have been impacted by the attack, including the Pentagon, the State Department, the Department of Homeland Security, the US Commerce Department, and Treasury Department in the US; NATO; the UK government; the European Parliament; and Microsoft.[16]

A TOTTERING ECONOMIC
HOUSE OF CARDS

Money is an exciting topic—if you don't think so, just try taking it away from someone. Jesus taught financial management—sixteen out of His thirty-eight parables deal with the topic of possessions. There are five hundred verses in the New Testament dealing with prayer, fewer than five hundred dealing with faith, and more than two thousand about how to handle our possessions.

At the end of 2019, most experts and all economic indicators told us that the US economy was stronger than ever and showed no signs of slowing down. In fact, America's steady financial stability has been called "the Goldilocks economy because it was neither too hot nor too cold."[17]

One respected financial website showed how leading economic indicators revealed a healthy economy of steady growth, low unemployment, and light inflation. The economy looked rosy and showed no cause for alarm. We could eat, drink, buy, sell, and be merry, for there was nothing on the horizon to interrupt our happy party.

But then came the COVID virus—a super-germ released into an unsuspecting world population. Fear, sickness, panic, and confusion overwhelmed many as the number of victims grew exponentially.

THE COVID-19 FISCAL FIASCO: CAUSE AND EFFECT

The Center for Risk and Economic Analysis of Terrorism Events (CREATE) is a Homeland Security think tank located at the University of Southern California (USC). Their projections, released in December 2020, reported on the effects COVID-19 will likely have on the US economy for the next two years. The study's introduction states the following:

> The study considers a comprehensive list of causal factors affecting the impacts, including: mandatory [business] closures and the gradual re-opening process; decline in workforce due to morbidity, mortality and avoidance behavior; increased demand for health care; decreased demand for public transportation and leisure activities; potential resilience through telework; increased demand for communication services; and increased pent-up demand.[18]

In early March of 2020, due to an increase in COVID-19 cases, several states ordered the closure of such nonessential businesses as restaurants, bars, salons, and multiple retail establishments. Many states also either halted or significantly restricted public services to limit the virus from spreading.

The researchers projected that these mandatory closures and subsequent partial reopenings could result in net losses somewhere between $3.2 and $4.8 trillion in US real gross domestic product (GDP) over the course of two years, depending on a multitude of factors. Noting that China had not suffered such astounding losses due to a shorter lockdown period, the team projected the US losses from the pandemic could dwarf those of China by more than 400%. And many people still believe this virus was an accident?

The USC researchers highlighted the following projections as a result of mandatory closures:

- Fifty-four million to 367 million work days would be lost due to people getting sick or [dying] from COVID.
- Two million to nearly 15 million work days would be lost due to employees staying home to care for sick loved ones.
- Job losses could range from 14.7 percent to 23.8 percent, and in the worst case, affect an estimated 36.5 million workers.
- Demand for health care has risen with COVID infections. Medical expenses due to COVID-19 from March 2020 to February 2022 could range from nearly $32 billion to $216 billion.
- A loss in demand for some services—such as the use of public transit and school attendance, restaurant dining and travel—as people avoid public places and services to reduce their risk of exposure.
- An uptick in demand for communication services, as

many employees during this pandemic have had to work from home.[19]

Another significant factor in the economy's decline was related to consumer behavior. The researchers assumed that certain people would strive to avoid the risk of infection by modifying their behavior: avoiding work; not attending classes in person; and staying away from restaurants, music venues, sporting events, church services, and other places where large groups might gather. Therefore, "because people have had to avoid activities, this has had a significant impact on economic losses,"[20] said Dan Wei, a CREATE research fellow and research associate professor at the USC Price School for Public Policy.

Despite estimating that in a worst-case scenario, avoidance behavior could result in nearly $900 billion losses in US GDP, the researchers asserted that such economic losses could be partly offset by the natural economic rebound that could occur after states reopened in efforts to return to a semblance of normalcy. "While the mandatory closures and partial reopenings drive most of the economic decline, the extent to which pent-up demand leads to an increase in consumption after reopening, can be crucial to the economic recovery,"[21] said Terrie Walmsley, a USC CREATE research fellow and adjunct assistant professor of practice in economics at the USC Dornsife College of Letters, Arts and Sciences.

Adam Rose, the study team leader who is the director of CREATE and a research professor at the USC Price School of Public Policy, posed this key question: "When will we see a complete reopening across this country? We simply cannot predict that, especially in light of the fact that we have not gained full control of the spread of the disease."[22]

STIMULUS CHECK OR SEISMIC SHIFT

A September 2020 *Forbes* magazine headline stated, "Thanks to Stimulus Spending, U.S. Debt Is Expected to Exceed the Size of the Entire Economy Next Year."[23] In other words, we are spending ourselves to ruin, and the seismic activity that will bring our demise is our national debt.

As of January 2021, the national debt—the total amount of outstanding treasury bonds, bills, and notes our government owes—stood at nearly $28,200,000,000,000.[24] That's more than 28 *trillion* dollars. A trillion is a difficult number to grasp. Think about it this way: If you went into business the day Jesus Christ was born, stayed open 365 days a year, and lost a million dollars every day, you'd have to work another 680 years from today before you'd lose a trillion dollars. In an attempt to describe the massive amount of money we are speaking of—one million dollars consists of a stack of one-thousand-dollar bills four feet high. One trillion dollars is one million million—and we currently owe more than 28 trillion!

It doesn't take a genius to look at the figures and see that it is mathematically impossible for our government to pay off the national debt. Here's why: Government spending is divided into three categories. The first is discretionary spending, which includes how much money each department will receive each year. The second category is mandatory spending, which includes programs such as Social Security and Medicare, where spending is set by law. The third category of spending is interest on the national debt, which grows annually with continuing deficit spending.

When you add the last two categories—mandatory spending and servicing the national debt—the total is almost as large as the government's entire annual tax revenue. This leaves little or nothing to run governmental departments or to handle emergencies or engage in military operations.[25] Then add to these categories the massive stimulus measure through the CARES Act (Coronavirus Aid, Relief, and Economic Security Act) that pushed $2.2 trillion into American households in March 2020 and then an additional $900 billion in late December—all in an attempt to hold back the economic crisis brought on by the COVID-19 pandemic. And in early 2021, President Biden and the US Congress passed the American Rescue Plan Act, another economic relief package which adds an additional 1.9 trillion dollars to our out-of-control debt.

Bottom line, our growing national debt will ultimately destroy the American dollar, our economy, and our nation.

THE RUMBLINGS HAVE BEGUN

The United States is standing in a line of dominoes that have begun to topple. To see how easily an economic collapse could occur, let's take a brief look at recent history. In the summer of 1997, the tiny nation of Thailand devalued its currency, the baht, and few Americans even noticed. But devaluation of any currency is serious business, and the global economy is so fragile and so interconnected that even the slightest nudge can set off the toppling dominoes. Thailand's Asian trading partners were affected and soon followed suit, devaluing their own currencies. Foreign investors panicked and pulled out of Asian investments.

Japan was the next country to be affected, because 40 percent of its trade was held in other Asian countries.[26] The loss of exports pushed its already weak economy into a terrible recession. Japanese banks were left with more than $500 billion in bad debts. Japanese pension funds suffered enormous losses, and their government bonds plunged into negative interest rates.

The investor exodus hit Latin America and Russia next. To stop investors from converting local currencies into dollars or another more stable currency, countries raised interest rates. But high rates mean slow economic growth; the dominoes had rattled almost half the world economy.

Korean banks that had invested heavily in the Russian market had to sell their positions in order to pay their own creditors. The Russian ruble began to fall while interest rates began to increase, hitting heights of 70–90 percent in July 1998. Finally, in mid-August, the Russian government literally ran out of dollars and announced it would no longer convert their unstable ruble into more dollars. Their stock market went into free fall; the Russian financial system collapsed.

Subsequently, the line of falling dominoes reached the United States. First in line for the devastating hits were the huge hedge funds, investment banks, and commercial banks that invest in foreign markets.[27] Few people paid attention when newspapers and magazines reported that the Federal Reserve Board had put together a multibillion-dollar rescue of a struggling hedge fund.

Newsweek magazine began its story about the hedge fund rescue by citing a flippant parody: "If you owe a bank a million dollars and can't pay, the bank owns you. But if you owe a billion dollars, you own the bank, because it doesn't dare foreclose and take a huge loss."[28]

That's the best explanation I've heard of what happened in October 1998. Long-Term Capital Markets, located in Greenwich, Connecticut, owed so much money to important institutions that the Federal Reserve and Wall Street didn't dare let it collapse. Why not? Because if Long-Term Capital failed, businesses to whom they owed money would go bankrupt, forcing still other businesses to go out of business. Who knows where the chain reaction would end? Talk about a domino effect!

When you see how easily the global economy can be disrupted by what seems to be a small, minor country, it's frightening to think what it would mean if the world's strongest economy suddenly faltered. As we have seen, not only could it easily happen, in the view of many economists, it is inevitable given the massive debt and insolvency of the US government.

How would such a scenario play out? What will America do when it runs out of money to pay for its entitlements? First, it will begin to default on its debts. Its creditors will go bankrupt, creating a worldwide domino effect. Confidence in the dollar will plummet, along with America's credit rating and the willingness of institutions to loan us money.

When the inevitable financial collapse hits us, how will the government attempt to pull out of it? According to Simon Black:

> Throughout history, inflation has been the option of choice for hopelessly indebted governments. Since the US dollar is nothing but an empty promise of the US government, they can simply create more dollars out of thin air . . . thereby devaluing every other dollar in circulation. This allows them to pay back their creditors with dollars that are worth 'less' . . . until the US dollar literally becomes worthless and everyone who holds it loses their purchasing power.[29]

In 2019, one economic blogger commented, "In the short-term, the Federal Reserve will undoubtedly attempt to stabilize things. In recent days they have begun wildly printing money once again."[30] As we have seen, we are at the point where all fixes are merely temporary. Like a man who trips on a curb, he may stumble on for a few more steps as he's going down, but inevitably he will hit the ground.

WHY WOULD GOD ALLOW AN ECONOMIC CRASH?

Long ago, America and the world set the God of Abraham, Isaac, and Jacob on the sidelines to worship the false god of Mammon. In Deuteronomy 28:17–18, God announced the curses that fall on the nation that does not heed His voice or obey His precepts: "Cursed shall be your basket and your kneading bowl. Cursed shall be the fruit of your body and the produce of your land, the increase of your cattle and the offspring of your flocks." The basket (for gathering grain), the kneading bowl (for making bread), the produce of the land, the increase of cattle and the offspring of flocks all have to do with a nation's source of supply. Men may think they control the economies of nations, but they do not— God does!

During the coming Tribulation, the Antichrist will demand a cashless society in which every financial transaction is electronically monitored. John, author of the book of Revelation, described the situation: "He causes all, both small and great, rich and poor, free and slave, to receive a mark on their right hand or on their foreheads, and that no one may buy or sell except one who has the mark or the name of the beast, or the number of his name" (Revelation 13:16–17). We are all too naive if we believe that this kind of monitoring doesn't exist currently.

But be sure of this, God Almighty will topple America's false god, Mammon. He esssentially says to us, "I am the Lord your God, and there is none other beside me. I am your shield, your buckler, your high tower, your provider." Remember this truth, America: the power to gain wealth does not come from the president, Congress, the Federal Reserve, or Wall Street. God rules in the affairs of men, and the power to get wealth comes from Him, "for it is He who gives you power to get wealth" (Deuteronomy 8:18).

GOD WILL TOPPLE AN
UNJUST GOVERNMENT

How did we evolve from being the *United States*—"*one* nation under God" to the laughingstock of the world? Why did this transition happen in such a short time? Because America has lost its moral footing and is spiraling steeply into a pit of immorality and degradation rivaling that of the ancient condemned cities of Sodom and Gomorrah. And with moral decline comes the crumbling of our political, economic, and social prowess.

In his October 2019 speech, from which I quoted earlier, former US Attorney General William Barr astutely identified the cause of the downturn of our principles:

> The problem is not that religion is being forced on others; the problem is that irreligion and secular values are being forced on people of faith. . . . This is not decay; it is organized destruction. Secularists and their allies . . . have marshaled all the force of mass communications, popular culture, the entertainment industry, and academia in an unremitting assault on religion and traditional values.[31]

Attorney General Barr obviously realizes that the United States is desperately locked in a war to the death—not a war of conventional weapons, chemical weapons, or even biological weapons, but a spiritual war in which the enemy seems to have gotten the upper hand. I fear that all too few of us—and I include American Christians—realize how grim and deadly serious the present situation is. It is past time for us to wake up to reality!

My friend, every time I watch the news, I grow more and more convinced that God's Prophetic Clock is ticking out the final minutes of the last hour of the End of the Age as we know it. News of mass murders in schools and churches, rioting, mayhem and anarchy in the streets of America, and targeted attacks against police officers are all on the rise. The traditional family unit—which consists of a father, mother, and children—is deteriorating rapidly. Perversions that would not have been spoken of a few decades ago are now acceptable mainstream lifestyles. The very concepts of "male" and "female" are being rejected and declared out of bounds for recognition.

Pornography is a national scourge. The internet hosts more than 24.5 million porn sites, which receive more than 68 million daily searches in the US—accounting for 25 percent of all daily searches. Statistics show that every second, more than 30,000 people are watching porn. And more tragically, more than 80 percent of children are unintentionally exposed to pornography.[32]

The gay lobby has largely succeeded in getting homosexuality accepted as a normal lifestyle. According to a 2019 Gallup poll, 63 percent of Americans think gay or lesbian relationships are morally acceptable.[33] The US Supreme Court established gay marriage as a civil right in 2015, and one of the Democratic candidates who campaigned for the 2020 presidential nomination is a gay man who is legally married to his male partner. Other candidates vowed to revoke the tax-exempt status of churches who fail to endorse gay marriage. Christians with businesses providing wedding services such as bakeries, photographers, florists, and printers are being sued and put out of business for declining to serve gay weddings. Several states have closed down Christian adoption agencies that refused to place children in homes of gay or lesbian couples.

Sexual immorality among heterosexuals has also become rampant. The 2019 Gallup poll shows that 71 percent of Americans believe unmarried sex is morally acceptable, and 64 percent see nothing wrong with having a baby outside marriage.[34] Given such attitudes, it's not surprising that 48 percent of US children are born to single mothers, and 43 percent have no father in the home.[35] Unmarried couples living together has become the norm. According to CDC statistics, more than 43 percent of married adults aged 18 to 44 had cohabited with one or more partners before marriage.[36]

Reason and sanity have been abandoned as several businesses, organizations, states, and municipalities have bowed to current political correctness and ruled that restrooms, school locker rooms, sporting events, and even protective facilities for abused and battered women be open to transgendered members. As of this writing, at least nine transgender athletes were hoping to earn a spot in the Tokyo Olympics.

As terrible as this evidence of decline is, perhaps none of it is as outrageous and deplorable as our nation's endorsement of abortion. Since the US Supreme Court legalized abortion in 1973, the lives of more than 62.8 million babies have been snuffed out by this insidious practice.[37] Several states have tried to put limitations on abortions, but so-called progressives are fighting them tooth and nail by demanding expanded abortion access up to the moment of birth and even beyond.

What does "beyond" mean? Virginia Governor Ralph Northam defended a bill in his state that would remove all restrictions on abortion, even allowing a woman to abort her child while she is in labor. Then he went one step further and said that babies with severe deformities could be allowed to die even after they are born alive.[38]

In October 2019, California governor Gavin Newsom signed a bill mandating all public universities in his state to provide students with free access to medical abortions.[39] All but one of the Democratic presidential candidates in the 2020 election supported unrestricted abortion on demand. According to one journalist, "The current Democratic baseline [is] that abortion ought to be legal throughout all nine months of pregnancy for any reason."[40] The statement Mother Teresa of Calcutta made at the 1994 National Prayer Breakfast in Washington, DC, is worth repeating: "Any country that accepts abortion is not teaching its people to love, but to use any violence to get what they want. This is why the greatest destroyer of love and peace is abortion."[41]

God instructed Joshua to destroy the tribes in the land of Canaan for indulging in the same despicable practices that have become common in our nation. In Leviticus 18, God listed the depraved practices of the Canaanites, which included rampant sexual immorality, adultery, cult prostitution, homosexuality, bestiality, incest, and sacrificing children to their god Molech. Then God added this warning:

> Do not defile yourselves with any of these things; for by all these the nations are defiled, which I am casting out before you. For the land is defiled; therefore I visit the punishment of its iniquity upon it, and the land vomits out its inhabitants. You shall therefore keep My statutes and My judgments, and

shall not commit any of these abominations . . . lest the land
vomit you out also when you defile it, as it vomited out the
nations that were before you.

(vv. 24–28)

Israel descended into depravity, and even though they were God's chosen nation, they were not spared from judgment. The fact that the United States was founded on godly principles and upheld them for most of two centuries will not save us. If God did not save His own nation from the consequences of their actions, how can we expect that He will spare us when we are descending so rapidly into the same pit of depravity?

Our national conscience is seared. American society, founded upon the principles of faith and freedom, has left its moral underpinnings and chased after the prevailing winds. We are like King Solomon, who said:

> *Whatever my eyes desired I did not keep from them.*
> *I did not withhold my heart from any pleasure,*
> *For my heart rejoiced in all my labor;*
> *And this was my reward from all my labor.*
> *Then I looked on all the works that my hands had done*
> *And on the labor in which I had toiled;*
> *And indeed all was vanity and grasping for the wind.*
>
> (Ecclesiastes 2:10–11)

America is a soulless travesty of what she once was. Our society, like ancient Rome's, is headed for destruction.

As I write this, God's Prophetic Clock reads 11:52. There is no turning back.

CHAPTER FOUR

11:53 PM

The Great Escape

Then we who are alive and remain shall be caught up together with them in the clouds to meet the Lord in the air. And thus we shall always be with the Lord.

1 Thessalonians 4:17

Most people have heard of "judgment day"; however, far too many see it as a manipulative myth created to keep people in line. For older Americans, Armageddon is merely a synonym for world war, while many others might immediately think of the movie with Bruce Willis, Billy Bob Thornton, and Ben Affleck. Few have heard of the Rapture, and even fewer fully understand it; nonetheless, it is the next event on God's Prophetic Clock.

We are hearing more and more chatter about the end of the world. Not since the approach of the year 2012, when many bought into the narrative of the ancient Mayan calendar's call for the cataclysmic destruction of the planet, has there been growing speculation that "the end" is near.

It is apparent not only with prophecy-aware Christians, but also among certain politicians, seismologists, nuclear physicists, and even ordinary citizens who are deeply disturbed by the signs of an impending collapse of national and world order—that something is coming. Many have even jumped on board with a novice congresswoman who recently predicted that climate change would end the world by 2030. Some are expecting the world to die by famine, pollution, or during an alien invasion. Others are expecting nuclear war with North Korea and Iran, biological terrorism from China, and cyber-devastation from radical extremists. Still others believe the COVID-19 pandemic is the beginning of the end.

The Doomsday Clock was set at two minutes to midnight in 2018 by its governing board due to the same concerns about climate change and the additional threat of nuclear weapons.[1] Many scientists in various disciplines expect the world to be destroyed by massive earthquakes or gigantic volcanic eruptions. Some astronomers believe that a collision between the earth and a massive asteroid is at some point inevitable. And concerned geologists warn that an explosion of the Yellowstone volcano is long overdue—an eruption they say would effectively end life on earth as we know it.

Bible believers are expecting none of the above. We are anticipating at any moment that "the Lord Himself will descend from heaven with a shout, with the voice of an archangel, and with the trumpet of God. And the dead in Christ will rise first. Then we who are alive and remain shall be caught up together with them in the clouds to meet the Lord in the air. And thus we shall always be with the Lord" (1 Thessalonians 4:16–17). Yes, my friend, the Son of God, Jesus Christ will come for His Church at the Rapture. Those who have placed their faith in Him will be instantly transported into heaven.

Thomas D. Ice, in his work "The Rapture in History and Prophecy," stated that "the rapture of the church is the first time that God will take a large group of people from earth to heaven without experiencing death." However, "it will not have been the first time that God takes individuals to heaven in this way." The first was Enoch, who "walked with God; and he was not, for God took him" (Genesis 5:24); Elijah was taken "by a whirlwind to heaven" (2 Kings 2:1 NASB); Isaiah was physically taken into the throne room of God and brought back to earth (Isaiah 6); Philip was not taken to heaven but was "snatched" away from the Judean wilderness by the Spirit of the Lord after evangelizing the Ethiopian eunuch and "found himself at Azotus" (Acts 8:39–40 NASB); Paul, in a situation similar to Isaiah's throne-room experience, was "caught up to the third heaven" and received "visions and revelations of the Lord" (2 Corinthians 12:1–4); and the two witnesses of Revelation will be summoned "into heaven in the cloud" during the Tribulation (Revelation 11:12 NASB).[2]

But the most referenced Rapture is still to come. It will be that of the Church of Jesus Christ and will occur before the beginning of the seven-year Tribulation.

Daniel, the prophet who saw the things to come, didn't mention the Rapture. He saw the "times of the Gentiles" and the future of Israel, but he never mentioned anything about a snatching away of believers. So how do we know the Rapture will occur?

THE MYSTERY OF THE RAPTURE

In 1 Corinthians 15:51–52, Paul wrote, "Behold, I tell you a mystery: We shall not all sleep, but we shall all be changed—in a moment, in the twinkling of an eye, at the last trumpet. For the trumpet will sound, and the dead will be raised incorruptible, and we shall be changed."

Paul found it necessary to explain this mystery to the church at Corinth because age and illness were beginning to claim church members—and they had expected Jesus to come back for them before they passed away. Believers wanted to know if those who had died would have a part in the eternal Kingdom to come. So Paul shared with them a *mystery*, a term used in Scripture to denote something God had not previously shared with men.

Paul gave them a succinct explanation of the Rapture: at the sound of the trumpet, the dead in Christ will rise instantly, in "the twinkling of an eye" with supernatural, immortal bodies. Those who remain alive will be caught up to meet the Lord, too, and also be given glorified bodies of absolute perfection. This word picture of the mass gathering of believers is commonly called the Rapture.

If you were to ask average church members in America what they thought of the Rapture, far too many would look at you with puzzled expressions on their faces. Some have never heard the word mentioned from their pulpits and don't have the faintest notion what it means. Though most evangelical churches have preached the doctrine of the Rapture for years, they are now falling under attack for teaching that a literal taking away of the Church will actually occur. Others are debating as to whether the Rapture will occur before, during, or after the Tribulation.

The doubting herd is bellowing, "There will never be a Rapture! We're going through the Tribulation, so prepare yourself!" Their position reminds me of a story of a small Midwestern town. A man came running down Main Street screaming, "The dam broke! Run for your life!"

Two ladies coming out of the grocery store heard him. "The dam broke?" They ran after him, squealing in panic as they spilled groceries all over the sidewalk.

A trio of men in the barber shop heard the commotion. They saw the panicked man and the frightened ladies, so they fled, too. "The dam broke," they shouted, the barber's aprons flapping on their chests as they sprinted for the edge of town. "Run for your life!"

At the firehouse on Main Street, the fire chief heard the noise and punched the alarm button. The siren echoed through the town, drawing more people into the frightened flood of evacuees. The police chief, the mayor, and the city clerk all deserted their posts and jumped into the fleeing mob.

An elderly fellow from the barber shop reached the corner of 14th Street and Main, then retreated into a sheltered spot, too breathless to run any farther. "I guess this is where it ends for me," he said, bracing himself for the rush of water. Then, from nowhere, a startling thought crashed into him: "Wait a minute. I've lived here all my life, and we don't have a dam!"

Misinformed preachers are running down Main Street screaming, "We're going through the Tribulation," and those who are more loyal to the message of a man than the Word of God are joining the stampede. Saints of God, stop running like lemmings over a cliff. Look up! Pray up! Pack up! We're going up! Your redemption draws nigh, for the King of kings is coming!

Let's review 1 Thessalonians 4:13–18:

But I do not want you to be ignorant, brethren, concerning those who have fallen asleep, lest you sorrow as others who have no hope. For if we believe that Jesus died and rose again, even so God will bring with Him those who sleep in Jesus.

For this we say to you by the word of the Lord, that we who are alive and remain until the coming of the Lord will by no means precede those who are asleep. For the Lord Himself will descend from heaven with a shout, with the voice of an archangel, and with the trumpet of God. And the dead in Christ will rise first. Then we who are alive and remain shall be caught up together with them in the clouds to meet the Lord in the air. And thus we shall always be with the Lord. Therefore comfort one another with these words.

At the time of the Rapture, both the dead and the living in Christ will be changed in a "twinkling of an eye"—a microsecond. Dead bodies will be revitalized; bodies still living will become immortal and supernatural. At this moment, the Christian will experience victory over death, hell, the grave, the world, the flesh, and the devil. Hallelujah!

WHEN AND HOW WILL JESUS COME FOR HIS BRIDE?

Jesus said, "But of that day and hour no one knows, not even the angels in heaven, nor the Son, but only the Father" (Mark 13:32). Despite the thousands of people who would like to predict the exact year, month, date, or hour of Christ's return, Jesus said no man knows—not even He knows. Only God the Father knows when He will send His Son to take His bride home. However, while we do not know the day and hour, we can know through prophetic Scripture that the Rapture is very, very near. Jesus said, "But as the days of Noah were, so also will the coming of the Son of Man be" (Matthew 24:37).

How was it in the "days of Noah"? Noah did not know the date nor the hour of the flood, but he knew it was very, very near. Why? Because God put Noah and his family on the ark with all the animals, and God Himself closed the door. When Noah heard the door close, he knew the flood was imminent.

Today, with the portrait of tomorrow clearly revealed in prophetic Scripture, the door of the Age of the Dispensation of Grace is closing, and the coming of King Jesus is approaching—it could happen before you finish reading this page!

When you merge the prophetic references with common sense, you can paint the following picture of the Rapture: Without warning, the trump of God will sound, announcing the appearance of royalty, for Jesus is the Prince of Glory, the King of kings, and Lord of lords. The voice of the archangel shall summon the righteous dead from their resting places, and all over the earth, graves will explode as their occupants soar into the heavens to meet the Lord in the air.

The impact on the earth will be indescribable. Empty cars will careen down the highway, their drivers and occupants gone. Homes of believers will stand empty with supper dishes on the dining table. The radiant bride, without spot or wrinkle, will have been snatched from this vale of tears to a place where there is no crying, no parting, and no death, to celebrate the marriage supper of the Lamb of God.

The next morning, headlines will scream "Millions are missing!" The Church of Jesus Christ—which includes every born-again believer—will be absent from the earth. New Age church members, secular humanists, and agnostics will remain on the earth in a state of shock and confusion. People throughout the planet will be frantically looking for their loved ones on all social media platforms, causing internet servers to collapse under the weight of traffic.

Over the next few hours, accounts of airline crashes, unmanned vehicles careening off highways, and a flood of missing-person reports will fill the network news. All the media outlets will interrupt regular programming to run specials with talking-head know-it-alls trying to report what has happened. Among the "experts" will be a New Age prophet who jabbers about an invasion of aliens who "beamed up" millions of earthlings. A psychologist will say the missing were victims of mass hysteria caused by a "disappearance disorder," while a left-behind theologian will say the world is better off without the "right-wing, Bible-believing, politically incorrect fundamentalist hatemongers" who believed in some nonsensical allegory called the Rapture.

In the following days after the Rapture, churches will be packed with weeping people who will have realized, far too late, that God's Prophetic Clock had advanced, shearing away another event on His timeline. The world, and everyone in it, will continues to move second by second toward the greatest time of suffering ever known.

OPPOSING VIEWS OF THE RAPTURE

The Rapture is defined as an occurrence when the Church—all believers, living and dead—will be translated or resurrected into heaven. The Tribulation is the seven-year "time of preparation for Israel's restoration and regeneration (Deuteronomy 4:29–30;

Jeremiah 30:4–11; Ezekiel 20:22–44; 22:13–22)."[3] Even though some may believe that both events will occur, there is debate as to when the Rapture and the Tribulation take place.

The following is a brief summary of five opposing views of the Rapture's occurrence in reference to the seven-year Tribulation:

1. The Partial Rapture

The partial Rapture position says that when Jesus comes in the clouds of glory, He will take only those who have had a second work of grace or who are sanctified in their daily lives. According to this view, the body of Christ will be divided into two parts: a sanctified part that will ascend into heaven and an unsanctified part that will be left to go through the Tribulation in the hope that their sins may be purged through this great time of trial.

This view must be rejected on the basis that the death of Jesus Christ removes *all* sin. The Bible says, "Their sins [those who repent] and their lawless deeds I will remember no more" (Hebrews 10:17). Because our redemption at Calvary was complete, God will receive everyone who has confessed Christ as Lord and accepted His substitutionary death at Calvary.

Another reason to reject this view is that the bride of Christ is one body, perfect and complete: "For by one Spirit we were all baptized into one body—whether Jews or Greeks, whether slaves or free—and have all been made to drink into one Spirit" (1 Corinthians 12:13). To suggest that part of the body must remain on earth while the other part is in heaven is contrary to Scripture.

This doctrine also implies that salvation comes by our works, which is also contrary to God's Word (Romans 11:6). We do not sanctify ourselves—there's no way we could. We are saved and sanctified only through the redeeming blood of Jesus Christ.

109

2. The Midtribulation Rapture

This view suggests that the Church will endure the first three and one-half years of the seven-year Tribulation and be raptured before the beginning of the second half, prior to the Great Tribulation.

The midtribulation Rapture view must likewise be rejected. The first three and one-half years of the Tribulation consist of wars, pestilence, famine, disease, desolation, and death, and they are the beginning of God's wrath poured out upon the earth. Theologian Arthur Pink said the following:

> We repeat, at the Rapture and during the Tribulation period everything on earth will be morally and spiritually rotten. Even God's judgments at that time will have no other effect than to cause earth's-dwellers to "blaspheme God" (Rev. 16:11 etc.). Hence, is it not evident that the whole of the salt . . . must have first been removed: that the church and the Holy Spirit which now make impossible this total corruption must first be "taken out of the way"![4]

3. The Post-Tribulation Rapture

This position holds that the Church will go through the entire seven-year Tribulation period. It will endure the judgment and the wrath of God and then will be caught up to meet the Lord in the air to return immediately with Him to the earth.

A verse often used to justify this position is John 16:33: "In the world you will have tribulation."

In Scripture, the word *tribulation* is used in two different ways. First, it is used to describe any severe trial that comes upon an individual in his walk with Christ. In this sense the believer must expect tribulation in his or her everyday life—I think we are all living testaments of this truth (John 16:33). Second, the word *tribulation* is used to describe that specific seven-year period (Daniel's Seventieth Week) when the wrath of God will be poured out upon men for their rejection of Jesus Christ and His gospel.

If one purpose of the Tribulation is to punish the Gentiles that have rejected the Word of God, and the Bible assures believers that there is "no condemnation [judgment] to those who are in Christ Jesus" (Romans 8:1), then the post-tribulation theory must be rejected for this reason, as well as the reasons cited earlier. It is not only unscriptural but illogical to consider that the Church would suffer through any part of the Tribulation.

4. The Pre-Wrath Rapture

The pre-wrath view teaches that the Rapture will occur five and one-half years into the Tribulation. In this view the Day of the Lord commences near the end of the Tribulation, not at the beginning.

First Thessalonians 5:1–3 states that the Day of the Lord will come unexpectedly, while people everywhere are saying "peace and safety!"

However, according to the pre-wrath view, the Sixth Seal will just have been broken, which will result in earthquakes and great cosmic disturbances that will bring incredible terror to the inhabitants of the earth (Revelation 6:12–17).

In fact, at this time, more than a quarter of the world's population will have been destroyed by famines, disease, and widespread warfare. No one will be proclaiming "peace and safety" when millions upon millions of souls have recently perished.

Placing the beginning of the Day of the Lord and the Rapture at this point in the Tribulation doesn't make sense. According to

Scripture, God's wrath is poured out on the earth from the very beginning of the Tribulation.

5. Pretribulation Rapture: God's Premillennial, Pretribulation Plan

The pretribulation Rapture position states that the Church will not go through any portion of the Tribulation. I believe this is the correct position for several reasons.

First, the very nature of the Tribulation precludes the Church from suffering any of it. The Tribulation is a horrendous time of wrath, judgment, indignation, darkness, destruction, and death—and it leads to the End of the Age. Paul wrote, "There is therefore now no condemnation [judgment] to those who are in Christ Jesus" (Romans 8:1).

The Church has been cleansed by the blood of Jesus and needs no other purification. Some ask, "Don't Christians need to be cleansed?" The answer is yes, but they are cleansed through confession of sin and the blood of Jesus Christ, not through personal suffering. "If we confess our sins, He is faithful and just to forgive us our sins and to cleanse us from all unrighteousness" (1 John 1:9).

Second, I believe the pretribulation Rapture position is scripturally correct due to Paul's teaching in 2 Thessalonians 2. The believers in Thessalonica were experiencing great persecution. They wanted to know whether the sufferings they endured were part of the Tribulation and questioned Paul's first letter, which stated that Christians would not go through the Tribulation.

Paul told them "not to be soon shaken in mind or troubled, either by spirit or by word or by letter, as if from us, as though the day of Christ [the Day of the Lord] had come" (2:2).

Paul said they were not in the Tribulation. He wrote, "that

Day will not come unless the falling away comes first, and the man of sin is revealed, the son of perdition" (v. 3).

The "man of sin" is the coming Antichrist, who will come from the federated states of Europe, the final form of Gentile world power. He will be the leader of the "ten toes" Daniel saw in his dream of the statue with the head of gold.

The Antichrist has not appeared yet, "for the mystery of lawlessness is already at work; only He who now restrains [hinders] will do so [keep on hindering] until He is taken out of the way" (v. 7).

Who is restraining Satan from presenting the Antichrist to the world? The Holy Spirit. On the day of Pentecost, the Holy Spirit entered believers (later known as the Church) and dwelled within them. When the Church leaves earth, the Holy Spirit leaves with it. Accordingly, when the Lord Jesus appears in the clouds of heaven to rapture the Church from the earth, God's restraint will be removed, and Satan can then accomplish his aim of dominating the world through the work of the Antichrist—but not until the Church and its abiding Spirit have been raptured.

Third, I believe that the pretribulation position is scripturally correct because of what we find in Revelation 4:4. John recorded, "Around the throne were twenty-four thrones, and on the thrones I saw twenty-four elders sitting, clothed in white robes; and they had crowns of gold on their heads."

Notice that these elders are seated, robed, and crowned. This is clearly symbolic of the Church. In Ephesians 2:6 we read that God has "made us sit together in the heavenly places in Christ Jesus." In Revelation 19:8 we read, "And to her [the Church] it was granted to be arrayed in fine linen, clean and bright." Also, we read in 2 Timothy 4:8, "Finally, there is laid up for me the crown of righteousness, which the Lord, the righteous Judge, will give to me on that Day, and not to me only but also to all who have loved His appearing."

The critical question is this: When is the Church seen in heaven in its glorified position? It is seen at the very beginning of the Tribulation that John described in Revelation 4–19. It is seen in heaven, seated, robed, and crowned. Thus, the Rapture must precede the Tribulation.

Fourth and finally, I believe the pretribulation position to be accurate thanks to what we read in 2 Thessalonians 1:7–8. Paul spoke of giving "you who are troubled rest with us when the Lord Jesus is revealed," and "taking vengeance on those who do not know God, and on those who do not obey the gospel of our Lord Jesus Christ." The wrath of God during the Tribulation is to be poured out on "those who do not know God," not on the Church.

God saved Lot from the destruction of Sodom and Gomorrah because he was a righteous man. Since he was a righteous man (2 Peter 2:7), the angels said, "Escape for your life! Do not look behind you nor stay anywhere in the plain. Escape to the mountains, lest you be destroyed. . . . For I cannot do anything until you arrive there" (Genesis 19:17, 22). The presence of one righteous man held back the wrath of God.

The same thing happened at the time of the Genesis flood. The earth was terribly wicked, entirely corrupt, but "Noah found grace in the eyes of the LORD" (Genesis 6:8). God planned a way for Noah to escape His wrath and waited until Noah and his family were safely aboard the ark. Then God shut the door, and the floodwaters covered the earth and consumed every living thing.

In the same manner, the Church and the Holy Spirit must be removed before the wrath of God can be poured out upon the earth.

Revelation 3:10 notes that the Tribulation will not be for the Church but for "those who dwell on the earth" (Revelation 3:10; 6:10; 8:13; 11:10 [twice]; 13:8, 12, 14 [twice]; 17:2, 8), as a judgment upon them for their rejection of Christ and His salvation. While the Church will experience tribulation in the universal definition during this present age (John 16:33), she is never mentioned as participating in the Day of the Lord, an unparalleled time of trouble.

Pretribulationalism aligns with the biblical references that the Church will experience the Rapture before the Tribulation begins.

THE EARLY CHURCH BELIEVED IN A PRETRIBULATION RAPTURE

The members of the early Church counted the doctrine of the Rapture as one of their most blessed beliefs. The writers of the Epistles spoke of the appearance of the Lord in terms of hope, joy, and comfort. They longed for His appearing.

The disciples who followed Jesus to the summit of the Mount of Olives saw Him rise majestically into the air until He vanished from their sight. Baffled, they stood squinting and searching the heavens, until an angel appeared and said, "Men of Galilee, why do you stand gazing up into heaven? This same Jesus, who was taken up from you into heaven, will so come in like manner as you saw Him go into heaven" (Acts 1:11).

The disciples probably ran back to tell the others what had happened, and in the telling they reiterated the angel's words: "He's coming back! Just like we saw him go, through the clouds!"

Though it occurred several years ago, I still remember being quite frustrated as I watched a particular religious program on

115

television. Some very respected preachers were on a panel, and the host asked one of them to give his reasons for believing in the Rapture. "Of course, you know," the host added, "that the early church fathers didn't believe in the Rapture."

That's false! The disciples saw Jesus ascend into heaven, and they believed He would return in the same way. They had also heard Jesus Himself say He would return to give His followers an escape from the coming Tribulation: "Watch therefore, and pray always that you may be counted worthy to escape all these things that will come to pass, and to stand before the Son of Man" (Luke 21:36).

The disciples knew the truth from firsthand experience, and they shared it with the other followers of Christ.

Grant Jeffrey completely debunked the notion that the early Church didn't believe in a pretribulation Rapture. He referenced an old manuscript from 373 CE, in which Ephraem the Syrian wrote, "For [at the Rapture] all the saints and Elect of God are gathered, prior to the tribulation that is to come, and are taken to the Lord lest they see the confusion that is to overwhelm the world because of our sins."[5]

FALSE CHRISTS WILL ARISE

If you don't believe in the Rapture, how will you know when the real Jesus comes for His bride? Anyone can stand on the Mount of Olives and say, "I'm Jesus." Anyone can wear a white robe and claim to be a descendant of King David. Any cult leader can have his followers crown him king of the "new Israel" on the Temple Mount in Jerusalem—but that doesn't make him Jesus.

A false messiah could have scars placed in his hands and feet and perform supernatural acts like witches and warlocks do. You can even turn on your television and watch a documentary about psychic healers performing surgery with their fingernails. But remember this: People who possess supernatural power are not necessarily from God. The devil has supernatural power, too, as do his demons.

God knew that imposters and frauds would claim to be Christ, especially in the last days. Look at Matthew 24:23–27, in which Jesus told His disciples about His return and the advent of false christs:

> *Then if anyone says to you, "Look, here is the Christ!" or "There!" do not believe it. For false christs and false prophets will rise and show great signs and wonders to deceive, if possible, even the elect. See, I have told you beforehand.*
>
> *Therefore if they say to you, "Look, He is in the desert!" do not go out; or "Look, He is in the inner rooms!" do not believe it. For as the lightning comes from the east and flashes to the west, so also will the coming of the Son of Man be.*

USA Today once ran a full-page ad that read, "Christ Is Now on the Earth." The *New York Times* carried a similar ad proclaiming, "Christ Is Now Here." Those ads ran in the early 1980s, and I quickly threw them away after showing them on national television.

In 2017, *National Geographic* magazine ran a story about five men who claimed to be Jesus Christ. The article profiled the men, who were proclaiming their divinity in diverse parts of the world, including Brazil, Siberia, Japan, South Africa, and Zambia. All had a following, and all presented a narrative to reconcile their claims with Scripture. One of them, known as the "Christ of Siberia," boasted of more than five thousand disciples.[6]

Claims like these should never be heeded. Christ isn't on the earth in bodily form, for when He comes again, the entire world will know it! The apostle John told us unequivocally that when Christ comes, "every eye will see Him" (Revelation 1:7).

One of our church members once told me, "Pastor Hagee, a lady told me she was driving in California and that suddenly Jesus appeared in the car with her. What do you think?"

"I don't believe it," I answered. "Because if Jesus were here, I'd be gone. I wouldn't be talking to you right now."

Jesus is not in California, New York, Siberia, or Brazil. He is seated at the right hand of God the Father, where He will stay until Gabriel blows the trumpet to call the dead in Christ from their dusty beds of slumber to mansions on high.

How will you be able to tell the real Jesus from the counterfeits? Jesus knew imitators would come, so God installed a fail-safe mechanism that is so staggering in supernatural power, so earth-shattering, that not even Satan himself could duplicate it. That fail-safe method is the Rapture.

SOME GLAD MORNING, I'LL FLY AWAY

The old hymn writers wrote of the Rapture and sang about it as they lifted their voices in praise. These gifted men and women knew, as I know, that just beyond the clouds the saints of God will soon gather in our heavenly home! From east and west, north and south we will come, ten thousand times ten thousand. God will wipe away every tear from our eyes, and there will be no more parting, no more suffering, no more pain, no more sorrow, no more death, no more disease.

My mother and father will rise. My grandparents will rise with resurrected, healthy bodies. My family and I will fly to meet them, our bodies changed and clothed in immortality. My glorified body will sail through the heavens past the Milky Way into the presence of God. I'll know I'm with the real Jesus when I stand in His glorious presence with my brand-new, disease-proof, never-dying, fatigue-free body that looks better, feels better, and *is* better than any version of Arnold Schwarzenegger or Brad Pitt in their heyday!

DOES IT MATTER IF I BELIEVE?

Some of you may be saying, "It is what it is. It doesn't really matter if I believe in the Rapture or not. It's just one of those prophetic things that can be interpreted a hundred different ways."

I beg to differ with you, friend. Just as the word *rapture* does not appear in Scripture, neither does the word *trinity*, yet over and over it refers to the "oneness" of God and the "threeness" of God.[7] Likewise, there are very clear references to this "snatching away" of believers, which I have detailed in this chapter. The term may not be in the Bible, but the truth of it certainly is.

Mark it down, take it to heart, and comfort one another with these words—believers in Christ will escape the Tribulation. This dire time of unprecedented pain and suffering is coming to nations and individuals that are left behind, but those who believe in Jesus as Lord and Savior will not be on earth to witness it.

The apostle Peter warned that doubters will arise at the End of the Age:

Knowing this first: that scoffers will come in the last days, walking according to their own lusts, and saying, "Where is the promise of His coming? For since the fathers fell asleep, all things continue as they were from the beginning of creation."

(2 Peter 3:3–4)

J. Vernon McGee said, "The prophecy in the Old Testament of Christ's coming was to establish His kingdom upon the earth; the prophecy in the New Testament of His coming was first to take His church out of the world and then to come to establish His kingdom upon the earth."[8] The fact that the teaching of the Rapture has fallen on unbelieving ears is actual proof that Jesus will be coming soon.

Other critics of the Rapture say that the doctrine is nothing but escapism or an attempt to flee from the real world. Well, right now I'm living in the real world, and if I wanted to escape it, I could think of no better way than working for the Kingdom of God while waiting for the coming of my Lord. I'm thrilled that Jesus Christ is my Lord and Savior, that heaven is my home, and that I'm not going to walk in the fires of an eternal hell. If that's escapism, so be it.

Let's face it: Everyone wants to escape from the coming doomsday (as they perceive it). Environmentalists want to escape extinction caused by pollution. The disarmament globalists want to escape obliteration due to a nuclear war.

The Bible teaches us to prepare for our escape, which will come at the Rapture: "How shall we escape if we neglect so great a salvation?" (Hebrews 2:3). How do we prepare? We accept Jesus Christ as our Savior and Lord, and we look for His coming.

Believe in this truth: Christ is coming for His bride at the Rapture. This glorious event is both literal and visible, for "every eye will see Him," and it could occur at any moment (Revelation 1:7).

THE BRIDEGROOM WAITS
FOR HIS BRIDE

In order to better understand the meaning behind some of the symbolic language used to describe the Rapture, we must also understand the Jewish roots of our faith. The mystery of the Rapture is explained in the nuptial chain of events of a traditional Hebrew wedding.

In the ancient biblical ceremony, the bridegroom or an agent of the bridegroom's father went out in search of a bride. An example is when Abraham sent his servant to secure a bride for Isaac. If it was a good match, the bride or her family would often agree to the marriage without ever seeing the future groom.

Next, a price would be established for the bride—twenty camels, a dozen silver bracelets, or whatever the groom had to offer. The agreed-upon price was called a *mohar*. The bride and groom were now betrothed and legally bound to each other, though they did not yet live together. Next, a scribe would draw up a *ketubah*, or marriage contract. The document would include the bride's price, the rights of the bride, and the promise of the groom to honor, support, and abide with his bride.

Finally, the groom would present the bride with gifts. Most grooms today give their brides a ring as evidence of love and commitment, but in ancient times the gift could have been almost anything. If the bride accepted her groom's gift, they shared a cup of wine called the cup of the covenant, and the betrothal was complete. Before leaving her home, however, the groom would tell his bride, "I go to prepare a place for you. I will return again to you."

In the biblical custom, the bridegroom then went to his father's house to prepare a *chuppah*, or wedding canopy. Meanwhile, the bride made herself ready, and she had to stay ready, for she had no idea when her groom would return. She was consecrated for her betrothal and set apart while she waited for her groom. The bride took a *mikvah*, or cleansing bath, to purify herself for the coming wedding. Often, she kept a light burning in the window and an extra jar of oil on hand, lest the bridegroom come in the night and find her unprepared.

No engraved invitations were sent out for the wedding. When the young bridegroom was asked for the date of his wedding, he could only reply, "No man knows except my father." Why? Because he could not go get his bride until his father approved of his preparations.

When the groom's father decided everything was in order, he released his son to fetch his bride. The groom arrived at the bride's house with a shout and the blowing of a trumpet, or *shofar*. Once announced, the bridegroom presented the previously agreed-upon marriage contract to the father of his intended bride. The groom claimed her as his own and took her to his father's house. His father received the couple and placed the hand of the bride in the hand of his son. At that moment, she became his wife. This act was called the presentation.

After the presentation, the bridegroom would bring his bride to the bridal chamber he had gone to prepare. There he would introduce her to his friends who had heard the trumpet and come to celebrate the marriage feast. In 2 Corinthians 11:2, Paul wrote to the Church, "For I am jealous for you with godly jealousy. For I have betrothed you to one husband, that I may present you as a chaste virgin to Christ."

In like manner, Christians are betrothed to Christ through the new covenant written on our hearts and sanctified by the blood of Christ. We love our Heavenly Groom, whom we have not seen but believe may come at any moment. This is a powerful word picture of what God has prepared for us! We are the betrothed bride of Christ, sought by the Holy Spirit and purchased at Calvary with the precious blood of Jesus. Paul said, "For you were bought at a price" (1 Corinthians 6:20). The Almighty Father looked down from heaven and accepted the price of our redemption. We, the bride, accepted the Groom and the evidence of His love for us. Our betrothal contract is the Word of God, for it contains every promise our loving Groom has made on our behalf.

We received gifts at our betrothal. When we accepted Him, Jesus gave us the gift of eternal life! God Himself has given us the Holy Spirit, who has bestowed His own gifts of grace, faith, love, joy, peace, longsuffering, kindness, goodness, faithfulness, gentleness, and self-control. Like the bride in her purifying *mikvah*, we have been baptized with water and by the cleansing power of the Holy Spirit (Luke 3:16; Acts 1:5).

As we wait for our Bridegroom, Jesus has returned to His Father's house to prepare everything for our arrival. Before He departed this earth, Jesus said, "In My Father's house are many mansions; if it were not so, I would have told you. I go to prepare a place for you. And if I go and prepare a place for you, I will come again and receive you to Myself; that where I am, there you may be also" (John 14:2–3).

How do we publicly demonstrate our acceptance of Christ? Just like the bride, each time we take the Communion cup and drink the wine, we proclaim our wedding vows to our beloved Lord. We demonstrate that we love only Him, that we are loyal to Him, and that we are waiting for Him. Like the eager bride, we keep our lamps burning in the interim and strive to be ready, for we don't know when He might arrive.

Our Bridegroom will soon come for us. Make no mistake; we must wait with our ears attuned to hear the trumpet sound.

Remember this truth—the Church is not going into or through the Tribulation. We're going home to the city where the Lamb is the Light, to the city where roses never fade, to the city inhabited by Abraham, Isaac, Jacob, and King Jesus.

We have not yet seen our Bridegroom face-to-face, but we love Him and "rejoice with joy inexpressible and full of glory" (1 Peter 1:8) for His return.

OUR WEDDING GARMENTS

What happened in an ancient Hebrew wedding after the bridegroom took his bride home? She stood before him and awaited his appraisal. If she was wise, she had prepared a trunk with her wedding clothes, and she adorned herself in the beautiful garments she had made out of her love for her bridegroom.

In biblical times the marriage feast was a celebration to honor not the bride, as is our custom, but the bridegroom. All the guests who assembled at the marriage supper were expected to compose poems and sing songs to honor him as they appreciated the beauty and grace of his bride.

Jesus, the blessed Bridegroom, will be honored, not because

of who we are, but because of who He has made us to be. In Ephesians 5:27, Paul referred to this analogy when he wrote that Christ gave Himself for the Church so that "He might present her to Himself a glorious church, not having spot or wrinkle or any such thing, but that she should be holy and without blemish."

We're not holy by nature. We're not holy by practice. But the bride is the Father's love gift to the Son in honor of His obedience to the Father's will. When Jesus, the Bridegroom, is presented with His bride, He will say, "She is beautiful, without spot or wrinkle," and He will rejoice as He leads her to the marriage banquet.

Imagine, if you will: After bringing the bride to his house, the bridegroom takes her into his chamber, looks her in the eye, and says, "Soon I will take you in to meet all my friends. They will want to praise you and exclaim over your beauty, so look into your trunk and pull out those garments you have prepared for our marriage feast."

What would you do if you looked into your hope chest and found nothing? Or if you found only poorly made garments? You would be embarrassed beyond words before your loving bridegroom, his father, and the assembled witnesses.

J. Vernon McGee asks a very important question of the bride:

> The wedding gown of the church is the righteous acts of the saints. . . . The wedding gown will be used only once, but we will be clothed in the righteousness of Christ throughout eternity. . . . Through the ages believers have been performing righteous acts which have been accumulating to adorn the wedding gown. By the way, what are you doing to adorn that wedding gown?[9]

THE JUDGMENT SEAT OF CHRIST

The analogy of wedding garments translates into the reality of Christ's judgment seat. Soon after the Rapture, all believers will stand before the judgment seat, the *"bema* seat" of Christ.

In ancient Greece, the *bema* seat was never used as a judicial bench where criminals were either pardoned or sentenced; instead it referred to a raised platform in the sports arena on which the umpire sat. From this platform the judge rewarded all contestants and winners.

As Christians, we run the race set before us. If we play by the rules established in the Word of God, we will be ushered to the *bema* seat to stand, not before heads of state, but before the Son of God.

Paul wrote, "For we must all appear before the judgment seat of Christ, that each one may receive the things done in the body, according to what he has done, whether good or bad" (2 Corinthians 5:10).

At this judgment seat, we are not judged on whether we are saved, for everyone before the *bema* seat is a believer. Paul wrote, "There is therefore now no condemnation to those who are in Christ Jesus" (Romans 8:1). Christ took all my judgment at Calvary. If He paid my penalty in full, there is no sin judgment to face at the *bema* seat of Christ. Paul said it is the believer's works that are brought into judgment, in order that they may be determined to be good or bad.

Concerning the word *bad* (*phaulos*), Dwight Pentecost observed that Paul did not use the usual word for *bad* (*kakos* or *poneras*), either of which would signify that which is ethically or morally evil, but rather a word that means "good for nothing" or "worthless." The Lord will reward our deeds done in His Name and the qualities under examination at the *bema* seat will be our character and faithfulness.

This is why Paul wrote, "But I discipline my body and bring it into subjection, lest, when I have preached to others, I myself should become disqualified" (1 Corinthians 9:27). Paul wasn't concerned about losing his salvation, but that his deeds might be found to be worthless.

When we appear before Christ's judgment seat, that which is within us will be revealed to all present. The Bible says, "Man looks at the outward appearance, but the LORD looks at the heart" (1 Samuel 16:7). It's not possible for us to know what motives drive people to serve God. For one it may be an absolutely altruistic expression of servanthood. Another, who works just as diligently, may serve to receive applause and recognition from others. Your motives will be revealed and exposed before all at the judgment seat of Christ. In 1 Corinthians 3:11–15, Paul wrote:

> *For no other foundation can anyone lay than that which is laid, which is Jesus Christ. Now if anyone builds on this foundation with gold, silver, precious stones, wood, hay, straw, each one's work will become clear; for the Day will declare it, because it will be revealed by fire; and the fire will test each one's work, of what sort it is. If anyone's work which he has built on it endures, he will receive a reward. If anyone's work is burned, he will suffer loss; but he himself will be saved, yet so as through fire.*

On display at the *bema* seat will be five great crowns bestowed upon the bride as the loyal and trustworthy servants of Christ. The bride will stand before the Lord for a final review

127

of our faithfulness. It is here that He will reward us for the lives we have lived. Our rewards will be partly based on how faithfully we served the Lord (1 Corinthians 9:4–27; 2 Timothy 2:5), how we obeyed the Great Commission (Matthew 28:18–20), and how we overcame sin (Romans 6:1–4):

1. To steadfast believers tested by prison and persecution even to the point of death, the Lord will give a crown of life (Revelation 2:10).
2. A never-fading, never-tarnishing crown of glory awaits the self-sacrificing pastor who shepherds his flock (1 Peter 5:2–4).
3. Everyone who ran life's race with patience, endurance, and perseverance will receive a crown of righteousness (2 Timothy 4:8).
4. Evangelists and soul winners can eagerly anticipate receiving the crown of rejoicing (1 Thessalonians 2:19–20).
5. Finally, those who overcame all for the sake of the gospel will be handed an eternal victor's crown (1 Corinthians 9:25).

It is at the judgment seat of Christ that we will receive our crowns symbolizing our righteous deeds. James described this astounding moment: "Blessed is the man who endures temptation; for when he has been approved, he will receive the crown of life which the Lord has promised to those who love Him" (James 1:12).

Yes, the bride of Christ will receive beautiful jewel-encrusted crowns, and our gowns will be adorned by our righteous deeds.

Which crown will you wear?

Which of your works will be burned, and which will endure?

Will you take your Bridegroom's arm with the scent of smoke upon you? Or will you join Him, dressed in dazzling white, with a radiant crown upon your head? John warned all believers, "Hold fast what you have, that no one may take your crown" (Revelation 3:11). We must all run the race and run it to win!

The marriage of the Lamb (Bridegroom) to His Church (the bride) will take place in heaven, after the judgment seat of Christ, and it will be immediately followed by the Marriage Supper celebration:

"Let us be glad and rejoice and give Him glory, for the marriage of the Lamb has come, and His wife has made herself ready." And to her it was granted to be arrayed in fine linen, clean and bright, for the fine linen is the righteous acts of the saints.

Then he said to me, "Write: 'Blessed are those who are called to the marriage supper of the Lamb!'"

(Revelation 19:7–9)

Of course, as of this moment, the Master's Son, Jesus Christ, waits to come for His bride. When He comes to fetch her away, anyone who has believed in Him and His lordship will go to the place He has prepared. If you are a believer in Christ, there is a place under the wedding canopy especially reserved for you.

CHAPTER FIVE

11:54 PM

Russia Invades Israel

Then you [Russia] will come from your place out of the far north, you and many peoples with you, all of them riding on horses, a great company and a mighty army. You will come up against My people Israel like a cloud, to cover the land. It will be in the latter days that I will bring you against My land, so that the nations may know Me, when I am hallowed in you, O Gog [Russia], before their eyes.
Ezekiel 38:15–16

You are a citizen of Iran. Your life has been made very difficult due to the sanctions against your country. Your wife no longer sings in the house; she spends every spare moment at the market, trying to barter yesterday's bread for cough syrup so your little ones can sleep through the night. These are dark days, but you and your countrymen endure them because the Ayatollah assures you that the day of victory will make all sacrifices worthwhile.

You come home from a long day's work, sit in your living room, and turn on the television. The face of the most powerful political and spiritual leader in Iran instantly fills the screen, and again he is denouncing America and Israel. "But the time has come," he says, his eyes brightening as the camera zooms in on his angry face, "for us to settle the old scores. The dead will be avenged, and Allah will be praised! We will march upon the settlement of Israel and rid the land of the invaders. Those who have distorted the faith and exchanged the gift of Allah for heresy and rebellion will be purged from the land!"

The camera pulls back, and you see rows of men—several in full military regalia, others wearing the traditional chafiyeh (headdress)—and alongside them is their president. All nod in unison at every word spoken by their Supreme Leader; then, in an instant, the screen flickers and changes to a jubilant group of your countrymen dancing in the streets of Tehran. "The invasion has begun!" The Ayatollah's voice underlines the celebration. "Our stalwart allies, the people of Russia, and our brothers in arms have united to cleanse Palestine once and for all! Victory to Allah!"

A tide of goosebumps races up your arms and collides at the back of your neck. In public, of course, you will praise the Ayatollah. But here, in the privacy of your small home, you cannot help but wonder if this time will end like the last time—with bombs, death, and humiliation in the face of Iran's enemies.

But surely the Supreme Leader has learned an important lesson. He would not attack again without a sure and certain confidence that this time he would be victorious. And surely, with Russian weapons, commanders, and technology behind him, this time he will be.

You breathe a sigh of relief as you consider the implications. Hitler needed to conquer all of Europe to destroy most of the Jewish people, but Iran need only to conquer a tiny territory, inhabited by fewer than 10 million people. What can the Jewish people do against the hundreds of millions who will remain loyal to Russia? Absolutely nothing.

But the God of Abraham, Isaac, and Jacob can do everything—and He will once again deliver Israel from her enemies.

THE CLOCK EDGES FORWARD

Make no mistake—at some moment in the countdown to the End of the Age, the above scenario or something very similar will occur. Russia, together with Iran, Turkey, Libya, and the radical Islamic Arab nations, will lead a massive attack upon the nation of Israel. It will take place after the Rapture of the Church and after the Antichrist is revealed. The coming battle is clearly described in the book of the prophet Ezekiel, chapters 38 and 39.

I believe this attack will happen three and a half years after the Antichrist makes a seven-year peace treaty with Israel, presenting himself as the prince of peace.

Please remember that the Rapture of the Church will cause a global economic crash as millions upon millions in the workforce instantly leave planet earth. The nations of the earth will be scrambling for economic stability and will welcome the charismatic and brilliant leader out of Europe who comes as a man of peace but is in fact the chief son of Satan. He is the Antichrist who will create a global Government of Ten to rule the earth. He will force every person on earth to take his mark, either on their forehead or right hand. Those who take the mark will lose their souls; those who don't take the mark will lose their lives at the hand of the Antichrist's ruling government.

THE VALLEY OF DRY BONES

In the thirty-seventh chapter of Ezekiel, the prophet was caught up by the Spirit of God and taken to a valley of dry bones. Ezekiel looked at a multitude of dry bones, scattered by wind, rain, and wild animals, and wondered what God had in mind by bringing him to such a place.

God then asked the prophet a strange question: "Son of man, can these bones live?" (v. 3).

Ezekiel lifted his brows. Perhaps it was a trick question because those bones had been dead a long time, but with God anything is possible. The prophet, ever a diplomat, gave a careful answer: "O Lord GOD, You know" (v. 3).

God then told Ezekiel to prophesy to the valley of dry bones, and as Ezekiel spoke, the bones began to clatter and clack. An arm bone rushed to join its wrist; a thigh bone snapped to a leg bone. Broken ribs came together; crushed skulls curved to their original state. And then, as the prophet watched, sinew grew over the bones, then skin appeared and covered it over. In moments, the bones were miraculously changed into human bodies, complete and whole, but they did not move or breathe (v. 8).

Then God spoke again. "Prophesy to the breath," He told Ezekiel. "Prophesy, son of man, and say to the breath, 'Thus says the Lord GOD: "Come from the four winds, O breath, and breathe on these slain, that they may live"'"(v. 9).

So Ezekiel obeyed, and breath came into the bodies, and they opened their eyes and lived. They stood, an exceedingly great army of men (v. 10).

And God said to Ezekiel:

Son of man, these bones are the whole house of Israel. They indeed say, "Our bones are dry, our hope is lost, and we ourselves are cut off!" Therefore prophesy and say to them, "Thus says the Lord GOD: 'Behold, O My people, I will open your graves and cause you to come up from your graves, and bring you into the land of Israel. Then you shall know that I am the LORD, when I have opened your graves, O My people, and brought you up from your graves. I will put My Spirit in you, and you shall live, and I will place you in your own land. Then you shall know that I, the LORD, have spoken it and performed it,' says the Lord."

(Ezekiel 37:11–14)

This prophecy is a message of hope regarding Israel's restoration. The Jewish people were scattered throughout the world like the bones in the valley, but God brought them back together in 1948. J. Vernon McGee noted, "They have a flag, they have a constitution, they have a prime minister, and they have a parliament. They have a police force and an army. They have a nation, and they even have Jerusalem [the eternal capital of Israel]."[1] In other words—they have come back to life!

GOG AND MAGOG ARE DRAWN TO ISRAEL

In Ezekiel 38 the prophecy continues: "Now the word of the LORD came to me, saying, 'Son of man, set your face against Gog, of the land of Magog, the prince of Rosh, Meshech, and Tubal, and prophesy against him'" (v. 1).

The leader is "Gog," and his kingdom is "Magog." Magog is referred to as one of the sons of Japheth in Genesis 10:2 and 1 Chronicles 1:5.

Who is Gog? He is called the prince of "Rosh, Meshech, and Tubal," which are provinces of Asia Minor.

Currently this geographical area is occupied by Iran, Turkey, and the southern provinces of the Commonwealth of Independent States (CIS)—the Russia-dominated confederation that arose in place of the former Soviet Union. Since its inception in 1991, the CIS has been plagued with infighting, ethnic and regional hostilities, and bloody civil wars.[2] The citizens of these disjointed states experience political upheavals, coups, and attempted assassinations on a regular basis. With the mounting turmoil and uncertainty of the future, the citizens are looking for someone to lead them—someone who appears confident and stable.

Vladimir Vladimirovich Putin has been both the president of the Russian Federation and its prime minister since 1999. He is a former KGB agent who seems determined to restore Russia to its former power and prestige, which it once possessed before the disintegration of the USSR. He has even managed to guarantee his longevity as president "after a controversial national referendum . . . paved the way for him to stay in power until 2036."[3] Mark my words, the Iron Fist of the KGB is more powerful than ever and is still actively silencing its opponents.

Consider the high-profile case of just one critic of Putin's government, from early 2021:

> Russian opposition leader and fierce Kremlin critic Alexei Navalny was sentenced to three and a half years in prison. . . .
>
> His supporters—more than 8,000 of whom have been detained by police at protests . . . —immediately called for a new show of support.
>
> Navalny, a 44-year-old anti-corruption investigator who's become an increasingly large thorn in Putin's side, was arrested . . . upon his return [to Russia] from Germany, where he spent five months recovering from poisoning with the Soviet-era nerve agent Novichok.
>
> He says the attack took place in Russia, on Putin's orders—an allegation the Kremlin has denied.
>
> Navalny was found guilty . . . of violating the terms of a previous 3.5-year suspended sentence, stemming from an earlier conviction that he has always dismissed as politically motivated.
>
> According to the prison service and Russian prosecutors, Navalny failed to check in with prison officials while he was recovering in Germany [from being poisoned!].[4]

By mid-2021, the Russian court labeled Navalny and his organization "extremist" and banned all their activities. The ruling prohibited Navalny's allies from running for office.[5] The Old Guard is still alive and well.

Meanwhile, Putin has taken several steps to increase Russian influence in the Middle East. Between 2000 and 2010, he sold arms valued at $1.5 billion to Syria. In 2017, Putin entered a long-term contract with Syria that allowed Russia to maintain troops and a naval presence in that country.

In late 2019, Putin and Turkey's President Erdogan signed a cooperative military deal, creating a safe zone along the Turkish-Syrian border with the intent of ending military action by separatist-controlled Syrian Kurdistan.[6] During the US conflict with Libya, Putin expressed strong support for Libya and condemned US intervention. In October 2019, he struck six trade agreements with the United Arab Emirates, totaling $1.3 billion and involving health, energy, and advanced technology.[7]

In Lebanon, Russia and Iran together sponsor Hezbollah, a highly trained and well-equipped terrorist organization with its stated purpose being to wipe Israel out of existence. Putin has a natural interest in Israel because of its strategic geographical crossroads position, its large natural-gas deposits, and its warm-water seaports.

Add all these ancient and modern factors together, and it makes perfect sense to think that Russia is the likely leader in a future major aggression against Israel.

A great military movement under the leadership of Gog, the leader of Rosh, is described in Ezekiel 38:4: "I will turn you around, put hooks into your jaws, and lead you out, with all your army, horses, and horsemen, all splendidly clothed, a great company with bucklers and shields, all of them handling swords."

Next God identified the invaders that will join Russia: Persia, Ethiopia, Libya, Gomer, and Togarmah (vv. 5–6).

Persia is easily identified as Iran. Ethiopia and Libya refer to the Arab Islamic nations of the Arabian Peninsula. I believe when Ezekiel spoke of Persia, Ethiopia, and Libya he was speaking of the contemporary extremist Arab states that are constantly calling for a holy war to exterminate Israel. Gomer and Togarmah most likely refer to the region now occupied by the nation of Turkey.

Since Israel is the fourth-greatest military power on the face of the earth, there is no way the Arabs could defeat Israel by themselves. So they will enter into an agreement with Russia, who will be more than willing to share their military organization, know-how, and weapons.

In brief summation, it is reasonable to assume that Russia will lead a massive pan-Islamic extremist military force to invade Israel. Russia's motive is to control the oil-rich Persian Gulf and the warm-water port at Haifa, while the fundamentalist Islamics have a burning passion to control Jerusalem. This Russian/pan-Islamic union is an unholy alliance that will lead to the invasion described by Ezekiel in chapters 38 and 39.

ISRAEL, THE KEY TO END TIMES

It is not possible to understand Bible prophecy without an understanding of Israel's past, present, and future. Israel will be the epicenter of the earth's shuddering travails in the last days, and all pivotal events will revolve around the Holy Land and the family of Abraham.

Israel was founded by a sovereign act of God. God said to Abraham:

> *Get out of your country,*
> *From your family*
> *And from your father's house,*
> *To a land that I will show you.*

> (Genesis 12:1)

Upon Abraham's arrival in the Promised Land, God repeated this promise: "To your descendants I will give this land" (Genesis 12:7).

There are presently two controversies concerning Israel: the first states that God's promise to Abraham was not a promise of literal land, but a promise of heaven. Those who embrace this position teach that Israel lost favor with God through disobedience, and the Church is now Israel. The second controversy holds that the promise to Abraham and his descendants is literal but also conditional, based on Israel's obedience to God.

This common confusion is instantly corrected by the clear teaching found in the Word of God. In Genesis 22:17, God told Abraham, "Blessing I will bless you, and multiplying I will multiply your descendants as the stars of the heaven and as the sand which is on the seashore."

God mentioned two separate and distinct elements: stars and sand. The "stars of the heaven" represent the Church. Stars, as light, rule the darkness, which is the commission of the Church. Jesus said, "You are the light of the world" (Matthew 5:14). Jesus is called the "Bright and Morning Star" (Revelation 22:16). And Daniel 12:3 tells us:

> *Those who are wise shall shine*
> *Like the brightness of the firmament,*
> *And those who turn many to righteousness*
> *Like the stars forever and ever.*

Stars are heavenly, not earthly. They represent the Church, Abraham's spiritual seed.

The "sand of the seashore," on the other hand, is earthly and represents an earthly kingdom with a literal Jerusalem as its capital city. Both stars and sand exist at the same time, and neither ever replaces the other. In the same way, the nation of Israel and the Church exist at the same time and do not replace each other.

The Bible clearly teaches that God's promise to Abraham was literal and unconditional. Let's examine the Scripture to verify beyond any doubt that God intended for Abraham and the Jewish people to possess a literal land.

In Genesis 13, God told Abraham, "Lift your eyes now and look from the place where you are—northward, southward, eastward, and westward; for all the land which you see I give to you and your descendants forever . . . Arise, walk in the land through its length and its width, for I give it to you" (Genesis 13:14–15, 17).

Genesis 15:18 states "On the same day the LORD made a covenant with [Abraham], saying: 'To your descendants I have given this land, from the river of Egypt to the great river, the River Euphrates.'" Then God listed the heathen tribes living in that area at that time. This is a very literal land. Heaven is not described, even allegorically, as the area between the river of Egypt (the Nile) and the Euphrates.

God told Abraham concerning the Jewish people in Egypt's bondage: "Know certainly that your descendants will be strangers in a land that is not theirs, and will serve them, and they will afflict them four hundred years. And also the nation whom they serve I will judge; afterward they shall come out with great possessions" (Genesis 15:13–14).

After four hundred years of slavery, Abraham's descendants became a nation of more than two million people, and they physically left a literal Egypt for a literal Promised Land. The books of Exodus, Leviticus, Numbers, Deuteronomy, and Joshua deal with Israel's return to the earthly Promised Land—not heaven.

The title deed to the Promised Land was passed to Isaac from Abraham. In Genesis 26:3, God said to Isaac, "Dwell in this land, and I will be with you and bless you; for to you and your descendants I give all these lands, and I will perform the oath which I swore to Abraham your father."

That same deed to the Promised Land was then passed to Jacob from Isaac. In Genesis 28:13, God told Jacob, "I am the LORD God of Abraham your father and the God of Isaac; the land on which you lie I will give to you and your descendants." You have to be in a very literal land to lie on it!

Was God's promise to Abraham conditional? Those who believe God's promise depended upon Abraham's obedience simply do not understand the blood covenant.

In the Old Testament, a blood covenant was the most solemn and binding of all covenants. The agreeing parties would sacrifice an animal or animals, split the carcasses in half down the backbone and place the divided parts opposite each other on the ground, forming a pathway between the pieces. Then the participants would join hands, recite the contents of the covenant, and walk between the divided halves of the slain animals.

The blood covenant meant they were bound until death, and if either one broke the terms of the covenant, his blood would be spilled just as the blood of the animals had been spilled. God gave to Abraham, Isaac, Jacob, and their descendants a permanent, unconditional agreement of a Promised Land in which they were to actually live forever, based on the blood covenant God made with Abraham.

In Genesis 15, God commanded Abraham to take a heifer, a female goat, a ram, a turtledove, and a pigeon. All were split in half except the birds. Because no man can look upon God and live, God placed Abraham in a deep sleep as He prepared to enter a blood covenant with him.

In his sleep, Abraham saw "a smoking oven and a burning torch that passed between those pieces" of the slain animals (v. 17). In the Old Testament, the burning lamp signified the presence of the shekinah glory of God. God was binding Himself by blood covenant to Abraham and his descendants forever, saying: "To your descendants I have given this land" (v. 18). Never did God suggest the covenant was conditional. Exactly the opposite is true; this covenant depends only on the faithfulness of God, not on man; and the Almighty is ever faithful.

Psalm 89:30–37 confirms this unconditional promise when God said:

> *If his [Israel's] sons forsake My law*
> *And do not walk in My judgments,*
> *If they break My statutes*
> *And do not keep My commandments,*
> *Then I will punish their transgression with the rod,*
> *And their iniquity with stripes.*
> *Nevertheless My lovingkindness I will not utterly take*
> *   from him,*

Nor allow My faithfulness to fail.
My covenant I will not break,
Nor alter the word that has gone out of My lips.
Once I have sworn by My holiness;
I will not lie to David:
His seed shall endure forever,
And his throne as the sun before Me;
It shall be established forever like the moon,
Even like the faithful witness in the sky.

God clearly said He would "not lie to David" and not break covenant with Israel, even though the nation disobeyed Him. He also said that the moon is a witness of this covenant. When you walk out at night and see the moon shining in the heavens, you are seeing God's eternal witness speaking to all men in all languages that His covenant with Israel is forever.

ISRAEL: REBORN, REBUILT
AND RESTORED

What about the future of Israel? Israel was reborn as a nation in a day on May 15, 1948, when the United Nations recognized the state of Israel. This was a fulfillment of Isaiah 66:8:

Who has heard such a thing?
Who has seen such things?
Shall the earth be made to give birth in one day?
Or shall a nation be born at once?
For as soon as Zion was in labor,
She gave birth to her children.

Through the prophet Ezekiel, God wrote, "I will bring you out from the peoples and gather you out of the countries where you are scattered, with a mighty hand, with an outstretched arm. . . . Then you will know that I am the LORD" (Ezekiel 20:34, 38).

Regarding the restoration of Israel, the prophet Amos wrote:

> *"I will bring back the captives of My people Israel;*
> *They shall build the waste cities and inhabit them;*
> *They shall plant vineyards and drink wine from them;*
> *They shall also make gardens and eat fruit from them.*
> *I will plant them in their land,*
> *And no longer shall they be pulled up*
> *From the land I have given them,"*
> *Says the LORD your God.*

(Amos 9:14–15)

The prophets declared that the nation of Israel would be reborn, rebuilt, and restored. The Jewish people will never again be removed from their covenant land, no matter who looks toward Israel with covetousness—Gog, Magog, Persia (Iran), or any Arab country. That is God's promise now and forevermore.

THE ABRAHAM ACCORDS

President Trump has always been a friend to Israel. In December 2017, under his administration, the US was the first country to recognize Jerusalem as Israel's capital. This historic event blazed a trail for other nations to follow. As of the spring of 2021, the nation of Kosovo officially opened its embassy in Jerusalem. Kosovo becomes the third country with an embassy in the Holy

City. The US was the first to move its embassy to Jerusalem in May of 2018, and Guatemala shortly followed. Kosovo, however, is the first predominantly Muslim nation to make this historic move. In June 2021 Honduras became the fourth country to relocate its embassy to Jerusalem.[8]

Since the 1970s, various attempts to establish peace between Israel and its Arab neighbors failed until President Trump and Prime Minister Benjamin Netanyahu met at the White House in September of 2020. It was on this day that they signed the historic Abraham Accords with the United Arab Emirates (UAE) and Bahrain.

I traveled to the UAE in mid-2021 to meet with their foreign minister, Sheikh Abdullah bin Zayed, the signatory to the Abraham Accords. I personally thanked him for signing the Accords and for showing commendable courage in defending Israel during the conflict with Hamas. It was also my distinct privilege to tour the "We Remember" Holocaust exhibition in Dubai—the first of its kind in the Arab world. Who could have imagined this would be possible?

Conversely, Iran, which represents the modern-day Persian Empire, has had an obsession to destroy the Jews since the days of Haman thousands of years ago. And it is still Iran's ultimate objective to create a nuclear weapon that will irradiate every Jewish person in Israel.

Shortly after taking office in June of 2021, Israel's newly elected government under Prime Minister Naphtali Bennett and Alternate Prime Minister Yair Lapid stated, "More than ever, Iran's nuclear program must be halted immediately, rolled back entirely and stopped indefinitely."[9]

Current Foreign Minister Yair Lapid, whom I had the pleasure of meeting while in Israel, noted that "Iran's newly elected president Ebrahim Raisi, known as 'The Butcher of Tehran,' is its most extreme president yet and committed to quickly advancing Tehran's nuclear program. An extremist, [Raisi] is responsible for the deaths of thousands of Iranians. He is committed to the regime's nuclear ambitions and to its campaign of global terror."[10]

After Ebrahim Raisi, Iran's judiciary chief, was declared to have won the election, the leaders of Russia, Turkey, Syria, and the Hamas terror group sent congratulations for his landslide victory. Russian President Vladimir Putin expressed hope for "further development of a constructive bilateral cooperation." A spokesperson at the Russian embassy in Tehran further stated, "We respect the choice of the Iranian people. We are ready to consistently strengthen cooperation with the Islamic Republic in all directions, as we did under previous Iranian presidents."[11]

During the Hamas rocket bombardment of Israel in the summer of 2021, Raisi praised Hamas for fighting against the Jewish state and called for the liberation of Jerusalem from Israeli control: "The heroic resistance of Palestine once again shone in a great and decisive test and forced the occupying Zionist regime to take another step [back] towards the lofty ideal of liberating Holy Qud ["city of Jerusalem" in Farsi]."[12]

The Gog-Magog union of Russia and Iran remains rock solid, and its fundamental message is clear: "Death to Israel!"

WHY WOULD RUSSIA WANT TO ATTACK ISRAEL?

There are several likely reasons why Russia would invade Israel.

First, the Russian economy may be dangerously weak due to the effects of coronavirus and oil price wars, but they do have some very valuable assets such as comprehensive knowledge in nuclear development, military skill, and a cache of weapons. Why not offer these assets to Iran and the Arab nations who desperately need them in exchange for Middle Eastern alliances, which will counter the economic clout of the European Union?

Second, although Russia is rich with oil reserves and other natural resources, these assets tend to be in remote areas that are difficult to reach. This makes the drilling and transportation of the oil to their refineries cost prohibitive. Therefore, Russia must establish alliances with the countries that control the world's vast oil fields—the Arab nations surrounding the Persian Gulf.

In order to efficiently transport that oil—and, in the future, effectively engage in shipping military weapons—Russia needs warm-water seaports. Historically, Russia has coveted warm-water ports, that is, ports that are free of ice all year round. Russian maps reveal that her seaports are primarily located in the frozen Arctic Ocean and to the east. Her navy is essentially iced-in-place for several months during the year.

Currently, Russian ships must travel through the Black Sea, then through the narrow Bosporus, to the Sea of Marmara and finally through the Aegean Sea before reaching the Mediterranean. Israel, however, is located right *on* the Mediterranean—and is considered a prime shipping area. Seaports in Israel offer access to the Atlantic Ocean through the Mediterranean, the Strait of Gibraltar, and to the Indian Ocean on to the Pacific southward through the Red Sea and the Gulf of Aden. In order to achieve its goal of military dominance, Russia must have direct access to these oceans.

Russia's lust for Israel increased in 2010 when geologists discovered enormous deposits of oil existing beneath Israel's Golan Heights area. They estimate the field to be plentiful enough to meet all of Israel's oil and gas needs for a century or more. Having this oil and gas would benefit Israel not only by providing an ample supply of fuel but also because it can disrupt Putin's political manipulation of natural gas sent to Europe.

Russia's interest in Israel and the Middle East is not a new development. As stated earlier, Russia's growing ambitions to regain the power it lost as the dominant state of the defunct USSR has been apparent for more than two decades. In 1996, Uri Dan and Dennis Eisenberg, writers for the *Jerusalem Post*, noted the following:

> [Russia] has reverted to the policies of the former Soviet Union and is aiming to become a dominant power in the Middle East once again. The Russian bear has already hugged Iran in a honeyed embrace by building a nuclear reactor for the mullahs of Teheran. It is also working hard to take Syria back into its bosom, holding out modern arms for Damascus as bait.[13]

Syria has taken the bait. In early 2017, Putin signed an agreement with Syria allowing the Russian military to expand its presence and exercise absolute control of their naval base at the port of Tartus. The treaty allows Russia to dock eleven warships—including nuclear vessels—and to maintain a military air base nearby. It also gives them sovereignty over the territory and administrative jurisdiction. This agreement is to last forty-nine years.[14]

After President Trump pulled US troops out of Syria, Putin wasted no time in convincing the Syrian government to allow Russian troops to deploy to the Turkish-Syrian border. This new alliance between Russia, Syria, and Turkey will ensure that Kurdish fighters leave the area, thus increasing Russia's growing influence in Middle Eastern affairs.[15]

As stated before, in addition to its solid foothold in Syria, Russia has also made significant inroads into Iran. As far back as the mid-1990s, Russia aided Iran's nuclear program by completing its reactor plant in Bushehr. Putin took advantage of the increasing tension between the US and Iran, mostly over its development of nuclear power, and increased Russia's relations with the Iranians.

Russia initially complied with the 2010 UN resolution that imposed sanctions against selling nuclear or military equipment to Iran. But in 2016, Putin defied the ban and delivered a mobile surface-to-air S-300 missile defense system to the Iranians, with plans for a $10 billion deal to supply helicopters, planes, and artillery.[16]

Russia and Iran have joined to sponsor the highly trained and well-equipped terrorist organization Hezbollah, which is based in Lebanon and has a significant presence in Syria, Iraq, and Yemen. Hezbollah's stated purpose is the same as the PLO's—the complete slaughter of all Jewish people. Hezbollah poses a serious danger to Israel, as they will attack in two contrasting ways: with guerrilla ambushes and raids at Israel's borders and with their vast arsenal of Iranian rockets.

Why do Israel's enemies need so many rockets? Because of the high effectiveness of Israel's Iron Dome—their all-weather defense system, which has been the bedrock of their defense since 2011. The moment an enemy rocket is launched toward Israel, the Iron Dome senses it and computes its route. If the system determines that the missile will hit a populated area, it instantly fires a defense missile, which intercepts and destroys the incoming warhead.

In one fifty-day span of conflict in 2014, Hezbollah fired 4,594 rockets into Israel, and the Iron Dome destroyed all but 70 of those that posed a danger to innocent people—a success rate of 90 percent.[17] Hezbollah, along with its backers Iran and Russia, are convinced their increased arsenal of a half-million rockets will overwhelm Israel's vaunted defense system.

More recently, in an eleven-day span (May 10–21, 2021), Hamas in Gaza launched more than 4,500 rockets toward Israel. Israel's Iron Dome once again came to the rescue by intercepting 90 percent of the rockets.[18] Remember, Israel is surrounded on three sides by hostile forces dedicated to its complete annihilation. Iranian and Syrian forces, backed by Russia, daily hover on the Israeli-Syrian border. Hezbollah is firmly ensconced on Israel's northern border with Lebanon. And Hamas, a brutal terrorist organization, has complete control of the Gaza Strip to Israel's southwest.

Jordan, which is divided from Israel only by the trickling Jordan River on the east, has enjoyed peace with Israel since signing a peace treaty in 1994. Egypt, which shares a border with Israel on the western side of the Sinai Peninsula, signed a treaty with Israel in 1980, which is still in effect at this writing. But all Arab treaties with Israel are fragile and tenuous, and the treaties with both of these nations have suffered many strains over real and perceived provocations.

Putin has visited King Abdullah of Jordan several times, and you can be sure he is ready to take immediate advantage of any breach in the Israel-Jordan relationship.

Putin's relationship with Egypt is much closer. In 2005 he promised to work with Egyptian President Mubarak to create a nuclear program in Egypt. Since the coup that made Abdel Fattah al-Sisi head of the Egyptian government, Putin's ties with Egypt are even closer. Military and economic cooperation have increased between the two countries, and in 2014, Putin signed a protocol that resulted in Russia delivering billions of dollars' worth of arms to Egypt.[19]

In other words, Putin is so eager to have a presence in the Middle East that he will practically give weapons away. Russia needs economic and military partners, strategic ports, and Israel's newly discovered oil reserves, and the Bear will stop at nothing to get them.

Not much has changed, Aleksandr Solzhenitsyn (1918–2008), Russian novelist, historian, and political prisoner whose works exposed the brutality of the Soviet labor camps, said, "Everything you add to the truth, subtracts from the truth." And of the Russian governmental mindset he said: "We know they are lying, they know they are lying and they know we know they are lying, we know they know we know they are lying—but they are still lying."

No matter how Russia explains away their aggressive actions in the Middle East, we know what they are up to. By joining forces with Russia, the radical Islamic nations, which despise Israel, benefit greatly from the strength of Russia's armed forces. The extremist Islamic nations have oil and cold, hard cash. Russia has military might and the organizational skills necessary to launch a military invasion. Together, they will make a treaty guaranteeing mutual support.

Russia will say to the Islamic nations, "You want Jerusalem and the Temple Mount as a holy site. We want the Persian Gulf and Israeli oil. Let's join forces. Each of us will get what we desire and together, we will rule the world!"

The final and most compelling reason for Gog and Magog to invade Israel is the "hook" that God will put in Gog's jaw. Regardless of the political or economic reasons, God will inexorably draw Gog and his forces toward Israel. It will soon be payday for the anti-Semitic nations who have historically tormented, tortured and murdered the Jewish people.

The end result? A massive pan-Islamic military force led by Russia's high command will come against Israel "like a cloud, to cover the land" (Ezekiel 38:16); and the God of Israel will kill five out of six in that invading army (Ezekiel 39:2 KJV).

THE GUARDIAN OF ISRAEL NEVER SLEEPS

Like so many of man's plans, what is intended for evil, God will turn for good. This monumental battle between Israel and the coalition of Islam and Russia is no exception. For while this dreaded collaborative army believes they have devised this battle of their own accord to serve their own ends, in fact it is God the Father who has brought them.

Ezekiel 38:4–6 declares:

> *I will turn you around, put hooks into your jaws, and lead you out, with all your army, horses, and horsemen, all splendidly clothed, a great company with bucklers and shields, all of them handling swords. Persia, Ethiopia, and Libya are with them, all of them with shield and helmet; Gomer and all its troops; the house of Togarmah from the far north and all its troops— many people are with you.*

In Ezekiel 38:16 we see again that the Lord has orchestrated this battle: "It will be in the latter days that I will bring you against My land."

Gog will not see the hand of God; he will see only Israel, "the land of those brought back from the sword and gathered from many people on the mountains of Israel, which had long been desolate; they were brought out of the nations, and now all of them dwell safely" (v. 8). As a result of Israel's peace treaties with the Palestinians in which she has traded valuable land for peace, she will appear to be more vulnerable than ever—a "'land of unwalled villages . . . a peaceful people, who dwell safely, all of them dwelling without walls, and having neither bars nor gates' . . . and against a people gathered from the nations, who have acquired livestock and goods, who dwell in the midst of the land" (vv. 11–12).

As a result, the coalition will "come from [its] place out of the far north, [it] and many peoples with [it], all of them riding on horses, a great company and a mighty army. [The coalition] will come up against My people Israel like a cloud, to cover the land" (vv. 15–16).

But what the invaders do not realize is that God has sworn by His holiness to defend Jerusalem. Since God created and defends Israel, those nations that fight against Israel fight against God Himself.

The invaders find an easy entry into the Promised Land. Whether in honor of Allah or in obedience to a Russian military commander, the attackers will embark on their plan to commit plunder and genocide.

The vast majority will never know what hit them. The defeat of Israel's enemies will be sudden, devastating, complete, and divine.

GOD'S RESPONSE TO THE THREAT

God said that when Gog sweeps down from the north, "My fury will show in My face" (Ezekiel 38:18). King David said, "Behold,

155

He who keeps Israel shall neither slumber nor sleep" (Psalm 121:4). After watching the Jews of the Holocaust walk into the gas chambers, after seeing the "apple of His eye" thrown into the ovens and their ashes dumped by the tons into the rivers of Europe, after seeing the "land of milk and honey" run red with Jewish blood in five major wars for peace and freedom, God will stand up and shout to the nations of the world. He will shatter His silence and say, "Enough!"

First, He will send a mighty earthquake so devastating it will shake the mountains and the seas, and every wall shall fall to the ground:

> *Surely in that day there shall be a great earthquake in the land of Israel, so that the fish of the sea, the birds of the heavens, the beasts of the field, all creeping things that creep on the earth, and all men who are on the face of the earth shall shake at My presence. The mountains shall be thrown down, the steep places shall fall, and every wall shall fall to the ground.*
>
> (Ezekiel 38:19–20)

Second, God will send massive confusion to the multinational fighting force, and "every man's sword will be against his brother" (v. 21). This is exactly what God did when He commanded Gideon to blow the trumpets and break the pitchers. The Midianites became divinely confused and turned their swords on each other. Gideon won a great military victory without one casualty. God will do it again in defense of Israel.

Third, God will open fire with His divine artillery: "And I will bring him to judgment with pestilence and bloodshed; I will rain down on him, on his troops, and on the many peoples who are with him, flooding rain, great hailstones, fire, and brimstone" (v. 22).

This passage could be interpreted in two ways: First, the "fire and brimstone" may refer to Israel's release of nuclear weapons in a last-ditch attempt to prevent annihilation. "Pestilence" might refer to a more nefarious implements of war—biological weapons. I can easily imagine a scenario in which the Russians fire biological weapons upon Israel, but God miraculously turns the missiles or causes them to misfire, so that the invaders are destroyed by their evil intention!

The second interpretation is that this event is a repeat of Sodom and Gomorrah. God will blast Israel's enemies into oblivion by raining fire and brimstone from heaven. In either case the results will be equally catastrophic. However, suppose Israel decides to launch a nuclear attack upon Russia in a desperate attempt to halt the approaching Russian-Arab army . . . what would Russia's response be?

WILL NUCLEAR BOMBS FALL ON THE UNITED STATES?

Ezekiel 39:6 presents a possible scenario that I find interesting in the light of today's technology. Let's look at the verse: "And I will send fire on Magog and on those who live in *security in the coastlands*. Then they shall know that I am the LORD" (emphasis added).

There's something you should know about the old USSR. During the height of the Cold War, Soviet scientists designed and built a "doomsday machine," which they named Perimeter, or Dead Hand. According to Dr. Bruce Blair of the Brookings Institution, this doomsday system, with backups and fail-safes aplenty, was designed to detect any attack upon Russia and automatically send

157

a message to a network of intercontinental ballistic missiles via orbiting communications satellites. In the event Russian commanders are wiped out by an American first strike, the Dead Hand would deliver orders to the weapons systems to retaliate in full. This system was built upon the doctrine of "mutually assured destruction" in the event of any nuclear exchange.[20]

In December 2018, Russian military expert and former rocket commander Viktor Yesin warned that if the US ever deploys intermediate-range missiles in Europe, "Russia will consider adopting a doctrine of a preemptive nuclear strike." He added this note, warning us that Dead Hand is not only being maintained today but it has been upgraded: "The Perimeter system is functioning, it has even been improved. But when it works, we will have little left—we can only launch those missiles that will survive after the first attack of the aggressor."[21]

Unfortunately, the preassigned targets assigned to the Perimeter system are American cities.

For certain we will sustain damage from this war, for God says: "All men who are on the face of the earth shall shake at My presence. The mountains shall be thrown down, the steep places shall fall, and every wall shall fall to the ground" (38:20). Whether this devastation arises from a nuclear war or a catastrophic earthquake, every person on the face of the planet will tremble as God wreaks destruction upon Israel's enemies during the End of the Age.

GOG AND MAGOG ARE ANNIHILATED

Ezekiel's graphic account of the battle's aftermath makes clear just how thorough and disastrous will be the defeat of this

Russian-Arab coalition. The prophet opened chapter 39 by stating: "Thus says the Lord GOD: 'Behold, I am against you, O Gog.'" This comment will go down in history as one of the greatest understatements of all time as the internet will be filled with pictures and reports of millions of bloated bodies lying in the hot, Middle Eastern sun.

Why is God against Russia? I can think of several reasons, including the fact that Soviet leaders imposed atheism upon millions of people for most of the twentieth century. For years during the Cold War we watched atheism emanate from Moscow and infiltrate scores of countries around the world. The late Tim LaHaye said:

> No nation in the history of the world has destroyed more flesh than Russia through the spread of Communism . . . but her greatest sin has not been the destruction of flesh, as serious as that is. Her greatest sin has been the soul damnation caused by her atheistic ideology. . . . No nation has done more to destroy faith in God than Communist Russia, thereby earning the enmity of God.[22]

The most crucial reason God is set against Gog, I believe, has to do with the fact that God promised Abraham, "I will bless those who bless you, and I will curse him who curses you" (Genesis 12:3). For years, Russia has cursed and persecuted the Jews.

The Russian word *pogrom*, which pertains to the persecution and massacre of a helpless people, passed into the international lexicon after the devastation of Russian Jews in the Ukraine in 1903. The Russian nation has been persecuting Jews since the time of the czars. In the span of time between the two world

159

wars, the entire Jewish population of the Russian Western Military District—including the old, the sick, and children—were forcibly evacuated into the interior of the country on twelve hours' notice.

In August 1924, *Dawn* magazine reported the following, quoting a 1923 statement from a Dr. Adler, the chief rabbi of Great Britain:

> Wholesale slaughter and burials alive, rape and torture, became not merely commonplace but the order of the day. There were pogroms that lasted a week; and in several cases the systematic and diabolic torture and outrage and carnage were continued for a month. In many populous Jewish communities there were no Jewish survivors left to bury the dead, and thousands of Jewish wounded and killed were eaten by dogs and pigs; in others the Synagogues were turned into charnel houses by the pitiless butchery of those who sought refuge in them. If we add to the figures quoted above the number of those indirect victims who in consequence of the robbery and destruction that accompanied these massacres were swept away by famine, disease, exposure and all manner of privations—the death total will be very near half a million human beings.[23]

The blood of at least 500,000 innocent Jews cries out for justice, and God will deliver it in His battle against Gog and Magog.

THE AFTERMATH OF THE BATTLE

Ezekiel did not tell us how many will die in the battle, but he told us how many will be left alive: only a "sixth part" (Ezekiel 39:2 KJV).

The casualty rate for this battle will be 84 percent, an unheard-of figure in modern warfare.

Then the people of Israel will set about burying the dead invaders in a mass grave eerily reminiscent of the huge trenches the Nazis used to bury Jewish dead in the Holocaust. They will call this killing field the "Valley of Hamon Gog," which means "the valley of the multitude of Gog [Russia]" (Ezekiel 39:11–16):

> *"It will come to pass in that day that I will give Gog a burial place there in Israel, the valley of those who pass by east of the sea; and it will obstruct travelers, because there they will bury Gog and all his multitude. Therefore they will call it the Valley of Hamon Gog. For seven months the house of Israel will be burying them, in order to cleanse the land. Indeed all the people of the land will be burying, and they will gain renown for it on the day that I am glorified," says the Lord GOD. "They will set apart men regularly employed, with the help of a search party, to pass through the land and bury those bodies remaining on the ground, in order to cleanse it. At the end of seven months they will make a search. The search party will pass through the land; and when anyone sees a man's bone, he shall set up a marker by it, till the buriers have buried it in the Valley of Hamon Gog. The name of the city will also be Hamonah. Thus they shall cleanse the land."*

(Ezekiel 39:11–16)

Some Bible scholars believe this valley of the dead might be in modern-day Lebanon. It is a country of mountains that run from north to south, with a valley in between two mountain ridges and a logical path for a Russian-led attack on Israel. The prophet Habakkuk mentioned Lebanon in a passage dealing with the End of the Age: "For the violence done to Lebanon will cover you" (Habakkuk 2:17). Zechariah 11:1 declares, "Open your doors, O Lebanon, that fire may devour your cedars." The dead bodies of the invaders will be strewn in the fields and mountains surrounding Israel, and the seven-month burial detail will involve every Israeli citizen as every last bone shall be buried.

Not only will there be tremendous carnage, but the weapons left by these devastated forces will provide fuel for Israel for seven years—through the years of the Tribulation:

> *"Then those who dwell in the cities of Israel will go out and set on fire and burn the weapons, both the shields and bucklers, the bows and arrows, the javelins and spears; and they will make fires with them for seven years. They will not take wood from the field nor cut down any from the forests, because they will make fires with the weapons; and they will plunder those who plundered them, and pillage those who pillaged them,"* says the Lord GOD.
>
> (Ezekiel 39:9–10)

Can you imagine weapons burning for seven years? I was in Israel during Operation Peace for Galilee led by General Ariel Sharon back in the eighties. I personally saw Israeli eighteen-wheel trucks bringing back the spoils of war in a convoy that stretched farther than my eye could see. These were supplies that had been stored in Lebanon by the Soviet Union and were said to be enough to keep 500,000 men in combat for six months. As great as those spoils were, it was only a matter of days before the Israeli army collected and stored them. But Ezekiel describes a war so vast it will take seven years to gather and dispose of the weapons of war.

Israel will derive an unexpected benefit from this. The prophet said the plunder from this massive invasion will provide Israel with fuel for seven years, and because of this the forest will be spared. In that verse alone, we find proof that this will occur in the Latter Days—even contemporary times. Prior to the State of Israel's establishment in 1948, the land was almost entirely deforested, a desert wasteland. But the Israelis have worked hard to make the Promised Land bloom again.

It has been my distinct honor over the years to plant a tree each time I go to Israel. We have a Night to Honor Israel forest that we systematically add to each time we visit. I'm happy to know that the invading armies will leave such a massive amount of fuel that "my" trees will survive the war!

THIS IS NOT ARMAGEDDON

Though the world will reel at the damage sustained in this battle, it is important to realize that this is not Armageddon. The battle that is to come at the end of the Great Tribulation (Ezekiel 38) involves only a select group of nations, while Armageddon will involve all the kings of the earth—a true world war.

Armageddon will involve a battlefield spanning two hundred miles from north to south and one hundred miles from east to west. The battle will be most intense in the Valley of Jehoshaphat (Joel 3:2, 12). The word *Jehoshaphat* means "God judges." Zechariah locates the final judgment of the invading nations near the city of Jerusalem (Zechariah 14:1–5). When Jesus returns to the Mount of Olives, He will lead His army down to Edom to rescue the Jewish remnant hiding there. His clothes will be stained with blood and His sword will be drenched in blood (Isaiah

163

34:6; 63:1–3). The wicked people of Bozrah will be slaughtered to such an extent that the mountains will flow and the land will be soaked with blood.

John the Revelator described the brutality of Armageddon in Revelation 14:17–20:

> *Then another angel came out of the temple which is in heaven, he also having a sharp sickle.*
>
> *And another angel came out from the altar, who had power over fire, and he cried with a loud cry to him who had the sharp sickle, saying, "Thrust in your sharp sickle and gather the clusters of the vine of the earth, for her grapes are fully ripe." So the angel thrust his sickle into the earth and gathered the vine of the earth, and threw it into the great winepress of the wrath of God. And the winepress was trampled outside the city, and blood came out of the winepress, up to the horses' bridles, for one thousand six hundred furlongs.*

God's promise to Abraham will be fulfilled, "I will curse him who curses you" (Genesis 12:3).

ISRAEL ACKNOWLEDGES THE HAND OF GOD

Why does God allow the nations to make war upon Israel? There is only one answer: for His glory. Ezekiel wrote, "I will magnify Myself and sanctify Myself, and I will be known in the eyes of many nations. Then they shall know that I am the LORD. . . . So the house of Israel shall know that I am the LORD their God from that day forward" (Ezekiel 38:23; 39:22).

Mankind worships a pantheon of so-called gods. Some worship Buddha, others Muhammad, some Satan. Some worship gods of their own making, but who is the Almighty God? When the God of Abraham, Isaac, and Jacob destroys the enemies of Israel, there will be no doubt that He is the One and only Jehovah God: "It will be in the latter days that I will bring you against My land, so that the nations may know Me, when I am hallowed in you, O Gog, before their eyes" (Ezekiel 38:16).

Truly the only way we can understand the significance of this incredible defeat is to accept it as an act of God. Ezekiel wanted the world to know that God supernaturally will neutralize the enemies of Israel that His name might be glorified.

A second reason for this great display of God's power is to testify to His beloved Jewish people that He alone is their God. Through their miraculous deliverance, the hearts of the Jewish people will begin to turn again to the God of Abraham, Isaac, and Jacob:

> "So the house of Israel shall know that I am the LORD their God from that day forward. The Gentiles shall know that the house of Israel went into captivity for their iniquity; because they were unfaithful to Me, therefore I hid My face from them. I gave them into the hand of their enemies, and they all fell by the sword. According to their uncleanness and according to their transgressions I have dealt with them, and hidden My face from them."
>
> Therefore thus says the Lord GOD: "Now I will bring back the captives of Jacob, and have mercy on the whole house of Israel; and I will be jealous for My holy name—after they have borne their shame, and all their unfaithfulness in which they were unfaithful to Me, when they dwelt safely in their own

land and no one made them afraid. When I have brought them back from the peoples and gathered them out of their enemies' lands, and I am hallowed in them in the sight of many nations, then they shall know that I am the LORD their God, who sent them into captivity among the nations, but also brought them back to their land, and left none of them captive any longer. And I will not hide My face from them anymore; for I shall have poured out My Spirit on the house of Israel," says the Lord GOD.

(Ezekiel 39:22–29)

The Israel of Ezekiel's vision of the valley of dry bones will know beyond all doubt that the God of Abraham, Isaac, and Jacob orchestrated Israel's victory in this coming Gog-Magog battle. I don't know exactly how it will happen, but I do know that Israel will rebuild her temple, and it is logical to assume her spiritual reawakening will be the result of seeing God's mighty hand in the defense of the Jewish nation. The Bible is very clear that this event will happen in the middle of the Tribulation, a moment yet to arrive in our study of God's Prophetic Clock.

CHAPTER SIX

11:55 PM

The Time of the Tribulation Begins

According to a 2016 poll conducted by LifeWay Research, 49 percent of all US pastors believe in a literal being called the Antichrist who will arise in the future. That percentage is much higher among evangelical Christians (Baptists: 75 percent; Pentecostals: 83 percent). The poll also revealed that 43 percent of evangelical pastors believe in the Rapture that will ignite a period called the Tribulation.
Bob Smietana, Baptist Press[1]

God's Prophetic Clock has advanced to 11:55 P.M. The time is the beginning of the seven-year period of tribulation, and this moment represents the first three and a half years. Many characteristics mark this interval, including war, pestilence, famine, earthquakes, and devastation.

THE PURPOSE OF THE TRIBULATION

The word *tribulation* strikes terror into the hearts of men, and justly so. God's portrait of the seven-year Tribulation reveals a time of unspeakable horror that can only be described as hell on earth. J. Dwight Pentecost provided ten descriptive biblical words that characterize the coming of this dreadful time: "wrath, judgment, indignation, trial, trouble, destruction, darkness, desolation, overturning, and punishment."[2]

Why does God allow this seven-year period to come to the world? The Bible give us at least three reasons for the Tribulation:

1. To prepare for Israel's regeneration and restoration, bringing the nation into complete submission to the God of Abraham, Isaac, and Jacob in anticipation for the coming Messiah (Jeremiah 30:11; Zechariah 12:10)
2. To punish the godless Gentile nations and all unbelievers for their sin of rejecting His Son, and for bowing before the Antichrist (Revelation 16:2)

3. To demonstrate God's ultimate power in crushing the wicked nations of the world—especially those that have come against Israel. History will repeat itself. The Pharaoh of Egypt, who refused to let God's people go, mockingly said, "Who is the LORD?" (Exodus 5:2). Ten monstrous plagues later, which left Egypt in economic ruin and mourning the death of every firstborn, Pharaoh received his answer and begged the children of Israel to leave.

In the coming Tribulation, God Almighty will pour out His awesome power on the whole world. There will be twenty-one separate acts of judgment on the earth associated with the Seven Seals, the Seven Trumpets, and the Seven Bowls (Revelation 1–6; 8–9; 11; 16). On one occasion, God will release four angels on a day certain to kill one third of humanity (Revelation 9:15). He will prove to a rebellious world that He alone is God, and there is no other.

One of the most graphic descriptions of this season is found in Zephaniah 1:12–18:

> "And it shall come to pass at that time
> That I will search Jerusalem with lamps,
> And punish the men
> Who are settled in complacency,
> Who say in their heart,
> 'The LORD will not do good,
> Nor will He do evil.'
> Therefore their goods shall become booty,
> And their houses a desolation;
> They shall build houses, but not inhabit them;

They shall plant vineyards, but not drink their wine."

The great day of the LORD is near;
It is near and hastens quickly.
The noise of the day of the LORD is bitter;
There the mighty men shall cry out.
That day is a day of wrath,
A day of trouble and distress,
A day of devastation and desolation,
A day of darkness and gloominess,
A day of clouds and thick darkness,
A day of trumpet and alarm
Against the fortified cities
And against the high towers.

"I will bring distress upon men,
And they shall walk like blind men,
Because they have sinned against the LORD;
Their blood shall be poured out like dust,
And their flesh like refuse."

Neither their silver nor their gold
Shall be able to deliver them
In the day of the LORD's wrath;
But the whole land shall be devoured
By the fire of His jealousy,
For He will make speedy riddance
Of all those who dwell in the land.

In Matthew 24:5–8, Jesus specifically described the first three and a half years of the Tribulation:

For many will come in My name, saying, "I am the Christ,"
and will deceive many. And you will hear of wars and rumors
of wars. See that you are not troubled; for all these things must
come to pass, but the end is not yet. For nation will rise against
nation, and kingdom against kingdom. And there will be fam-
ines, pestilences, and earthquakes in various places. All these
are the beginning of sorrows.

In the fifth chapter of Revelation, the apostle John was even more specific about the beginning of the Tribulation. In his vision, a scroll sealed with Seven Seals was in the right hand of Him who sat on the throne of heaven. A voice proclaimed, "Who is worthy to open the scroll and to loose its seals?" (v. 2). John wept when no one in heaven or on the earth or under the earth was able to open the scroll.

But one of the elders comforted John: "Do not weep. Behold, the Lion of the tribe of Judah, the Root of David, has prevailed to open the scroll and to loose its seven seals" (v. 5).

John watched as Jesus Christ, the perfect sacrificial Lamb, came forward before the host of believers, numbering "ten thousand times ten thousand, and thousands of thousands" out of every tribe and tongue and people and nation (v. 11). While the redeemed Church sang praises to Him, Jesus stepped forward and opened the scroll. At this time, the world's doomsday scenarios move from the realm of mere possibility to stark reality.

THE FIRST SEAL—THE RIDER
ON THE WHITE HORSE

After Jesus Christ opened the scroll, He broke the First Seal. John saw a white horse: "He who sat on it had a bow; and a crown was given to him, and he went out conquering and to conquer" (Revelation 6:2).

The man on the horse will be a master imitator. Because prophecy tells us Jesus will return on a white horse at His Second Coming (19:11), this man will ride a white horse, but he will be no savior. He will be given a bow, a weapon of war, and a crown, and he will go forth to conquer the world.

And he will be successful.

The first and most noticeable sign of the Tribulation's advent is the rise of a global personality, a man whose name will be on everyone's lips. He will be called the Antichrist.

Is the Antichrist a literal man? For some, he is just an allegory. Look at this quote from the *Dallas Morning News*:

> Many scholars argue that the Bible's authors never intended their work to be interpreted as literal prophecy. The Antichrist in Revelation, for example, alludes to the Roman emperor Nero, who represented evil to early Christians. The passage predicting Armageddon, scholars say, refers to the final victory of good over evil, not a literal battle. The Rapture, mentioned in 1 Thessalonians, is an expression of the apostle Paul's confidence that Christians will spend eternity with Jesus.[3]

My reaction to the above statement? Poppycock! First of all, any so-called scholar who talks about the Bible's "authors" doesn't understand how the Bible was written. You could talk about the Bible's "writers," "scribes," or even "secretaries," but you don't dare talk about the Bible's "authors." An author is one who writes words he has created in his mind or imagination. The Bible was authored by the Holy Spirit of God, not by man. Men recorded the words of God under the absolute control of

173

the Holy Spirit so that the finished product was simply the *Word of God*!

Secondly, the men who wrote what the Holy Spirit dictated were not creating allegories or fables. John the Revelator wasn't tactfully trying to describe the Roman emperor Nero, nor was he being metaphorical when he described Armageddon with great and vivid detail. And if Paul merely wanted to reassure Christians that they would spend eternity with Jesus, why didn't he just say so? No, my friend. The Rapture is going to occur exactly as it is described, Armageddon is an actual battle, and the Antichrist is a living, breathing person whom the Bible calls the "son of perdition" (2 Thessalonians 2:3).

John wasn't the only biblical writer to mention the Antichrist. He was shown to Daniel not once, but three times through God's prophetic visions. Let's look at the story beginning in Daniel's tenth chapter.

DANIEL'S FASTING AND PRAYER

"In the third year of Cyrus king of Persia a message was revealed to Daniel," also known by his Babylonian name Belteshazzar (Daniel 10:1). The year was about 534 BCE, four years after Daniel received the vision of the Seventy Weeks.

In the first few verses of the tenth chapter, Daniel said that he had been in a mournful fast for three full weeks: "I ate no pleasant food, no meat or wine came into my mouth, nor did I anoint myself at all, till three whole weeks were fulfilled" (Daniel 10:3).

Something had shaken Daniel to his core. We're not told why Daniel was in mourning, but we can chance a guess. Daniel told us it was the third year of Cyrus's reign, and we know that in his first year Cyrus proclaimed a decree that allowed any able and willing Hebrew to return to the land. Daniel may have been upset because so few of his people returned to Jerusalem (this was prior to the time when Nehemiah and his co-laborers formed a committee to rebuild the walls).

Daniel may have also been in mourning because he realized he would not return to his beloved Jerusalem, God's holy city. He was nearing ninety and perhaps felt he could be of more use to his people in his powerful palace position.

After twenty-one days of prayer and fasting, Daniel went outside to the banks of the Tigris River and had a vision unlike any he had ever seen. Some Bible scholars believe he saw the transfiguration of Jesus Christ:

> I lifted my eyes and looked, and behold, a certain man clothed in linen, whose waist was girded with gold of Uphaz! His body was like beryl, his face like the appearance of lightning, his eyes like torches of fire, his arms and feet like burnished bronze in color, and the sound of his words like the voice of a multitude.
>
> And I, Daniel, alone saw the vision, for the men who were with me did not see the vision; but a great terror fell upon them, so that they fled to hide themselves. Therefore I was left alone when I saw this great vision, and no strength remained in me; for my vigor was turned to frailty in me, and I retained no strength. Yet I heard the sound of his words; and while I heard the sound of his words I was in a deep sleep on my face, with my face to the ground.
>
> (vv. 5–9)

Daniel's description of this heavenly visitor is strikingly similar to that of John, who saw Jesus and recorded his impression in Revelation:

One like the Son of Man, clothed with a garment down to the feet and girded about the chest with a golden band. His head and His hair were white like wool, as white as snow, and His eyes like a flame of fire; His feet were like fine brass, as if refined in a furnace, and His voice as the sound of many waters.

(Revelation 1:13–15)

Though others were with Daniel, they did not see the vision, but they were frightened enough to retreat and hide in the bushes along the river. The apostle Paul had a similar experience on his way to Damascus. He saw Jesus and heard His voice while his frightened companions saw nothing. But the supernatural power of God was clearly evident on the Damascus Road (Acts 9:1–8).

Overcome with the power and significance of what he had seen, Daniel, already weak from fasting, fainted dead away:

Suddenly, a hand touched me, which made me tremble on my knees and on the palms of my hands. . . .

Then he said to me, "Do not fear, Daniel, for from the first day that you set your heart to understand, and to humble yourself before your God, your words were heard; and I have come because of your words. But the prince of the kingdom of Persia withstood me twenty-one days; and behold, Michael, one of the chief princes, came to help me, for I had been left alone there with the kings of Persia. Now I have come to make

you understand what will happen to your people in the latter
days, for the vision refers to many days yet to come."
(Daniel 10:10, 12–14)

This nameless angel—who most believe to be Gabriel—explained that he was hindered by the prince of Persia, the satanic ruler over the kingdom of Persia, the god of this world. The holy angel was given his marching orders on the first day of Daniel's fasting and prayer but was blocked for twenty-one days by this demonic prince! We are not given a name for this being, but he was a high-ranking principality assigned by Satan to control the demonic activities in the kingdom of Persia where Daniel lived.

Satan, you see, has a host of fallen angels under his command, just as God has a host of angels. The fallen angels are organized into hierarchies, and the mighty prince of Persia was able to hinder God's angelic messenger until the archangel Michael arrived to help clear the way.

Demons are earthbound creatures who walk the earth (Matthew 12:43) and crave the habitation of a body. When Jesus cast the demons out of the demoniac (Matthew 8:28–34), they begged to be permitted to enter the swine. When Lucifer led the rebellion in heaven, one-third of the angels joined him and were banished—these are the fallen angels spoken of in the book of Jude, verse 6: "And the angels [fallen] who did not keep their proper domain, but left their own abode, He [God] has reserved in everlasting chains under darkness for the judgment of the great day."[4] Therefore, demons and fallen angels are two different satanic battalions with the same commander-in-chief, Satan himself!

Why would Satan want to block an angel from appearing to Daniel? God wanted to give Daniel important prophetic

177

information, and Satan didn't want Daniel to have it. In sharing this information about Satan's restraint and struggle via the prince of Persia, the heavenly messenger lifted the curtain on the invisible warfare going on all around us. Paul wrote "For we do not wrestle against flesh and blood, but against principalities, against powers, against the rulers of the darkness of this age, against spiritual hosts of wickedness in the heavenly places" (Ephesians 6:12). A principality in Satan's high command is a chief ruler of the highest rank (Ephesians 1:21; Colossians 2:10).

Interestingly enough, before he left, the angel told Daniel, "And now I must return to fight with the prince of Persia; and when I have gone forth, indeed the prince of Greece will come. . . . (No one upholds me against these, except Michael your prince. Also in the first year of Darius the Mede, I, even I, stood up to confirm and strengthen him)" (Daniel 10:20–11:1).

There's a wealth of assurance in the angel's parenthetical comment. "It was I," the angel confided in a daring whisper, "who strengthened King Darius after you were thrown into the lions' den. Do you remember how distraught the king was? He spent a sleepless night worrying about you and beseeching God, so it was I who gave him the strength to trust that God would save your life."

The angel also mentioned that soon he would not only encounter the prince of Persia again, but also the prince of Greece. Why? Because the prophecy the angel related was concerning Greece.

The angel began the prophecy by explaining that it had to do with Daniel's people: "Now I have come to make you understand what will happen to your people [the nation of Israel] in the latter days, for the vision refers to many days yet to come" (Daniel 10:14).

Immediately *after* the Church is taken up in the Rapture,

God's Prophetic Clock will begin to tick again, and the world will enter Daniel's Seventieth Week. The phrase "The vision is for many days," lets Daniel know that a long period of time was involved in the vision's fulfillment.

What followed was the most detailed account of history in all the Bible, yet it was prophetic when written. The angel's words covered events from approximately 529 to 164 BCE, and we will see how they were exactly fulfilled. It also covered events that will be precisely achieved in the seven-year Tribulation that is just before us.

THE LAW OF DOUBLE REFERENCE

As we look at the next passage in Daniel, it's important to understand the prophetic law of double reference. This very important principle means simply this: "Two events, widely separated as to the time of their fulfillment, may be brought together into the scope of one prophecy. This was done because the prophet had a message for his own day as well as for a future time. By bringing two widely separated events into the scope of the prophecy both purposes could be fulfilled."[5]

Daniel's vision in chapters 10–12 was a prophecy of double reference. It pertained to what would come in the near future, as well as what would come to pass at the End of the Age. Chapter 11 contains a remarkable example of prewritten history. The angel explained exactly what would happen in Greece, Egypt, and Syria during the years between the Old and New Testaments. When you read Daniel's prophecy and compare it to world history, you'll see why prophecy should never be confused or equated with allegories or metaphors.

Many Bible scholars speak of the intertestamental period (the four hundred years between the Old and New Testaments) as a time of prophetic silence, but God was not silent at all about this time period. With absolute omniscience, He predicted the rise of fall of great empires and described the nations that would oppress the children of Israel for generations to come. He foretold the rise of a ruler, Antiochus Epiphanes, who would be a picture, or type, of the prince to come referred to in Daniel's vision of Seventy Weeks. Antiochus Epiphanes, however, was by far the lesser of two evils.

Since we are primarily concerned about events of the Tribulation, let me summarize the now-historical events included in the vision of Daniel 11:

- Four Persian kings would rule after Cyrus. The fourth, King Xerxes, who married Esther, was the wealthiest of the four.[6]
- "A mighty king" would stand up (v. 3). This was Alexander the Great of Greece.
- This king would be uprooted, and his kingdom divided into four pieces and given to people not of his posterity (v. 4). Alexander died at age thirty-two, and his kingdom went to his four generals.[7]
- "Also the king of the South shall become strong, as well as one of his princes" (v. 5). One of the generals, Ptolemy, began a dynasty in Egypt, while Seleucus did the same in Syria.[8]
- "They shall join forces" (v. 6). Egypt and Syria made an alliance in 250 BCE, after both generals had died. Ptolemy II gave his daughter Berenice in marriage to the grandson of Seleucus, Antiochus II, which forced Antiochus II to divorce his first wife, Laodice I. After Ptolemy's death, in a series of vicious political maneuvers, Laodice had Antiochus II

poisoned, Berenice and her young son murdered, and her own son, Seleucus II, appointed to the throne.[9]

- "But from a branch of her roots one shall arise in his place" (v. 7). Berenice's brother, Ptolemy III, now ruled Egypt. To avenge his sister's death, Ptolemy III invaded Syria, dramatically pillaging its vast wealth.[10]

- "And he shall also carry their gods captive to Egypt" (v. 8). Ptolemy III plundered tons of Syrian treasure, including forty thousand talents of silver and twenty-five hundred golden idols.[11]

- "Also the king of the North shall come" (v. 9). Prior to his planned invasion of Egypt, Seleucus II died in 225 BCE. He was succeeded first by his eldest son, Alexander, who took the name Seleucus III Ceraunus, and later by a younger son Antiochus III the Great in 222 BCE.[12]

- "And the king of the South shall be moved with rage" (v. 11). The next few verses describe continuing warfare between Egypt and Syria. During this period Antiochus III won control of Palestine at a battle outside Sidon. He eventually gave his daughter Cleopatra (not the famous one) in marriage to Ptolemy V. Cleopatra turned out to be a loyal wife . . . just as Daniel had predicted (v. 17).[13]

- "After this he shall turn his face to the coastlands" (v. 18). Advised by Hannibal, the great Carthaginian general, Antiochus III eventually invaded Greece, where Roman warriors soundly defeated him.[14]

- "There shall arise in his place one who imposes taxes" (v. 20). Seleucus IV ruled in his father's stead but was soon murdered by his own commander Heliodorus after he returned from Jerusalem seeking to impose taxes on its citizens.[15]

ANTIOCHUS EPIPHANES:
A PROTOTYPE OF THE ANTICHRIST

Antiochus Epiphanes was the youngest son of Antiochus III, and at best, the angel of the Lord described him as a "vile person" who would "seize the kingdom by intrigue":

> *And in his place shall arise a vile person, to whom they will not give the honor of royalty; but he shall come in peaceably, and seize the kingdom by intrigue. With the force of a flood they shall be swept away from before him and be broken, and also the prince of the covenant. And after the league is made with him he shall act deceitfully, for he shall come up and become strong with a small number of people. He shall enter peaceably, even into the richest places of the province; and he shall do what his fathers have not done, nor his forefathers: he shall disperse among them the plunder, spoil, and riches; and he shall devise his plans against the strongholds, but only for a time.*
>
> (Daniel 11:21–24)

Bible Scholar Harold Willmington has said that those who knew Antiochus Epiphanes best nicknamed him "Epimanes," a word meaning "madman." Apparently, he "pretended to be a second century Robin Hood,"[16] as in stealing from one party and doling out plunder to others.

> *He shall stir up his power and his courage against the king of the South with a great army. And the king of the South shall be stirred up to battle with a very great and mighty army; but he shall not stand, for they shall devise plans against him. Yes,*

those who eat of the portion of his delicacies shall destroy him;
his army shall be swept away, and many shall fall down slain.
Both these kings' hearts shall be bent on evil, and they shall
speak lies at the same table; but it shall not prosper, for the end
will still be at the appointed time.

(vv. 25–27)

In 170 BCE, Antiochus Epiphanes defeated the Egyptian king
Ptolemy Philometor at a battle east of the Nile delta. Ptolemy lost
the battle because he was betrayed by counselors who sat at his
own dinner table (v. 26).

While returning to his land with great riches, his heart shall be
moved against the holy covenant; so he shall do damage and
return to his own land.

At the appointed time he shall return and go toward the
south; but it shall not be like the former or the latter. For
ships from Cyprus shall come against him; therefore he shall
be grieved, and return in rage against the holy covenant, and
do damage.

So he shall return and show regard for those who forsake
the holy covenant.

(vv. 28–30)

Antiochus advanced in a second military campaign against
Egypt but was stopped by Roman ships sailing from Cyprus.
In his fury, he turned toward Palestine, breaking his peace
treaty with the children of Israel. He wooed and flattered certain nonobservant Jews who were willing to "forsake the holy
covenant."

And forces shall be mustered by him, and they shall defile the sanctuary fortress; then they shall take away the daily sacrifices, and place there the abomination of desolation.

(v. 31)

Armed with information from disloyal spies, Antiochus came against Jerusalem in 171 BCE. In a violent rage of frustration, he murdered over forty thousand Jews and sold an equal number into slavery. He forbid the worship of the God of Israel in Zerubbabel's temple that had been erected by the returned exiles and offered pigs upon the altar. And in an act of ultimate desecration, Antiochus Epiphanes set up an image of the Hellenistic god Zeus, to be deified in Jerusalem's holy place.

THE ORIGIN OF HANUKKAH

Ever wonder where the Jewish holiday of Hanukkah originated? You'll find the answer in Daniel's prophetic timeline.

Antiochus began his anti-Jewish campaign on September 6, 171 BCE and it continued until December 25, 165 BCE when Judas Maccabeus and his followers restored true worship in Jerusalem's Second Temple through their famous revolt. The 2,300 days of Daniel 8:14 accounts for the time between the desecration of the temple by the Greek-Syrian oppressors and the Maccabees' rededication of it.

Hanukkah, or Chanukah, is the eight-day celebration on the twenty-fifth day of the Hebrew month of Kislev, commemorating the Maccabee victory over the forces of Antiochus Epiphanes. Hanukkah is not mentioned in the Old Testament because the Torah was written before the events that inspired the festival.

However, it is referred to in the New Testament when Jesus attends the "Feast of Dedication" (John 10:22–23).

According to the Talmud, Judah Maccabee and the other observant Jews that rededicated the temple witnessed a miracle. Judah ordered the cleansing of the temple, the rebuilding of its altar, and the lighting of the seven-branched golden candelabrum, which represented God's knowledge and creation. There was only enough unpolluted oil (not offered to idols) to keep the menorah lit for one day, but miraculously the menorah stayed lit for eight days.[17]

TIME OF GREAT SUFFERING

Those who do wickedly against the covenant he shall corrupt with flattery; but the people who know their God shall be strong, and carry out great exploits. And those of the people who understand shall instruct many; yet for many days they shall fall by sword and flame, by captivity and plundering. Now when they fall, they shall be aided with a little help; but many shall join with them by intrigue. And some of those of understanding shall fall, to refine them, purify them, and make them white, until the time of the end; because it is still for the appointed time.

(Daniel 11:32–35)

In this portion of Daniel's prophecy, we can see that the years ahead were to be a time of great suffering. Gentile nations will continue to batter the nation of Israel—Syria from the north, Egypt from the South, Rome from the West. Many people will fall away from the faith and try to immerse themselves in the predominant culture. Others will remain faithful to the God of Abraham, Isaac, and Jacob. These people, like the Maccabees, will be strong and "carry out great exploits." Some would fall and get up, being purged, refined, and strengthened as the End of the Age approaches.

THE WILLFUL KING

Now the angel took Daniel over a prophetic gap of time. He moved from foretelling the future about Antiochus Epiphanes to speaking about a man who will be very much like the pagan Seleucid king. The angel began to speak of the Antichrist, and Daniel dutifully recorded the description:

> *Then the king shall do according to his own will: he shall exalt and magnify himself above every god, shall speak blasphemies against the God of gods, and shall prosper till the wrath has been accomplished; for what has been determined shall be done. He shall regard neither the God of his fathers nor the desire of women, nor regard any god; for he shall exalt himself above them all. But in their place he shall honor a god of fortresses; and a god which his fathers did not know he shall honor with gold and silver, with precious stones and pleasant things. Thus he shall act against the strongest fortresses with a foreign god, which he shall acknowledge, and advance its glory; and he shall cause them to rule over many, and divide the land for gain.*
>
> (vv. 36–39)

Daniel had seen this *willful prince* before, in his vision of the four beasts (Daniel 7). He heard the man speak pompous words and watched "its body [the beast's] destroyed and given to the burning flame" (Daniel 7:11).

186

Daniel had also learned about the Antichrist in his vision of the ram and goat. Here the angel told Daniel:

> *A king shall arise,*
> *Having fierce features,*
> *Who understands sinister schemes.*
> *His power shall be mighty, but not by his own power;*
> *He shall destroy fearfully,*
> *And shall prosper and thrive;*
> *He shall destroy the mighty, and also the holy people.*
>
> *Through his cunning*
> *He shall cause deceit to prosper under his rule;*
> *And he shall exalt himself in his heart.*
> *He shall destroy many in their prosperity.*
> *He shall even rise against the Prince of princes;*
> *But he shall be broken without human means.*
>
> *And the vision of the evenings and mornings*
> *Which was told is true;*
> *Therefore seal up the vision,*
> *For it refers to many days in the future.*
>
> (Daniel 8:23–26)

The Antichrist will make his debut upon the stage of world history with hypnotic charm and charisma. In Revelation 13:1, John described him: "Then I stood on the sand of the sea. And I saw a beast rising up out of the sea, having seven heads and ten horns, and on his horns ten crowns, and on his heads a blasphemous name."

Notice that the beast rose from the sea—the sea, in prophetic symbolism, represents the Gentile nations of the world. He will come from a confederation that was once part of the Roman Empire. At one point in history, the Roman Empire stretched from Ireland across to Germany, Switzerland, down to Egypt and included Turkey, Iran, and Iraq. In Daniel's vision of the four beasts, the fourth beast had ten horns, which represented ten kingdoms (Daniel 7:19–25). The little horn (the Antichrist), sprouted from among the other ten, which is believed to be the ten divisions of the old Roman Empire.

In his rise to power, the Antichrist will first weave his hypnotic spell over one nation in the ten-kingdom federation, then over all ten. He will conquer three of the ten nations, (the seven heads and ten crowns of Revelation 13:1) then he will assume dominance over all of them. The Bible states that after the Antichrist's position is secure in the ten-nation federation, he will turn his predatory destruction toward the apple of God's eye—Israel.

The Antichrist will enter the world stage with a reputation of being a powerful negotiator, a military expert and a man of peace. However, Daniel 8:25 says that by peace he "shall destroy many." Like Hitler, the Antichrist will make peace treaties he doesn't intend to keep although he will guarantee peace for Israel and the Middle East.

This Willful Prince, having already amalgamated his control in Europe, will rule over his federation with absolute authority (Daniel 11:36). And by guarding Israel, the Antichrist will secure his chance to become a dominant military force in the Middle East. He will be a man who has paid his dues in the military and the political sense, and many will willingly follow him. The Antichrist's Middle East peace treaty will catapult him onto the world stage, and all will wonder after him.

It is a sad fact that those who deny the existence of God

eagerly believe in anything else. For example, no philosophy is more falsely contrived, highly improbable, blatantly foolish, or anti-science than the theory of evolution. Yet evolution has become the widely accepted secular explanation for the origin of mankind. The end-of-the-world scenario of manmade global warming was swallowed by many of the US populace almost the moment it was announced. Many who reject Christianity turn around and embrace New Age philosophy, astrology, Scientology, or some other form of occult spirituality.

As the familiar saying goes, "Those who stand for nothing fall for anything." The failure of the Western nations to stand strong in our Judeo-Christian beliefs explains why the world will fall so quickly for the lies of the Antichrist.

First John 2:18 boldly declares, "Little children, it is the last hour; and as you have heard that the Antichrist is coming, even now many antichrists have come, by which we know that it is the last hour." The Antichrist—capital A—is coming. Though many people through the years have been *against* Christ, there is coming a man who is the devil incarnate, the son of Satan, evil personified, and many will readily and eagerly accept him as their savior.

The Antichrist's three-point plan for world domination consists of a one-world economic system, a one-world government, and a one-world religion that will eventually focus its worship on the Antichrist himself.

THE ONE-WORLD ECONOMY

The idea of a one-world monetary system with a single universal currency has been seriously considered since the end of World

War II. It was proposed at the Bretton Woods conference shortly after the war when global financial experts met to discuss rebuilding war-torn Europe.

In 2009, the United Nations proposed a one-world system with a single currency. According to a report by the UN Conference on Trade and Development, "the system of currencies and capital rules which binds the world economy is not working properly, and was largely responsible for the financial and economic crises." In addition, "the present system, under which the dollar acts as the world's reserve currency, should be subject to a wholesale reconsideration."[18] It was the first time a major multinational institution had ever made such a vast proposal.

The Antichrist's economy is making this proposal a reality. His economy will be a totally cashless society in which every financial transaction will be electronically monitored. John, inspired by the Holy Spirit to write the book of Revelation, described the situation:

> *He causes all, both small and great, rich and poor, free and slave, to receive a mark on their right hand or on their foreheads, and that no one may buy or sell except one who has the mark or the name of the beast, or the number of his name.*

(Revelation 13:16–17)

When the Euro was first introduced, it existed only electronically, not in cash. If you traveled in Europe at that time, all your transactions were by credit card and not in actual currency because the Euro did not yet exist.[19] There is even a greater interest today in reverting the Euro back to a cashless medium due to the fear initially created by the spread of the coronavirus.

In early spring of 2020, when the World Health Organization released a statement recommending that people turn to cashless transactions to fight the spread of COVID-19, several governments and retailers across the world immediately acted on the warning. At the first hint that paper money was a potential carrier of the coronavirus, a growing number of businesses and individuals stopped using physical currency, fearing it could be a path for spreading the deadly virus.

Why was this ban on paper currency so readily accepted? Could it be that the public worldwide has been willingly indoctrinated to deal in cashless transactions through the exclusive use of credit cards, debit cards, and smartphone apps such as Zelle, Venmo, Apple Pay and Google Pay as means to transfer digital financial information via a smartphone?

Will the global pandemic make cash obsolete? With increasing frequency, you hear the terms digital dollar, digital wallet, digital currency, or digital cash—all describing cashless transactions. The US was on the verge of issuing a digital dollar as part of the early draft for the COVID-19 stimulus package distribution. Separate House and Senate bills were proposed, creating digital dollars as an effort to reduce the shock of the economic lockdown due to the spread of the novel coronavirus. Why is this important? Because a "cashless transaction" is the forerunner to a global currency.

It's important to note that China has already transitioned to an almost completely cashless society where its citizens generate 80 percent of all expenditures digitally. Nearly everyone in China uses QR (quick read) codes to exchange virtual money in person or through digital wallets online.

The People's Bank of China will soon issue a digital currency electronic payment (DCEP) system using blockchain technology, which is a decentralized, distributed ledger that records the origin of all digital assets. China plans to roll out DCEP globally, especially throughout Asia and Africa. As this digital currency is used, the Red Communist state will have direct insight into the finances of everyone in the country and beyond.[20]

A day is coming when those left behind will not be able to buy a pack of gum without having a chip in their hand or a mark on their forehead and proper authorization from the Antichrist and his one-world government. If you think this prediction seems extreme or far-fetched, let me point out that we are seeing exactly this on a limited scale as a result of the COVID-19 crisis.

Local governments shut down businesses, church worship services, and schools for fear remaining open could spread the coronavirus. Professors have been fired for endorsing Intelligent Design. Adoption agencies have been closed down for refusing to place children in LGBTQ households. Certain lawmakers propose denying hospital privileges to doctors who refuse to perform abortions. At the same time, the giant tech companies that control most of the electronic information and access in the world have recently taken to "de-platforming" any person or organization they don't like or agree with.

The message here is either comply with the official politically correct agenda or be denied the right to work in your chosen profession. Given the anti-God direction of our nation and the world today, it doesn't take much imagination to envision a time in the near future when everyone must either submit to all the government's decrees or be denied the right to work, buy, or sell. And to enforce its tyrannical rule, the government could well take the additional step of branding every citizen with indelible identification to ensure compliance.

ONE-WORLD GOVERNMENT

Never in history has one government completely ruled the world, but the false man of peace will "devour the whole earth" (Daniel 7:23). He will rule over them by their own consent and with absolute and total authority (Daniel 11:36). His personality will be marked by great intelligence, persuasiveness, subtlety, and economic prowess. His mouth will speak "pompous words" (Daniel 7:8), and he will be a "master of intrigue" (Daniel 8:23 NIV). The Antichrist will be the world's most prominent, popular, and powerful personality.

The world—which will no longer have the salt and light of the true Church sprinkled throughout its nations—will not hesitate to give this man its full attention. The Antichrist will be free to set up his one-world government, but there's nothing new about his New World Order!

Satan has been scheming to institute a New World Order since Nimrod proposed building a mighty tower on the plains of Shinar. The purpose of the city of Babel was to defy God's authority on earth by setting up the government of man and to institute a new religion with the Tower of Babel at its center. While God commanded men to "be fruitful and multiply, and fill the earth" (Genesis 9:1), the people of that day had a different idea:

> Now the whole earth had one language and one speech. And it came to pass, as they journeyed from the east, that they found a plain in the land of Shinar, and they dwelt there. . . . And they said, "Come, let us build ourselves a city, and a tower whose top is in the heavens; let us make a name for ourselves, lest we be scattered abroad over the face of the whole earth."
>
> (Genesis 11:1–2, 4)

But in His all-encompassing knowledge and power, God scattered the inhabitants of Babel.

After World War I, "the war to end all wars," President Woodrow Wilson crafted the League of Nations to uphold peace through a one-world government. Adolf Hitler told the German people he would bring a new order to Europe. He did exactly that, by dragging Europe into the bowels of a living hell and turning its streets crimson with rivers of blood.

The communists of the former Soviet Union pledged to institute a new world order and erected an atheistic empire that collapsed like a house of cards. And now the United Nations is crying out for a new world in the name of unity and brotherhood.

What does this mean? It means the end of our freedom of speech, the end of our freedom of thinking, the end of our freedom of worship. Brock Chisholm, director of the United Nations World Health Organization in the mid-twentieth century, said, "To achieve One-World Government, it is necessary to remove from the minds of men their individualism, their loyalty to family traditions and national identification."[21]

It is astounding what can happen in the name of unity through one-world thought. The cancel culture, or call-out culture, which boycotts an individual or business who is considered to have acted or spoken in a manner that counters the acceptable philosophy of the day, is the new trend. The consequences of cancel culture lead not only to the death of individual thinking and freedoms but also to irreparable loss of reputation and income.

I believe a deadly combination of desperation, weariness, and indifference will be the prime force that draws the masses to the Antichrist. As nations tire of struggling to pick up the pieces after the Rapture, they will look to the one who promises peace, economic prosperity, and order. Why not hand the reins of control to the man who has the answers to all the world's problems?

THE ANTICHRIST'S ONE-WORLD RELIGION

What is the Antichrist's chief desire? He is, above all, a false Christ—he will counter everything Jesus embodies. Satan knows that one day every knee will bow before Jesus Christ, but so great is his hatred toward God the Father that he's determined to oppose His divine plan by keeping as many people from salvation as possible. The Antichrist will proceed deliberately, solidifying his positions in politics by maintaining his facade as a global peacemaker. However, during the Antichrist's limited time on earth, he will want to be worshiped as a god.

And to accomplish this end, nowhere is he more vigilant and diplomatic than in Jerusalem. The Jewish temple will be rebuilt in the Holy City shortly after the Antichrist's rise to power. He will allow the Jews to make daily sacrifices to their God. They will rejoice, and some of the people will believe him to be their messiah. Moses Maimonides, a Jewish rabbi of the thirteenth century who wrote part of the Talmud, prophesied about the temple of the End of Days: "In the future, the Messianic king will arise and renew the Davidic dynasty, restoring it to its initial sovereignty. He will rebuild the Beis Ha Mikdash [the temple] and gather in the dispersed remnant of Israel."[22] Why not this man of peace?

It could very well be that Maimonides was prophesying about Jesus and the Millennial temple, but thousands of Jews may also link it to the Great Deceiver, the Antichrist, who has brought peace and allowed them to resume their daily temple sacrifices.

I wouldn't be surprised if, in a show of false humility, the Antichrist visits the temple himself, accompanied by the Jewish leadership of Israel.

THE SEVEN SEALS OF
THE TRIBULATION

The opening of the first six Seals of the Tribulation begins in Revelation chapter six. The Seals mark a progressive path to the End of the Age referred to in Daniel's Seventieth Week (9:20–27), as well as the Lord's End of the Age seminar of Matthew 24. The Seven Seals represent the terrible judgments that come to earth after the Rapture of the Church.

The First Seal: The Rider on the White Horse

John the Revelator saw approaching dark clouds of thunder signaling the beginning of turbulent times. A rider was seen on a white horse wielding a bow, conquering those in his path. John knew this rider was "the beast from the sea" of Revelation 13, "the prince that shall come" of Daniel 9:26 (KJV), the leader of the revived Roman Empire and the prophetic world ruler of the Tribulation. John Walvoord called him "Satan's masterpiece and the counterfeit of all that Christ is or claims to be."[23] The man John saw was the Antichrist:

> *And I saw when the Lamb opened one of the seals, and I heard,*
> *as it were the noise of thunder, one of the four beasts saying,*
> *Come and see.*

And I saw, and behold a white horse: and he that sat on
him had a bow; and a crown was given unto him: and he went
forth conquering, and to conquer.

(Revelation 6:1–2 KJV)

The Second Seal: The Rider of the Red Horse

Shortly after the First Seal of Revelation 6:2 was opened, which introduced the Antichrist onto the world stage, John the Revelator saw Jesus break the Second Seal:

Another horse, fiery red, went out. And it was granted to the
one who sat on it to take peace from the earth, and that people
should kill one another; and there was given to him a great
sword.

(Revelation 6:3–4)

American essayist Robert Kaplan stated that the world has become an infinitely more dangerous place as distinctions weaken "between states and armies, armies and civilians, and armies and criminal gangs."[24] We are currently experiencing this kind of social upheaval in America.

Due in part to the breakdown of the traditional family, the drug epidemic, and the open borders, there are more than twenty thousand gangs in the US spanning all fifty states and consisting of more than one million members. Lawlessness is ruling our streets, but it will get worse. Under the Red Horseman, anarchy will reign as world societies completely break down.

The Antichrist's "peace" will be false and short-lived, for the Second Seal will propel the world toward increasing violence. I believe the rider on the red horse will instigate actual warfare

197

between countries as well as violence between man and his neighbors. As this rider takes peace from the earth, people will kill one another on battlefields, in subways, on highways, in cities, and in country fields.

Concepts such as common decency and human kindness will fade to vague memories from another age. Nation will rise against nation, man will rise against his friend, children will rise against their parents. As towns turn into armed camps, anarchists will burn down major cities, nations will hurl weapons at each other, and the world will fall under a cloud of hopelessness and despair.

Remember the post-apocalyptic visions of a future world in movies like *Mad Max*, *I Am Legend*, and *The Book of Eli*? Welcome to the world under the Red Horseman.

The Third Seal: The Rider on the Black Horse

John looked again and saw a black horse:

> *Its rider was holding a pair of scales in his hand. Then I heard what sounded like a voice among the four living creatures, saying, "Two pounds of wheat for a day's wages, and six pounds of barley for a day's wages, and do not damage the oil and the wine!"*

(Revelation 6:5–6 NIV)

According to a 2018 United Nations report at that time, global hunger had risen for the third year in a row. The causes varied, but most of the problem was due to extreme weather disasters, including heat, drought, floods, and storms, which had doubled between 1990 and 2016. Another driver of hunger was civil conflicts, which occurred disproportionately in poorer countries. Military action destroyed cropland and drove farmers from the soil.[25]

In 2013, an alarming *Washington Post* article asserted that "we're not growing enough food to feed the world." The article pointed out that the global population was predicted to rise from 7 billion to 9.6 billion by 2050. Virtually all arable land is being used, and to cut down more forests to increase farmland is not tenable because it could create droughts, mudslides, and erosion.[26]

Farmers are searching for ways of squeezing more production out of existing lands, but that solution tends to deteriorate the soil. Synthetic fertilizers and modern agricultural techniques help, but crop yields are not rising fast enough to keep pace with the increasing demand. And there is a natural limit to how much production increase is possible.[27]

At some point, farmers will hit a biological wall past which the soil simply cannot go. Adding to the problem, some climate scientists are predicting extreme heat waves and more frequent droughts in the near future, which would further acerbate the anticipated world food shortage.[28] It will be interesting to see how the pandemic of 2020 will also affect the world's future food supply since crops were not planted or harvested and much of what was stored spoiled and was disposed.

Make no mistake; global famine is on its way. The Tribulation will mark a dearth "such as has not been since the beginning of the world until this time, no, nor ever shall be" (Matthew 24:21). The rider on the black horse represents the deep mourning that will fall upon every living creature. Listen how the prophet Jeremiah described death by famine:

> *Now their appearance is blacker than soot;*
> *They go unrecognized in the streets;*
> *Their skin clings to their bones,*
> *It has become as dry as wood.*

Those slain by the sword are better off
Than those who die of hunger;
For these pine away,
Stricken for lack of the fruits of the field.

(Lamentations 4:8–9)

While the Antichrist keeps himself aloof from the trouble, violence and havoc will envelop every nation in the aftermath of war and anarchy. Men, women, and children will die of starvation because there will be little food supply but also no money to buy even a piece of bread much less the luxuries of oil and wine. Lamentations 5:9–10 paints a picture of this time of suffering:

We get our bread at the risk of our lives,
Because of the sword in the wilderness.

Our skin is hot as an oven,
Because of the fever of famine.

The Fourth Seal: The Rider on a Pale Horse

As John the Revelator watched, Jesus broke open the Fourth Seal and a living creature beckoned John to "come and see":

So I looked, and behold, a pale horse. And the name of him who sat on it was Death, and Hades followed with him. And power was given to them over a fourth of the earth, to kill with sword, with hunger, with death [pestilence], *and by the beasts of the earth.*

(Revelation 6:7–8)

J. Vernon McGee explained the pairing of Death and Hades: "While death takes the body, hades is the place where the spirit of a lost man goes."[29]

Think of it—one-fourth of the earth's population will die as the rider on the pale horse goes forth. As anarchy, war, and famine continue to take lives, two new factors will be added to the scenario: pestilence and wild animal attacks. The agents of biological warfare certainly could account for both outbreaks. For the same reason a crazed rabid raccoon will attack almost anything in its path, a biological or chemical attack could affect animals so that they lose their natural fear of man and attack without provocation.

Dr. Frank Holtman, head of the University of Tennessee's bacteriology department, said, "While the greater part of a city's population could be destroyed by an atomic bomb, the bacteria method might easily wipe out the entire population within a week."[30]

The prophet Ezekiel foretold of the pale rider's path: "For thus says the Lord GOD: 'How much more it shall be when I send My four severe judgments on Jerusalem—the sword and famine and wild beasts and pestilence—to cut off man and beast from it?'" (Ezekiel 14:21).

Please note that the order of the first four Seals exactly follows Jesus' prediction about the beginning of the Tribulation: "For nation will rise against nation, and kingdom against kingdom [the red horse]. And there will be famines [the black horse], pestilences [the pale horse], and earthquakes in various places. All these are the beginning of sorrows" (Matthew 24:7–8).

The Fifth Seal: the Martyrs

When Jesus opened the Fifth Seal, John saw something remarkable under the heavenly altar in God's throne room:

The souls of those who had been slain for the word of God and for the testimony which they held. And they cried with a loud voice, saying, "How long, O Lord, holy and true, until You judge and avenge our blood on those who dwell on the earth?" Then a white robe was given to each of them; and it was said to them that they should rest a little while longer, until both the number of their fellow servants and their brethren, who would be killed as they were, was completed.

(Revelation 6:9–11)

The scene now moves from earth to heaven as John witnesses a vision of those precious souls who will receive white robes of righteousness after being killed for refusing to worship the Antichrist and declaring their faith in Christ. Martyrdom during this time of trouble will be commonplace as thousands will be murdered, sealing their testimony with their own blood.

The Sixth Seal: Nature Revolts

Jesus broke the Sixth Seal, and John recorded:

Behold, there was a great earthquake; and the sun became black as sackcloth of hair, and the moon became like blood. And the stars of heaven fell to the earth, as a fig tree drops its late figs when it is shaken by a mighty wind. Then the sky receded as a scroll when it is rolled up, and every mountain and island was moved out of its place. And the kings of the earth, the great men, the rich men, the commanders, the mighty men, every slave and every free man, hid themselves in the caves and in the rocks of the mountains, and said to the mountains and rocks, "Fall on us and hide us from the face of Him who sits on the throne and from the wrath of the

Lamb! For the great day of His wrath has come, and who is able to stand?"

(Revelation 6:12–17)

For the most part, the judgments of war, famine, and death, will be self-imposed by the morally corrupt choices of evil-hearted men and women. However, the judgment delivered by the Sixth Seal will be a divine rebuke on an ungodly world.

John described what seems much like a meteor or asteroid shower striking the earth. Scientists tell us that a collision with a huge asteroid would result in an explosion containing "more than 10,000 times the energy locked up in the world's nuclear arsenals at their peak," accompanied by enormous tidal waves, hurricanes moving at six hundred miles per hour (nearly the speed of sound), and months of darkness caused by thick clouds of dust.[31]

Our planet and various kinds of space debris—comets, asteroids, dust, and ice—intersect in space all of the time. Many small objects enter the earth's atmosphere continually and are burned up by friction before they hit the earth itself. Many others, some fairly large, occasionally pass close by the earth, sometimes within the orbit of the moon. For example, in July 2019 a "football-field-sized asteroid" came within 40,400 miles of the earth—that's one-fifth the distance to the moon.[32]

God Almighty has already demonstrated His awesome power to control the stars of the heavens. On February 15, 2013, a meteor struck Russia moving at a speed of at least 40,000 miles per hour. Three thousand buildings were damaged with 1,100 people severely injured.[33] Imagine the crushing impact of thousands of meteors striking the earth at the same time. It could make the effects of a nuclear war pale by comparison.

After John's in-depth depiction of God's fury, Revelation 6

ends with a very important question, "Who shall be able to stand?" (v. 17 KJV). I can assure you that unbelievers will not endure the wrath of God, and those who profess the Lordship of Christ will be protected by the grace of God even though martyred. There is no doubt that it is wiser to share in the grace of God now with the assurance that the Lord will be coming for His own than to wait until after the End of the Age and suffer a martyr's death in this future tragic period called the Tribulation.

The Seventh Seal: Silence in Heaven

The Seventh Seal and its judgments, to include the Seven Trumpets and the Seven Bowls of the wrath of God, pave the way for the glorious Second Coming of Christ. In advance of the breaking of the Seventh Seal, John saw the 144,000 servants of the Lord. Before the judgments are unbridled, God seals each of them on the forehead. In biblical times, a seal represented ownership, protection, and authority—and protection is exactly what this Seal affords each of the 144,000.

These servants represent the children of Israel, 12,000 from each tribe, who will spread the gospel throughout the entire world during the Tribulation. In Matthew 24, when Jesus described this time of unparalleled suffering, He spoke about the martyrs (v. 9), false prophets (v. 11), and a great evangelistic work: "And this gospel of the kingdom will be preached in all the world as a witness to all the nations, and then the end will come" (v. 14).

The mention of the twelve tribes of Israel counters the idea that the tribes of Israel are lost or that they have been replaced by the Church. None of the tribes of Israel are ever lost to the God of Abraham, Isaac, and Jacob. John's vision proves that God has a future purpose for Israel, and, despite Satan's persecution, a godly remnant will be protected in the Tribulation to be present on earth when Christ returns (Revelation 14:1–50).

But before the sound of the first trumpet, John described a time of silence: "When He opened the seventh seal, there was silence in heaven for about half an hour" (Revelation 8:1).

John Walvoord described this remarkable prelude:

> Though thirty minutes is not ordinarily considered a long time, when it is a time of absolute silence portending such ominous developments ahead it is an indication that something tremendous is about to take place. It may be compared to the silence before the foreman of a jury reports a verdict; for a moment there is perfect silence, and everyone awaits that which will follow.[34]

This all-embracing silence is akin to the quiet before the tempest of the coming judgment.

Then John saw "seven angels who stand before God and to them were given seven trumpets" and "another angel, having a golden censer, came and stood at the altar." And the angel offered incense "with the prayers of all the saints upon the golden altar which was before the throne" (Revelation 8:2–3). The prayers offered by the martyred saints is what breaks the period of eerie stillness.

Next John saw a great multitude of those who had come "out of the great tribulation, and washed their robes and made them white in the blood of the Lamb" (Revelation 7:14). Remember that the Great Tribulation is "the hour of trial which shall come upon the whole world" (Revelation 3:10).

This scene describes the martyrs of those executed by the Antichrist for "the word of their testimony" (Revelation 12:11).

This is also the same Great Tribulation described by Daniel right before the coming of Christ: "And there shall be a time of trouble, such as never was since there was a nation" (Daniel 12:1). And Jesus referred to it as "great tribulation, such as has not been since the beginning of the world until this time, no, nor ever shall be" (Matthew 24:21).

People will come to Christ during the Tribulation who did not hear the gospel during the Dispensation of Grace. They will hear the gospel preached by angels flying through the heavens saying, "Fear God and give glory to Him, for the hour of His judgment has come; and worship Him who made heaven and earth" (Revelation 14:7). They will refuse to take the mark of the Antichrist, and they will be killed.

Perhaps the Antichrist will charge them with treason. Perhaps he will condemn them for following what he might call "a dead religion for dead people." In any case, these martyrs will die for their faith, and their souls will wait in heaven until the Lord's purpose is complete.

This half hour of silence is not an unforeseen delay or a moment of vacillation—this is the deliberate lull before the storm. The host of heaven saw what God is about to do on earth, and they stood in absolute awe, in total silence, of His impending judgment of mankind.

And the clock ticks on.

CHAPTER SEVEN

11:56 PM

For Then Shall Come Great Tribulation

I have read the Book of Revelation and, yes, I believe the world is going to end—by an act of God, I hope—but every day I think that time is running out.

Caspar Weinberger, *New York Times*, August 23, 1982

God's overriding purpose since the beginning of time is the establishment of His Eternal Kingdom on earth (Revelation 21). Associated with this divine objective is man's redemption (John 17:1–5). Our new birth in Christ Jesus is produced by the Word of Life (1 John 1:1–2) and the Holy Spirit (John 3:5–6), and as born-again believers, it is our destiny to reign with the Son of God as coheirs in His Kingdom. And because of these truths, it is no wonder that John, the disciple that Jesus loved, was chosen as the scribe for the book of Revelation.

John, who dropped his fishing nets by the shores of Galilee to follow a radical rabbi named Jesus of Nazareth. John, who was in Christ's inner circle along with Peter and James. John, who was commissioned by the Lord to care for His mother as He hung on the cross. John, who played a pivotal role in the early Church at Jerusalem after Christ's death and resurrection. John, who encouraged the churches of Asia with the triumphant message of their Redeemer. John, New Testament writer of the fourth gospel and three letters. John, the one who was exiled to a small penal colony on the Isle of Patmos for his testimony of Jesus Christ. John, beloved disciple and friend who knew the voice of the Lord. It was this John who would pull back the veil to reveal the End of the Age.

The title of the book "The Revelation of Jesus Christ" in itself reveals its purpose, which is to tell of the glory, wisdom, power, and the ultimate rule of the Son of God. Know this: the "testimony of Jesus is the spirit of prophecy" (Revelation 19:10), for all biblical prophecy is reliant on His work as revealed by the Holy Spirit.

The book of Revelation illustrates Christ's person. He is seen as the glorified Son of Man (1:13); the Lion of the tribe of Judah and the root of David (5:5); the worthy Lamb (5:12); the Ruler with the rod of iron (12:5); the Bridegroom (19:7–9); the conquering King of kings and the Lord of lords (19:16); and the rightful Ruler of both the earthly (20:4–6) and heavenly kingdoms (22:1, 3).

Because John witnessed the life, death, and resurrection of Christ, it was natural for him to understand the remarkable visions he was shown. John remembered what the Lord had said to him during His earthly ministry and was able to comprehend Christ's directive to believers, His warning to unbelievers, His judgment on the sinful world, His one-thousand-year reign, and His eternal rule.

The book of Revelation is an example of "apocalyptic literature," which is an unveiling or revealing by a supernatural being. John made it clear that he was the writer (scribe) and the author was the angel of the living God. The writing speaks of the events that were happening at the moment, but it also looks to the future giving the reader the opportunity to choose to live according to the dictates of God's Word. Revelation is a study of the End of the Age in reference to "the things which you have seen, the things which are [2–3], and the things which will take place [1:7; 4–22]" (1:19).

John's book was not written in strict chronological order. Chapters 6 through 18 deal with the Tribulation period, but chapters 12 and 13 take a sidetrack to supply brief biographical sketches of several key characters that also have prominent roles in Daniel's Seventieth Week account. And remember—while

God's judgment is being poured out through the Seven Trumpets and Seven Vials, the Antichrist will continue to implement his scheme of world domination. To better understand this time, you must see these events from both an earthly viewpoint and a heavenly one.

TRIBULATION CHARACTER SKETCH: THE WOMAN, THE CHILD, AND THE DRAGON

In Revelation 12:1 John wrote, "Now a great sign appeared in heaven." This is not a literal depiction; by using the word *sign* John let us know the images were actually symbols. For example, the woman described in Revelation 12:1–17 is Israel, from whom came the Child, Christ the Messiah, and the dragon is Satan, who will persecute Israel during the Great Tribulation.

The dragon's tail drew a third of the stars of heaven and threw them down to earth, symbolizing the angels who rebelled with Lucifer and were cast out of heaven before the creation of the world.

Please note that though the Antichrist appears to be personally charting the path the world's taking during the Tribulation, he is actually inspired and dominated by the spirit of Satan.

THE ANTICHRIST: HIS CHARACTER REVEALED

Let's look back and see what Daniel had to say about the End of the Age and the evil man who will influence it:

Then the king shall do according to his own will: he shall exalt and magnify himself above every god, shall speak blasphemies against the God of gods, and shall prosper till the wrath has been accomplished; for what has been determined shall be done. He shall regard neither the God of his fathers nor the desire of women, nor regard any god; for he shall exalt himself above them all.

(Daniel 11:36–37)

The Antichrist is a future world ruler who will govern ten nations, make and break a peace treaty with Israel, and later become dictator over the entire earth. Though the Antichrist will come to the forefront under a banner of peace and tolerance, he will soon reveal his true colors. This Prince of Darkness will persecute those who do not accept his mark, cunningly created to allegedly solve global economic problems.

The Antichrist will portray those who refuse to take his mark or swear allegiance to him as dangerous subversives. His campaign of terror against Jews and Christians (those who accept Christ as Lord after the Rapture) will escalate as he condemns Judeo Christian–based worship in all its forms. He will stop the daily sacrifices in the newly rebuilt holy temple in Jerusalem and will demand that he be worshiped as God as he establishes his New Age concept of a one-world religion.

The Antichrist will do as he pleases. His advisors will be mere window dressing, for in the end he will do only what he wants, directed by Satan. Contrast the Wicked One's spirit with that of Jesus—the One the Antichrist will attempt to imitate. Jesus said, "I can of Myself do nothing. As I hear, I judge; and My judgment is righteous, because I do not seek My own will but the will of the Father who sent Me" (John 5:30). In the garden of Gethsemane,

Jesus prayed, "O My Father, if it is possible, let this cup pass from Me; nevertheless, not as I will, but as You will" (Matthew 26:39). Jesus submits to the total good of His Father and the son of perdition submits to the total evil of his father.

Both the Old and New Testaments record the existence, nature, and purpose of this diabolical End of the Age protagonist.[1] He is "the fleeting serpent" (Job 26:13; Isaiah 27:1). The Psalms refer to him often: he is "the bloodthirsty and deceitful man" (5:6); "the wicked [one]" (9:17); "the man of the earth" (10:18); the "mighty man" (52:1); and "the adversary" (74:10), to name a few.

Isaiah described him as the king of Babylon—the "abominable branch" (14:19), the "spoiler" (16:4), and the lord of Assyria (30:31–33). Jeremiah called him "the destroyer of nations" (4:7) and the "enemy" and the "cruel one" (30:14). Ezekiel referred to him as the "profane, wicked prince of Israel" (21:25) and the "prince of Tyre" (28:2). Daniel provided a full outline of the Antichrist's career through his visions and dreams. Hosea spoke of him as "the king of princes" (8:10) and the "cunning Canaanite [merchant]" who holds "deceitful scales" and who "loves to oppress" (12:7). Joel described him as the commander of the "northern army" who has done "monstrous things" (2:20). Amos described him as the "adversary" who will break Israel's strength and plunder her palaces (3:11). Micah's prophecy referred to the Antichrist as the "Assyrian" (5:6). Nahum told of his destruction and referred to him as the "wicked one" who has been "utterly cut off" (1:15). Habakkuk spoke of him as "a proud man" who "is like death, and cannot be satisfied" (2:5), and Zechariah described him as "the worthless shepherd" (11:17).

In the New Testament, Jesus said the Antichrist would come "in his own name" and be "received" by Israel (John 5:43). The

213

Lord also referred to him as "the ruler of this world" (John 14:30). The apostle Paul gave a full-length representation of him in 2 Thessalonians 2, where he is called "the man of sin . . . the son of perdition" (v. 3). The apostle John mentioned him by name and declared that he is a "liar" who "denies the Father and the Son" (1 John 2:22). Later in Revelation he called him the "beast" and referenced him by "the number of its name . . . let him who has understanding reckon the number of the beast, for it is a human number, its number is six hundred and sixty-six" (13:17–18 RSV).

All these prophetic verses converge in the Antichrist who will finally be cast into the lake of fire with the False Prophet, there to be joined a thousand years later by Satan, to suffer forever in that fire specially prepared by God.

THE ANTICHRIST WILL CENTER HIS CULT IN JERUSALEM

Jerusalem! There is no city on the face of the earth like the Holy City of God.

There are cities renowned for their massive size, their climate and beauty, their military prowess or industrial proficiency, but none can compare to the majestic city of Jerusalem. Why? Because Jerusalem is the city of God, the capital city of the nation God created by His spoken word (Genesis 12:1–3; 13:15). All other nations were created by acts of men, but Israel was created by God Himself. A nation whose title deed He later transferred to Abraham and his descendants through an unconditional and eternally binding blood covenant (Genesis

15:8–18). And Jerusalem is the heart of Israel, its eternal and undivided capital.

This is the city God has chosen as His habitation: "Yet I have chosen Jerusalem . . . that My name may be there forever; and My eyes and My heart will be there perpetually. . . . In this house and in Jerusalem, which I have chosen . . . I will put My name forever" (2 Chronicles 6:6; 7:16; 33:7). King David, the man after God's own heart, wrote of the City of God:

> Great is the LORD, and greatly to be praised
> In the city of our God . . .
> Beautiful in elevation,
> The joy of the whole earth,
> Is Mount Zion . . .
> The city of the great King. . . .
>
> God will establish it forever.
>
> (Psalm 48:1–2, 8)

The most passionate Scripture concerning Jerusalem was also penned by the psalmist David, the conqueror of the former hilltop Jebusite stronghold:

> If I forget you, O Jerusalem,
> Let my right hand forget its skill!
> If I do not remember you,
> Let my tongue cling to the roof of my mouth—
> If I do not exalt Jerusalem
> Above my chief joy.
>
> (Psalm 137:5–6)

215

David was a musician and singer, so he was stating that as much as he loved music, if he forgot Jerusalem and God's eternal purpose for that city, may his right hand no longer have the skill to play the harp, and may he no longer be able to sing. A musician who cannot play and a singer who cannot sing have no purpose in life. Similarly, the man who forgets Jerusalem, the heart and soul of Israel, has no reason to exist.

Jerusalem is a monument to the faithfulness of God. David wrote:

> Those who trust in the LORD
> Are like Mount Zion,
> Which cannot be moved, but abides forever.
> As the mountains surround Jerusalem,
> So the LORD surrounds His people
> From this time forth and forever.
>
> (Psalm 125:1–2)

Jerusalem is a living testimonial to Jews and Christians alike. We are sheltered in the arms of God just as Israel is cradled by the surrounding mountains and defended by God Himself.

Knowing all this, the Antichrist will decide to center his religious cult in Jerusalem, to include the very heart of the temple itself. He will know full well that his actions are an affront to Almighty God and His Chosen people, the Jews.

Jesus confirmed that Satan's messiah would demand worldwide worship in Jerusalem when He said:

> "Therefore when you see the 'abomination of desolation,'
> spoken of by Daniel the prophet, standing in the holy place"

(whoever reads, let him understand), "then let those who are in Judea flee to the mountains."

(Matthew 24:15–16)

THE ANTICHRIST'S COHORT: THE FALSE PROPHET

The Antichrist will not be alone in his diabolical deeds. He will have an assistant who is as thoroughly committed to evil as he is. Remember this principle: Satan loves to mimic God's truth. He will continue doing so until the End of the Age and after. Thus, the Antichrist will be part of a perverted satanic trinity that will endeavor to function in much the same way as the Father, Son, and Holy Spirit. Satan, the first person of this evil triune, will supply power to the Antichrist, who will be aided by the deceitful False Prophet:

And he [the False Prophet] deceives those who dwell on the earth by those signs which he was granted to do in the sight of the beast, telling those who dwell on the earth to make an image to the beast who was wounded by the sword and lived. He was granted power to give breath to the image of the beast, that the image of the beast should both speak and cause as many as would not worship the image of the beast to be killed.

(Revelation 13:14–15)

The image of the Antichrist will speak and when it does, most people will bow and worship him straightaway. Robotics have come a long way since Disney World first introduced its animatronic Hall of the Presidents in the 1960s. Today, Japanese robotic engineers have created android robots that can walk, use their

217

hands, speak in response to questions, follow movement with their eyes, and even vacuum your floor. The evolution of animatronics has been astounding to say the least.

With today's technology, the creation of a lifelike talking statue is no big feat, and people are not likely to be impressed unless this image also possesses powers beyond what we're accustomed to seeing. Still others will worship the statue because they fear the consequences of *not* doing so.

The book of Daniel recounts how Nebuchadnezzar commissioned his craftsmen to create a golden image of himself, ninety feet tall and nine feet wide. The king then commanded everyone to fall prostrate and worship the stature whenever they heard the musical prompt (Daniel 3). Three Hebrew young men, Shadrach, Meshach, and Abed-Nego, refused to bow and soon found themselves within the fiery furnace. But God delivered them from the roaring flames, sending His own Son to deliver Daniel's righteous friends.

Nebuchadnezzar was rightfully astonished and praised the Hebrews by saying, "Blessed be the God of Shadrach, Meshach, and Abed-Nego, who sent His Angel and delivered His servants who trusted in Him . . . [because they would] not serve nor worship any god except their own God!" (Daniel 3:28).

In the same way, the False Prophet will erect an image or statue of the Antichrist, and everyone will be commanded to worship it. In order to fully understand the Antichrist's agenda, it is important to grasp Satan's overall strategy. His goal is to be "like the Most High" (Isaiah 14:14), and his burning passion is to be worshiped. He wants, in fact, to dethrone the Great I AM, the God of Abraham, Isaac, and Jacob.

Before the dawn of time, Lucifer (called Satan after the fall) convinced one-third of the angels to join him in his reckless attempt to overthrow God as the ruler of all. Though he was decisively defeated in a supernatural war, Satan has continued in open opposition to God, seeking every possible opportunity to lash out and attempt to destroy, deceive, or discredit that which is important to the One True God of the universe.

The very name *Antichrist* hints at Satan's agenda. The Greek prefix *anti* has two meanings. The first and most obvious signifies "against." The second is far more interesting: *anti* also means "in place of." Both definitions apply here. Satan and his unholy conspirators are both against God and are seeking to take His place.

Since Satan and his demons know what the Word of God says about their ultimate doom, why do they persist in this futile endeavor? Part of the answer undoubtedly lies in their evil, malicious character. Perhaps they truly believe they can alter their destiny and somehow dethrone God Almighty—after all, Satan's defining sin is destructive pride.

To further delineate Satan's evil nature, let's contrast Jesus in the Millennium with Satan in the Tribulation:

- Jesus will rule a world of peace and prosperity; the Antichrist will reign through seven years of war, violence, and chaos.
- Jesus offers eternal salvation to those who believe in Him; the Antichrist offers death to those who denounce him and eternal damnation for those foolish enough to follow him.
- The Holy Spirit testifies of Jesus and provides truth, comfort, joy, and strength to those who trust the Savior; the False Prophet testifies of the Antichrist and enforces allegiance to him through threats, deception, and ruthless violence.

TRIBULATION CHARACTER SKETCH: THE BEASTS FROM THE SEA AND THE EARTH

The two beasts, one from the sea (Revelation 13:1–10) and one from the earth (13:11–18), are personalities we have met before. The beast from the sea is the Antichrist, and the beast from the earth is the False Prophet, who institutes the apostate religious worship of the beast from the sea.

At some point in the Great Tribulation, the Antichrist will be seemingly fatally wounded, perhaps by an assassination attempt, but he will not die. John said, "I saw one of his heads as if it had been mortally wounded, and his deadly wound was healed. And all the world marveled and followed the beast" (Revelation 13:3).

The Antichrist is a counterfeiter, and he will attempt to emulate the death and resurrection of Jesus Christ. Just as he entered the stage of world prophecy riding a white horse to replicate Christ, he will also appear to die and miraculously rise again.

THE NUMBER OF A MAN

In Daniel, as you will recall, the Antichrist was the little horn of chapter 7, the king of "fierce features" of chapter 8, the "prince who is to come" of chapter 9, and the willful king of chapter 11. John the Revelator gave us another way to identify him: "Here is wisdom. Let him who has understanding calculate the number of the beast, for it is the number of a man: His number is 666" (Revelation 13:18).

John Walvoord offered the following explanation of the number of man:

Triple six is the number of a man, each digit falling short of the perfect number seven. Six in the Scripture is man's number. He was to work six days and rest the seventh. The image of Nebuchadnezzar was sixty cubits high and six cubits broad. Whatever may be the deeper meaning of the number, it implies that this title referring to the first beast, Satan's masterpiece, limits him to man's level which is far short of the deity of Jesus Christ.[2]

Another explanation for the Antichrist's number lies in the ancient Jewish practice of *gematria*. As the apostle John wrote Revelation, he certainly knew that his readers were familiar with this practice, which involves substituting letters for numbers. In both Hebrew and Greek, each letter of the alphabet was assigned numeric value, not unlike the way some Roman letters also represent numbers. Fully aware of this practice, members of the early Church simply had to convert a number into a name or a name into a number.

In Revelation 13:18, John made it possible for the world to identify the Antichrist by the number 666. This cryptic puzzle is not intended to point to some obscure person, but rather to confirm exactly who the Antichrist is.

The identity of the Antichrist is of no practical value to the Church because we will be watching from the balconies of heaven by the time this lawless ruler is revealed. But for anyone reading this book after the Church has been taken away, you will know which personality arising out of a European federation is the devil incarnate, the son of Satan—the Antichrist.

During the late 1930s and early 1940s a flurry of pamphlets identified Adolf Hitler as the Antichrist. Others declared that Mussolini was the Antichrist because of his close relationship to Rome, and contemporary conspiracy theorists have done the same with several world personalities. However, no one who lives from the time of Pentecost until the Rapture of the Church can possibly know who the Antichrist is because he will not make his appearance on the world stage until the Church is removed from the earth by the Rapture.

This so-called man of peace, this false messiah, is very likely alive now and may even know his predestined demonic assignment. Although we do not know who he is, we certainly know what he will do.

THE ANTICHRIST AGENDA

Like Lucifer, the Antichrist desires to exalt himself. He will set up his image in the city of Jerusalem and demand that the nations of the world worship him—or face death by decapitation (Revelation 20:4). Daniel made it clear that the temple offerings will stop three-and-one-half years (1,290 days) before the end of the Tribulation. Why? Just like his forerunner, Antiochus Epiphanes, the Antichrist will introduce idolatrous worship inside the holy temple and set himself up as the god of Israel and the world:

> "[He] will make a treaty with the people for a period of one set of seven [seven years], but after half this time, he will put an end to the sacrifices and offerings. And as a climax to all his terrible deeds, he will set up a sacrilegious object that causes desecration, until the fate decreed for this defiler is finally poured out on him."

> (Daniel 9:27 NLT)

Paul also understood what would happen during the time of the Great Tribulation:

He [the Antichrist] will exalt himself and defy everything that people call god and every object of worship. He will even sit in the temple of God, claiming that he himself is God.

. . . And you know what is holding him back, for he can be revealed only when his time comes.

(2 Thessalonians 2:4, 6 NLT)

The Antichrist will speak so artfully, with such deception, that those who heard the gospel and rejected it before the Rapture will be caught up in his lies. Paul told us:

The coming of the lawless one is according to the working of Satan, with all power, signs, and lying wonders, and with all unrighteous deception among those who perish, because they did not receive the love of the truth, that they might be saved. And for this reason God will send them strong delusion, that they should believe the lie, that they all may be condemned who did not believe the truth but had pleasure in unrighteousness.

(vv. 9–12)

Listen carefully, friend: the Rapture has not yet happened, and salvation through Jesus Christ is still available to you. However, if you reject His Lordship now, you will not be able to accept it after the Rapture without being martyred.

We have established that the son of Satan is a deceiver and he will attempt to counterfeit the Son of God and His exploits. But we learn even more about the personality and plan of the

223

Antichrist by understanding how completely opposite he is from Jesus:

- Christ came from heaven (John 6:38); the Antichrist will come from hell (Revelation 11; 17).
- Christ came in His Father's name (John 5:43); the Antichrist will come in his own name (John 5:43).
- Christ humbled Himself (Philippians 2:8); the Antichrist "shall exalt himself in his heart" (Daniel 8:25).
- Christ was despised and rejected (Isaiah 53:3); the Antichrist will be admired, lauded, and worshiped (Revelation 13:3–4, 8).
- Christ came to do His Father's will (John 6:38); the Antichrist will do as he pleases (Daniel 11:36).
- Christ came to save (Luke 19:10); the Antichrist brings death and destruction (Daniel 8:24; Revelation 19:21; 20:15).
- Christ is the Good Shepherd (John 10); the Antichrist is "the worthless shepherd" (Zechariah 11:16–17).
- Christ is the Truth (John 14:6); the Antichrist is a liar (2 Thessalonians 2:11; 1 John 2:22).
- Christ is the "mystery of godliness" (1 Timothy 3:16); the Antichrist is the "mystery of lawlessness" (2 Thessalonians 2:7).

TRIBULATION CHARACTER
SKETCH: THE TWO WITNESSES

As powerful as the Antichrist is, there will be opposition. Along with those who refuse to submit to his evil agenda, God will send two witnesses who will be a thorn in his side. Many Bible scholars believe the two witnesses who will appear on the earth during the Great Tribulation are Elijah and Enoch (Revelation 11:1–15).

In writing about the End of the Age, the prophet Malachi wrote, "Behold, I will send you Elijah the prophet before the coming of the great and dreadful day of the LORD" (Malachi 4:5). In the observance of the Jewish Passover feast, a special cup is set for Elijah because the prophet is to return as a forerunner of the Messiah. A cup of wine is traditionally poured in the hope that Elijah will appear, thus announcing the Messiah's coming. Jesus Himself referred to this prophecy when He said, "Indeed, Elijah is coming first and will restore all things" (Matthew 17:11).

Hebrews 9:27 says, "And as it is appointed for men to die once, but after this the judgment." Neither Enoch nor Elijah experienced death but were transported to heaven. The Bible records that "Enoch walked with God; and he was not, for God took him" (Genesis 5:24), and, as the prophet Elijah was walking with Elisha, "suddenly a chariot of fire appeared with horses of fire, and separated the two of them; and Elijah went up by a whirlwind into heaven" (2 Kings 2:11).

God's emissaries will prophesy for 1,260 days during the Great Tribulation. They will testify of the truth concerning the coming Messiah: "'Not by might nor by power, but by My Spirit,' says the LORD of hosts" (Zechariah 4:6). These men will have miraculous powers. They will destroy those who persecute them with fire from their mouths, they will have the power to stop the rains like Elijah did in his earthly ministry, and they will turn water into blood and bring plagues like Moses in Egypt. They will be supernaturally protected until their assignment is

225

complete; then God will allow Satan to kill them (Revelation 11:7).

John describes their bodies as they lie in the streets of Jerusalem for three and a half days, and because of today's technology, the entire world will see them.

The witnesses will lie in the streets of the Holy City like dead animals while "those who dwell on the earth will rejoice over them, make merry, and send gifts to one another, because these two prophets tormented those who dwell on the earth" (v. 10). No one will recommend that they be given a proper burial. Human decency and kindness will not be found in Satan's kingdom nor will it prevail in the Antichrist's Jerusalem.

But three-and-one-half days later, God will raise His prophets from the dead and take them to heaven right before their enemies. They will stand to their feet, brush the dust and dried spittle off their sackcloth garments, and lift their faces to heaven. The sky will thunder with a loud voice saying, "Come up here!" and up they'll go, courtesy of a heavenly cloud: "And great fear fell on those who saw them" (v. 11).

Why will people be stricken with fear when they see the resurrection of Elijah and Enoch in the streets of Jerusalem? Because their miraculous rising from the dead will be proof positive that the God of heaven is in total control. He is sending His Son to rule the world, the Antichrist and the False Prophet will be "cast alive into the lake of fire," and the godless who took the mark of the Beast will be "killed with the sword which proceeded from the mouth of Him who sat on the horse. And all the birds were filled with their flesh" (19:20–21). Just as He promised.

THE VIEW FROM HEAVEN:
THE SEVENTH SEAL LEADS
TO SEVEN TRUMPETS

The first four Seals release the four Horsemen and their mission. The Fifth Seal ushers in the cries of the martyrs while the Sixth Seal introduces massive earthquakes and other catastrophic events.

The Seventh Seal will inaugurate the Seven Trumpet judgments of Revelation (8:7–9:16; 11:15–19), which are reminders of the ten plagues God poured out on Egypt (Exodus 7–11):

> *When He opened the seventh seal, there was silence in heaven for about half an hour. And I saw the seven angels who stand before God, and to them were given seven trumpets. . . .*
> *So the seven angels who had the seven trumpets prepared themselves to sound.*
>
> (Revelation 8:1–2, 6)

The first four judgments will affect the natural world; the last three will affect the unredeemed people of the earth. Everyone except the 144,000 Jewish evangelists will be subject to the plagues of the trumpet judgments. The horror announced by the first six trumpets will be beyond comprehension, but the seventh trumpet will announce the glory of the coming Kingdom of Christ.

In the Old Testament we learn that God commanded that trumpets be used for calling the congregation together, either for the purpose of war or to sound an alarm of impending danger. In Numbers 10:9 we read, "When you go to war in your land against the enemy who oppresses you, then you shall sound an alarm with

227

the trumpets, and you will be remembered before the LORD your God, and you will be saved from your enemies."

J. Vernon McGee said, "As the trumpets of Israel were used at the battle of Jericho, so the walls of this world's opposition to God will crumble and fall during the Great Tribulation."[3] And to that I say, "Amen!"

THE TRUMPET JUDGMENTS

At the beginning of the Great Tribulation, the angels of heaven will blow the trumpets, sounding the alarm, for God is about to pour out the full fury of His wrath:

The first angel sounded: And hail and fire followed, mingled with blood, and they were thrown to the earth. And a third of the trees were burned up, and all green grass was burned up.

(Revelation 8:7)

This first judgment will be against the earth itself. Burning hail will strike the earth and destroy one-third of all plant life—trees, shrubs, grass, forests, gardens, parks. God used a flood in His first judgment against the earth; now He will use fire. Plants were the first life forms to be created; now they will be the first to be destroyed:[4]

Then the second angel sounded: And something like a great mountain burning with fire was thrown into the sea, and a third of the sea became blood. And a third of the living creatures in the sea died, and a third of the ships were destroyed.

(vv. 8–9)

As God moves His mighty hand, a massive meteor will strike the earth, causing tidal waves and vast pollution that will contaminate our oceans.

I don't know if you've seen a red tide before, but when it strikes, hundreds of thousands of dead fish wash up on the shore, polluting the air for miles. This judgment will be far worse than a red tide; it will be a supernatural act of a wrathful God. One-third of all living creatures in the sea—dolphins and sharks, jellyfish and squid, microscopic plankton and great whales will perish.

Whereas the second trumpet will affect the salt-water seas, the third trumpet will affect fresh water, without which human life cannot exist:

Then the third angel sounded: And a great star fell from heaven, burning like a torch, and it fell on a third of the rivers and on the springs of water. The name of the star is Wormwood. A third of the waters became wormwood, and many men died from the water, because it was made bitter.

(vv. 10–11)

According to *The New York Times*, two-thirds of the world regularly face water shortages. About four billion people deal with severe water shortages at least one month of every year. These shortages affect not only China, India, Bangladesh, Pakistan, Nigeria, and Mexico, but also the southern United States, particularly California, Texas, and Florida. In affluent countries like the US, the shortages often mean rationing water for showers, lawns, or gardening. But in poorer countries, finding adequate drinking water can become a critical problem.[5]

When the angel poisons the waters, the situation will become life threatening. "Water wars" will break out between countries who share lakes and rivers with the Holy Land. According to Washington's Worldwatch Institute, many of the skirmishes between Israeli settlers and Arabs have been exacerbated by the conflict over water rights.[6]

If water is such an urgent concern now, can you imagine how horrible the situation will be when Wormwood pollutes one-third of the world's fresh water?

Like the heavy darkness that fell on Egypt when the lives of the Jewish people were made miserable by the ravages of Pharaoh's bitter bondage, darkness will cover the earth when the fourth angel sounds his trumpet:

> *Then the fourth angel sounded: And a third of the sun was struck, a third of the moon, and a third of the stars, so that a third of them were darkened. A third of the day did not shine, and likewise the night.*
>
> (v. 12)

In Matthew 24:29, Jesus predicted that the heavens would declare the Tribulation: "Immediately after the tribulation of those days the sun will be darkened, and the moon will not give its light; the stars will fall from heaven, and the powers of the heavens will be shaken."

Whether from supernatural delivery or as a result of the fire, the hail, and the meteor, God will allow a veil of thick fog to dim the light of sun, moon, and stars. He will not totally blot out sunshine and starlight, for He specifically made such a promise in Genesis 8:22:

> *While the earth remains,*
> *Seedtime and harvest,*

Cold and heat,
Winter and summer,
And day and night
Shall not cease.

God will keep His covenant with man. The earth will still know day and night, but it will be darkened under a black cloud that will bring deep depression and chilling emotional torment to humanity.

Then there will be an ominous announcement:

And I looked, and I heard an angel flying through the midst
of heaven, saying with a loud voice, "Woe, woe, woe to the
inhabitants of the earth, because of the remaining blasts of the
trumpet of the three angels who are about to sound!"

(Revelation 8:13)

The angel was warning that the judgments brought by the next three trumpets would be far worse than the previous. The first four were judgments upon creation; the next three terrors will be judgments upon mankind.

THREE TRUMPETS OF TERROR

The fifth angel will reveal unspeakable and unrelenting terror:

Then the fifth angel sounded: And I saw a star fallen from
heaven to the earth. To him was given the key to the bottomless
pit. And he opened the bottomless pit, and smoke arose out of
the pit like the smoke of a great furnace. So the sun and the air

231

were darkened because of the smoke of the pit. Then out of the smoke locusts came upon the earth.

(Revelation 9:1–3)

These unnatural destructive creatures will be released on earth from the very pit of hell to torment humanity. The "star fallen from heaven" will be Satan himself, and he will be given the authority to release these locusts. Normal locusts eat plants, but this demonic swarm will sting those who are not sealed with the seal of God. Their agonizing bite will make their victims beg to die, but they won't be able to. For five months these locusts, led by king Abaddon, will torment all mankind (vv. 4–11).

John described these locusts as being the shape of a horse prepared for battle, their faces like the faces of men, their teeth like lion's teeth, and the sound of their wings like the sound of chariots with many horses running into battle (Revelation 7–10). These are intelligent spiritual beings capable of commands as they follow the demonic leadership of Abaddon.

The sixth angel will raise the alarm about four of his evil counterparts:

Then the sixth angel sounded: And I heard a voice from the four horns of the golden altar which is before God, saying to the sixth angel who had the trumpet, "Release the four angels who are bound at the great river Euphrates." So the four angels, who had been prepared for the hour and day and month and year, were released to kill a third of mankind.

(Revelation 9:13–15)

Whereas the fifth trumpet brought torture, the sixth trumpet will bring death. At God's precise timing, "prepared for the hour and day and month and year" (Revelation 9:15), He will release four angels who are bound at the Great River Euphrates, near the original eastern border of the Promised Land (Genesis 15:18).

Just beyond the eastern boundary of the Euphrates, a massive army of two hundred million strong, comprised of God's enemies will invade Israel. Many prophecy scholars believe this to be the Chinese army for the following reason: They will come from the east; they are the only nation who could amass such an enormous military force, and the colors of the Civil Ensign of the Republic of China are "fiery red, hyacinth blue, and sulfur yellow" (Revelation 9:17).

It is interesting to note that this great demonic army will arise from the vicinity of the Euphrates River. J. Vernon McGee pointed out that this area has great spiritual significance:

> The Garden of Eden was somewhere in this section. The sin of man began here. The first murder was committed here. The first war was fought here. Here was where the Flood began and spread over the earth. Here is where the Tower of Babel was erected. To this area were brought the Israelites of the Babylonian captivity. Babylon was the fountainhead of idolatry. And here is the final surge of sin on the earth during the Great Tribulation.[7]

Even though more than half of the world's population will die in the Tribulation, those still living will persist in idolatry, immorality, and rebellion against God (vv. 20–21). Harold Willmington said we should not marvel at the callousness of those who continue to rebel against God. The Bible provides several examples of prideful unbelief and unrighteousness:

- All but eight of the people before the flood were destroyed because they refused to heed the Lord (1 Peter 3:20).[8]
- Sodom did not have even ten righteous people within their city (Genesis 18:32).[9]
- All but two of the Exodus Israelites died for their unbelief (Numbers 14:29–30).[10]

THE ANGEL AND THE LITTLE BOOK

An interlude falls between the sixth and seventh trumpet judgments. In Revelation 10:1–11, John prophesied the completion of the mystery of God concerning the nation of Israel. God's Kingdom on earth would be established, but at a high cost to those who reject Him.

At this point in his vision, an angel gave John a "little book" and cried with a loud voice. He was answered by seven thunders, but John was not allowed to write the words he heard. This part of his revelation is the only part that remains sealed.

The angel planted one foot on the land and one on the sea—claiming God's dominion over both—and swore by God the Creator that the seventh trumpet was about to sound and the "mystery of God would be finished" (v. 7). Then John was commanded to take the book from the angel's hand and eat it: "It will make your stomach bitter," he was told, "but it will be as sweet as honey in your mouth" (v. 9).

So John ate. To that point he had seen the destruction of Gentiles, but from this point on, he would see judgment on his own people. At the beginning of Revelation 11, an angel told

John to measure the temple of God, the altar, and the worshipers. He added that the outer court had been given to the Gentiles, who "will tread the holy city underfoot for forty-two months" (v. 2).

These forty-two months correspond to the three-and-one-half years the Antichrist will control the temple (Daniel 12:11).

THE SEVENTH TRUMPET

At the blowing of the seventh trumpet, loud voices in heaven will cry out, "The kingdoms of this world have become the kingdoms of our Lord and of His Christ, and He shall reign forever and ever!" (Revelation 11:15–16). The end of the Great Tribulation will be approaching. The world's suffering will be nearly done, and Jesus Christ will be ready to claim His Kingdom.

The twenty-four elders on their thrones will fall on their faces and worship God, saying:

> *We give You thanks, O Lord God Almighty,*
> *The One who is and who was and who is to come,*
> *Because You have taken Your great power and reigned.*
> *The nations were angry, and Your wrath has come,*
> *And the time of the dead, that they should be judged,*
> *And that You should reward Your servants the prophets and*
> *   the saints,*
> *And those who fear Your name, small and great,*
> *And should destroy those who destroy the earth.*

(vv. 17–18)

235

TRIBULATION CHARACTER SKETCH: THE THREE ANGELIC EVANGELISTS

The three angelic evangelists (Revelation 14:5–13) are heavenly beings sent to preach the message of God's righteous judgment on all the nations of the earth. They will invite people to fear and glorify God before final judgment; they will announce the ultimate downfall of wicked Babylon, and they will warn against worshiping the Antichrist.

"How tragic," wrote Harold Willmington, "that Christ [at Calvary] once drank this same cup for the very unrepentant sinners who are now forced to drink it again."[11]

TRIBULATION CHARACTER SKETCH: THE GREAT HARLOT

There is a vast difference between ignoring Scripture and interpreting Scripture. To ignore the prophetic teaching of Revelation 17 would be irresponsible. Yet anyone who accurately interprets Revelation 17 runs the risk of being labeled bigoted, extremist, and of course, politically incorrect.

In the New Testament, we find a clear presentation of an apostate church that professes Christ without possessing Him. In 1 Timothy 4:1, Paul wrote, "Now the Spirit expressly says that in latter times some will depart from the faith, giving heed to deceiving spirits and doctrines of demons." And in 2 Peter 2:1–2, Peter told us:

> But there were also false prophets among the people, even as
> there will be false teachers among you, who will secretly bring

in destructive heresies, even denying the Lord who bought
them, and bring on themselves swift destruction. And many
will follow their destructive ways, because of whom the way
of truth will be blasphemed.

After the Church is raptured into heaven, which removes all
believers in Christ, the apostate church will remain on earth. This
worldwide false religious system yields much power and influence. Revelation 17:1 labels this heretic church of the last days
as "the great harlot who sits on many waters." And later John
describes it as influencing many "peoples, multitudes, nations,
and tongues" (v. 15).

A harlot is one who has been unfaithful in her wedding vows.
Here John described an apostate church that professed to be loyal
to Christ but in fact cleaved to idols and a false religious system,
making it guilty of spiritual adultery. In verse 2 we discover that
this great harlot had seduced "the kings of the earth," not just
the general population. The kings of the earth "were made drunk
with the wine of her fornication." They were stupefied and mes-
merized by this global religious system.

John further wrote, "So he carried me away in the Spirit into
the wilderness. And I saw a woman [the apostate church] sitting
on a scarlet beast which was full of names of blasphemy, having
seven heads and ten horns [the Antichrist system]" (v. 3).

A few verses later, John gives us an all-inclusive portrayal of
the End of the Age, the character of the Antichrist, and the one-
world government he will lead:

The beast that you saw was, and is not, and will ascend out of
the bottomless pit and go to perdition. And those who dwell
on the earth will marvel, whose names are not written in the

237

Book of Life from the foundation of the world, when they see
the beast that was, and is not, and yet is.

(Revelation 17:8)

John F. Walvoord breaks down this passage's meaning
perfectly:

The angel first gives a detailed description of the beast in his
general character. The beast is explained chronologically as
that which was, is not, and is about to ascend from the abyss
and go into perdition. "The bottomless pit" . . . is the home of
Satan and demons and indicates that the power of the political
empire is satanic in its origin as is plainly stated in Revelation
13:4. The word *perdition* . . . means "destruction" or "utter
destruction," referring to eternal damnation. The power of the
political empire in the last days is going to cause wonder as
indicated in the questions: "Who is like unto the beast? Who
is able to make war with him?" (Revelation 13:4). The over-
whelming satanic power of the final political empire of the
world will be most convincing to great masses of mankind.

There is a confusing similarity between the descriptions
afforded Satan who was apparently described as the king over
the demons in the abyss (Revelation 9:11), "the beast that
ascends out of the bottomless pit" (11:7), the beast whose
"deadly wound was healed" (13:3), and the beast of 17:8. The
solution to this intricate problem is that there is an identification to some extent of Satan with the future world ruler
[the Antichrist] and identification of the world ruler with his
world government [the revived Roman Empire]. Each of the
three entities is described as a beast. Only Satan himself actually comes from the abyss. The world government which he

promotes is entirely satanic in its power and to this extent is identified with Satan. It is the beast as the world government [European confederation] which is revived. The man who is the world ruler [Antichrist], however, has power and great authority given to him by Satan. The fact that Satan and the world ruler are referred to in such similar terms indicates their close relationship one to the other.[12]

BEAUTIFUL BUT DEADLY

In Revelation 17:4, John described the apparel of the great harlot: "The woman was arrayed in purple and scarlet, and adorned with gold and precious stones and pearls." She had the outward appearance of royalty; she was wearing gold and an array of jewels, meaning she had unlimited wealth. In her hand was "a golden cup full of abominations and the filthiness of her fornication." Outwardly the great harlot was beautiful, but the contents of her cup were poison to the nations of the world.

John identified the great harlot by saying, "And on her forehead a name was written: MYSTERY, BABYLON THE GREAT, THE MOTHER OF HARLOTS AND OF THE ABOMINATIONS OF THE EARTH" (v. 5).

The word *mystery* in the New Testament does not refer to something secretive, but to a truth not previously made known by God. The mystery God was revealing is that in the last days there will be a worldwide apostate church that will reject Christ, dishonor God, and join forces with the Antichrist.

To identify Babylon, we must go to Genesis 10 and read about Nimrod, the archapostate of the postdiluvian world. Nimrod lived four generations after the flood and was called "a mighty hunter before the LORD. . . . And the beginning of his kingdom was Babel [meaning the 'gate of God']" (vv. 9–10).

It was Nimrod's generation that built the Tower of Babel for the purpose of casting God and His influence out of the earth. They proposed to build a great tower that would reach into heaven so they could have the benefits of God without submitting to Him. In response to their presumptuous action, God confounded their language and scattered them over the earth.

This is the critical point—the first organized, idolatrous religious system in the history of the world was introduced at Babel. That's why John called Babylon the mother of Harlots. Babylon was the birthplace of spiritual adultery. Consequently, the spiritual adultery at the End of the Age is also called Babylon, the mother of harlots.

What is the demise of the great harlot? Look carefully at Revelation 17:16–17:

> And the ten horns which you saw on the beast [the European confederation that will produce the Antichrist], these will hate the harlot, make her desolate and naked, eat her flesh and burn her with fire. For God has put it into their hearts to fulfill His purpose, to be of one mind, and to give their kingdom to the beast, until the words of God are fulfilled.

John was saying that in the middle of the Tribulation, members of the European confederation that arise from the revived Roman Empire will not want to share global power with the great harlot. The Antichrist, who will rule over the confederation, will share his power with the great harlot for a time, but then he will destroy her with a vengeance. By eliminating the apostate church, the Antichrist will be clearing the way for his own apostate religion and his own worship.

THE SEA OF GLASS AND
THE SEVEN VIALS

The final set of judgments described in Revelation arrive with the Seven Vials (Revelation 16:1–21). A vial is a bowl, and these Seven Bowls of fierce judgment will be poured out in rapid succession at the end of the Great Tribulation. As the Seventh Seal introduced the Seven Trumpet judgments, the Seventh Trumpet judgment will introduce the Seven Bowl judgments. The Seven Bowl judgments are similar to the trumpet judgments; however, whereas the trumpet judgments are partial in their effects, the bowl judgments will be complete and final. The seventh and final bowl judgment signals the great battle of Armageddon and foretells the final ruin of the Antichrist.

In Revelation 15:1–8, John the Revelator saw another seven angels preparing to pour out the seven last plagues. He described something "like a sea of glass mingled with fire," and told us that those who had been victorious over the Beast were standing on the sea of glass, singing the song of Moses and the song of the Lamb. While John listened to their praise songs, the "temple of the tabernacle of the testimony in heaven was opened" (v. 5) and out stepped the seven angels clothed in pure white linen, their chests girded with golden bands.

Without any delay, the angels were commanded to pour out the bowls of God's wrath upon the earth. These terrible plagues followed one another in quick succession:

- The first angel poured out "foul and loathsome sore[s]" on those who took the mark of the Beast (Revelation 16:1–2).
- The second angel poured his bowl on the sea, and it became

241

like the thick, coagulated blood of a dead man. "Every living creature in the sea died" (v. 3).

- The third angel poured his bowl on the rivers and springs of fresh water, and they, too, became as blood. The angel of the waters made a telling comment: "You are righteous, O Lord. . . . For they have shed the blood of saints and prophets, and You have given them blood to drink. For it is their just due" (vv. 5–6).

- The fourth angel poured his bowl on the sun, which began to burn hot enough to "scorch men with fire." Men cursed God, but they did not repent or give Him glory (vv. 8–9).

- The fifth angel poured his bowl on the throne of the Beast, "and his kingdom became full of darkness." His followers chewed their tongues in pain from the sores, the heat, and their thirst, but they did not repent (vv. 10–11).

- The sixth angel poured out his bowl on the great river Euphrates, and its waters dried up so the "kings from the east" could march across the dry riverbed and join God's other enemies for battle. At this time, three demons went forth to entice the kings of the world to gather at Armageddon. "You want a fight?" Satan was saying to God. "We're going to give You one" (vv. 12–16).

- The seventh angel poured his bowl into the air, and a voice from heaven proclaimed, "It is done!" (v. 17). A mighty earthquake unlike any other shook the earth. Every city was destroyed; every mountain was laid low. Every island vanished into the sea as seventy-five-pound hailstones (each as heavy as the weight of one talent) fell from the sky (vv. 17–21).

Yet men still continued to curse and blaspheme God.

TRIBULATION CHARACTER SKETCH:
THE REAPING ANGELS

The reaping angels (Revelation 14:14–20) are angels who will go forth at God's command to bring the wrath of God on the unbelieving world. In this "sneak preview" of Armageddon, John saw Christ return to earth and, joined by these two reaping angels, begin to harvest the earth with sharp sickles, resulting in a river of human blood two hundred miles long and one hundred miles wide up to the horse's bridle. When a horse drinks water, his bridle gets wet in six inches of water. When you say, "as high as a horse's bridle" that would equate to blood up to six inches in depth for two hundred miles in length and approximately one hundred miles in width.

The Old Testament prophets often spoke of the Latter Days in terms of harvest. Joel wrote:

> *Put in the sickle, for the harvest is ripe.*
> *Come, go down;*
> *For the winepress is full,*
> *The vats overflow—*
> *For their wickedness is great*
>
> (Joel 3:13)

Isaiah 63, the passage that inspired "The Battle Hymn of the Republic," the glorious old hymn sung throughout the Civil War, shares Joel's vision of a vat of ripe grapes, ready to be trampled underfoot:

> *Who is . . .*
> *This One who is glorious in His apparel,*
> *Traveling in the greatness of His strength? . . .*

243

Why is Your apparel red,
And Your garments like one who treads in the winepress?

"I have trodden the winepress alone,
And from the peoples no one was with Me.
For I have trodden them in My anger,
And trampled them in My fury;
Their blood is sprinkled upon My garments,
And I have stained all My robes.
For the day of vengeance is in My heart,
And the year of My redeemed has come."

(vv. 1–4)

This is no passive, mild-mannered, politically correct Jesus who comes to pay the earth a condolence call. This is a furious Christ, who has just destroyed the armies of the world on a plain called Armageddon.

The first time He came to earth, Jesus was the Lamb of God, led in silence to the slaughter—a death He willingly endured for our redemption. The next time He comes, He will be the Lion of the tribe of Judah who will trample His enemies until their blood stains His garments, and He shall rule with a rod of iron.

Even so, come Lord Jesus!

CHAPTER EIGHT

11:57 PM

Inching Toward Armageddon

I sometimes believe we're heading very fast for Armageddon right now.

Ronald Reagan, from a conversation with Jerry Falwell (May 2, 1982)

The battle of Armageddon, the greatest bloodbath in the history of civilization, will be fought in Israel on the plains of Megiddo. Though most Americans couldn't tell you which battle the word *Armageddon* actually refers to, the name nevertheless carries connotations of catastrophe that staggers the mind.

Imagine, if you will, that you are one of the 144,000 children of Abraham living in the city of Jerusalem during the time of the Tribulation. You were among the selected servants of the living God that were first seen at the beginning of the Great Tribulation (Revelation 7:3–8) and then again at its end (14:1–5). You were faithful and devout and refused to bow down to the Antichrist and his false religion, staying true to God. And because of this loyalty, you were protected during the dreadful days of persecution by the seal of the Almighty.

You didn't take the mark for two reasons—first, swearing allegiance to anyone but the God of Abraham, Isaac, and Jacob was unthinkable. Second, you remembered the time when another evil man tattooed your people with a number, persecuted them, and led six million of them to the slaughter and you took a stand—*never again!*

The last three and a half years have been relentless—it's as if the enemy knows he has a short time left. There have been rumblings in the streets of a great battle—greater than the previous ones of Gog-Magog. It seems as if the world's armies are gathering throughout the covenant land with many of Israel's enemies converging at the valley of Megiddo.

As has been your daily practice since you can remember, you read the Word of God. During the last years, however, you and the others who actually lived its prophecies have a deeper appreciation of its message. You open your tattered leather Torah and read the words of the prophet Zechariah as if it were today's headlines:

"Behold, I will make Jerusalem a cup of drunkenness to all the surrounding peoples, when they lay siege against Judah and Jerusalem. And it shall happen in that day that I will make Jerusalem a very heavy stone for all peoples; all who would heave it away will surely be cut in pieces, though all nations of the earth are gathered against it. In that day," says the LORD, "I will strike every horse with confusion, and its rider with madness; I will open My eyes on the house of Judah, and will strike every horse of the peoples with blindness. And the governors of Judah shall say in their heart, 'The inhabitants of Jerusalem are my strength in the LORD of hosts, their God.' In that day I will make the governors of Judah like a firepan in the woodpile, and like a fiery torch in the sheaves; they shall devour all the surrounding peoples on the right hand and on the left, but Jerusalem shall be inhabited again in her own place—Jerusalem.

"The LORD will save the tents of Judah first, so that the glory of the house of David and the glory of the inhabitants of Jerusalem shall not become greater than that of Judah. In that day the LORD will defend the inhabitants of Jerusalem; the one who is feeble among them in that day shall be like David, and the house of David shall be like God, like the Angel of the LORD before them. It shall be in that day that I will seek to destroy all the nations that come against Jerusalem.

"And I will pour on the house of David and on the inhabitants of Jerusalem the Spirit of grace and supplication; then they will look on Me whom they pierced. Yes, they will mourn for Him as one mourns for his only son, and grieve for Him as one grieves for a firstborn. In that day there shall be a great mourning in Jerusalem, like the mourning at Hadad Rimmon in the plain of Megiddo."

(Zechariah 12:2–11)

You know in your spirit that the Day of the Lord is coming soon as mentioned by Isaiah, Ezekiel, Joel, Amos, Obadiah, Zephaniah, and Malachi. And you are also confident that the Lord will go forth to be victorious against Israel's enemies once and for all as the prophets recorded. Though the sky is dark and oppressive overhead, your heart pounds with anticipation for He is faithful and true. You have seen God's sheltering hand work on your behalf as you and the others have remained dedicated to the Holy One's assignment. You and the other servants of God have been protected from the plague of boils and stinging locusts sweeping the city, and miraculously, the sun has not burned your skin. And just as before, when these coming horrors arrive, Israel's Messiah will defend His people and His holy city.

And yes, the "battle of the great day of God Almighty will take place" and there the nations of the earth will be judged by Him for their persecution of the Jewish people. Soon the 144,000 will stand victoriously with the Lamb in Jerusalem in His Millennial Reign.

I have been many times to the Prayer Wall in Jerusalem and witnessed hundreds of rabbinical students dance in worship to the Lord before the remnant of Solomon's wall. I want you to look into the theater of your mind and imagine the 144,000 dancing in euphoric praise as the Messiah joins His servants on Mount Zion at the beginning of His reign—what a glorious sight that will be.

STEP ONE: THE NATIONS WILL RISE AGAINST THE ANTICHRIST

Unlike Jesus Christ, whose throne will know no end, the Antichrist's days are numbered. While God readies the armies of heaven, the nations of earth will rise against the Antichrist. Daniel told us the Antichrist will constantly be at war with nations who rise against him:

> *At the time of the end [End of the Age] the king of the South shall attack him [Antichrist]; and the king of the North shall come against him like a whirlwind, with chariots, horsemen, and with many ships; and he shall enter the countries, overwhelm them, and pass through. He shall also enter the Glorious Land [Israel], and many countries shall be overthrown; but these shall escape from his hand: Edom, Moab, and the prominent people of Ammon. He shall stretch out his hand against the countries, and the land of Egypt shall not escape. He shall have power over the treasures of gold and silver, and over all the precious things of Egypt; also the Libyans and Ethiopians shall follow at his heels.*
>
> (Daniel 11:40–43)

The Antichrist will do battle with Egypt, just as his precursor Antiochus Epiphanes did. He will defeat the Egyptians and take their treasures for his own use. He will also send his armies to the Holy Land, where he will have trouble conquering the

Arabs. Libya and Ethiopia, however, will surrender to him, virtually guaranteeing his control over Africa. Revelation states the Antichrist's empire will rule the world "and authority was given him over every tribe, tongue, and nation" (13:7).

STEP TWO: THE ANTICHRIST
WILL BLASPHEME GOD

Scripture tells us that "news from the east and the north shall trouble" the Antichrist (Daniel 11:44). China has always sought world domination and the Antichrist's military intelligence will report an army of two hundred million Asians marching down the dry bed of the Euphrates River to engage him in a titanic struggle for world supremacy. The Antichrist's one-world religious cult, headquartered in Jerusalem, will be the focus of the invading armies.

Revelation 13:6 says that the Antichrist will open "his mouth in blasphemy against God, to blaspheme His name, His tabernacle, and those who dwell in heaven." As the Antichrist, indwelled by Satan, marshals his massive army for the battle of Armageddon, he will look into heaven at the angels who did not follow him in his first rebellion against God. He will look at Christ, to whom Satan once offered the kingdoms of the world. He will look up at the raptured believers who stand with their Lord, and he will say, "Look, all of you! Look where you would be if you had followed me! You would be rulers of the earth! I am the supreme one here! I rule and reign in this city! Jerusalem is mine."

Why does the Antichrist covet Jerusalem? One of Satan's purposes in this battle is to exterminate every Jew in the world. What inspires his hatred for the Jews? The answer is simple: Satan's

251

hatred for Israel and the Jewish people stems from God's eternal love for them. The Antichrist also wants Jerusalem because God Almighty has placed His Name there to be remembered forever (Psalm 45:17).

God chose the nation of Israel so He would have a repository of divine truth for generations to come. Through Israel God has given the world the Word of God, the patriarchs, the prophets, Jesus Christ, and the apostles. Where would Christianity be without the Jewish contribution? Look at the word *Judeo-Christianity*. Judaism does not need Christianity to explain its existence; Christianity, however, cannot explain its existence without Judaism.

The Lord Jesus Christ will return to earth to rule over the seed of Abraham, Isaac, and Jacob. If Satan, through the Antichrist, can destroy the Jews, there is no reason for Jesus to return, and Satan could continue as the world ruler. But the Antichrist cannot stop what God has already decreed.

STEP THREE: GOD WILL DRAW
THE NATIONS TO MEGIDDO

In Joel 3:2, God said, "I will also gather all nations, and bring them down to the Valley of Jehoshaphat." Speaking through Zechariah, God said, "Behold, I will make Jerusalem a cup of drunkenness to all the surrounding peoples, when they lay siege against Judah and Jerusalem. . . . I will gather all the nations to battle" (Zechariah 12:2; 14:2).

The battle of Armageddon will begin on the plains of Megiddo to the north, continue down through the Valley of Jehoshaphat on the east, cover the land of Edom to the south and east, and revolve around Jerusalem. Fighting will begin almost immediately. The Antichrist's enemies will lay siege to Jerusalem, then overrun her city defenses and wreak the havoc as Zechariah so vividly described. They will take captives, murder, rape, and pillage until the streets run red with blood.

The Antichrist will not pursue the thousands of Jews who are fleeing Jerusalem for Petra, as "tidings from the east . . . trouble him." What is the troubling news? The Antichrist must direct his military juggernaut toward Armageddon to face the two-hundred-million-man army advancing from China to capture the oil-rich Persian Gulf:

> But tidings out of the east and out of the north shall trouble him: therefore he shall go forth with great fury to destroy, and utterly to make away many.
> And he shall plant the tabernacles of his palace between the seas in the glorious holy mountain [Jerusalem].
>
> (Daniel 11:44–45 KJV)

After hearing about the advancing eastern army and the attack on Jerusalem, the Antichrist will advance from the territory of the defeated king of the South to Armageddon, a natural battlefield, to face the armies of the North and East.

STEP FOUR: GOD WILL DISPATCH THE CAVALRY

Then God, who has silently borne the blasphemies of the Antichrist, will say, in effect, "My Son, take the armies of heaven—the angels and the church—and return to earth as the King of kings and

253

Lord of lords. Go and make your enemies your footstool. Go and rule the earth with a rod of iron. Go and sit upon the throne of your forefather, King David."

Then will come the final invasion, not from the north, south, east, or west, but from heaven. It is the invasion described in Revelation 19, the attack led by Jesus Christ, the Lamb of God, the Lion of Judah, and the Lord of Glory!

The Lion of Judah shall mount His milk-white stallion, followed by His army wearing crowns and dazzling robes of white. Every righteous child of God will be in that army, for it is composed of the loyal angels of God and the raptured church! Enoch, the first prophet, prophesied about this day: "Behold, the Lord comes with ten thousands of His saints" (Jude 1:14).

Mounted upon a white horse, the King of kings will descend onto the battlefield at Armageddon. As He comes, His eyes will be like blazing fire, and the armies of heaven will follow Him. Out of the Messiah's mouth will come a sharp, two-edged sword, the Word of God with which He created the world, raised Lazarus from the dead, and rebuked the unruly wind and waves on the Sea of Galilee. This very same spoken Word will crush Israel's enemies at Armageddon, for He is the Mighty Conqueror, and of His Kingdom there shall be no end!

CHRIST'S BATTLE DRESS

In Revelation 19:12, John wrote that Jesus had a name "written that no one knew except Himself." As a Jew, John knew that the Lord appeared to Abraham, Isaac, and Jacob in the name of God Almighty, *El Shaddai*. But God did not reveal Himself by the name of Jehovah (Yahweh). The patriarchs knew God as the

Almighty One, but they had no concept of Him as an intimate friend and master, the One who delights to walk with His children "in the cool of the day" as God walked with Adam in the Garden of Eden (Genesis 3:8).

Christ, wearing His robe dipped in the blood of the enemies of Israel and His prayer shawl whose tzitzit (tassels) spell "God is One" in Hebrew, fulfills the prophecy that He is the King of kings and Lord of lords (Revelation 19:13, 16).

When Jesus begins His descent to the Mount of Olives in His Second Coming, two opposing forces will be drawn up in battle array on the mountains of Israel—the armies of the Antichrist and the army of the kings of the East. Jesus told us, however, that before this battle begins there will be a sign in the heavens: "Then the sign of the Son of Man will appear in heaven, and then all the tribes of the earth will mourn, and they will see the Son of Man coming on the clouds of heaven with power and great glory" (Matthew 24:30).

We don't know what this sign will be, but it will be something so clear and obvious that it leaves no room for doubt—Jesus Christ, Messiah and Lord, is returning to earth to reign as King of kings and Lord of all lords.

At that point, the two armies will turn from fighting each other and direct their weapons toward Christ Himself. John the Revelator said, "And I saw the beast, the kings of the earth, and their armies, gathered together to make war against Him who sat on the horse and against His army" (Revelation 19:19).

Jesus Christ, leading the armies of heaven, will dismount from His white horse and step out onto the Mount of Olives, cleaving the mountain in two. The terrified inhabitants of Jerusalem, who have been brutalized by the invading armies, will flee the city through the gap in the ancient mountain.

John the Revelator wrote that the mire of mingled blood and mud will form a lake that reaches to the bridle of a horse: "And the winepress was trampled outside the city, and blood came out of the winepress, up to the horses' bridles, for one thousand six hundred furlongs [180 miles]" (Revelation 14:20). This blood will flow from the veins of men who came to destroy Israel but were themselves destroyed by God Almighty. God's promise to Abraham still stands: "And I will curse him who curses you" (Genesis 12:3).

Daniel foretold the outcome of the Antichrist's encounter with Jesus: "He [the Antichrist] shall even rise against the Prince of princes [Jesus]; but he shall be broken without human means" (Daniel 8:25).

Paul also gave us a word of prophecy: "And then the lawless one [the Antichrist] will be revealed, whom the Lord will consume with the breath of His mouth and destroy with the brightness of His coming" (2 Thessalonians 2:8).

The Antichrist doesn't stand a chance!

Then the beast [Antichrist] was captured, and with him the false prophet who worked signs in his presence. . . . These two were cast alive into the lake of fire burning with brimstone. And the rest were killed with the sword which proceeded from the mouth of Him who sat on the horse. And all the birds were filled with their flesh.

(Revelation 19:20–21)

He who invaded Jerusalem, who murdered and killed the righteous Jews who would not worship him, who conquered the world, will be cast alive and forever into the lake of fire with the False Prophet! And "that serpent of old, who is the

Devil and Satan" will be bound by an angel and cast "into the bottomless pit, and shut him up and set a seal on him so that he should deceive the nations no more till the thousand years were finished" (Revelation 20:2–3).

Returning to the earth with His bride, the Church, Jesus will clean house. Not only will the Antichrist and the False Prophet be thrown into hell, but Satan himself will be put away for a thousand years. Every hostile force that would challenge Christ's right to rule the earth will have been eradicated.

ARMAGEDDON'S AFTERMATH

J. Dwight Pentecost, in his book *Things to Come*, surveyed Armageddon's campaign results:

1. The armies of the South are destroyed.
2. The armies of the Northern Confederacy are smitten by the Lord.
3. The armies of the Beast and the East are slain at the Second Coming.
4. The Beast and the False Prophet are cast into the lake of fire (Revelation 19:20).
5. Unbelievers have been purged out of Israel (Zechariah 13:8).
6. Believers have been refined as a result of these invasions (Zechariah 13:9).
7. Satan is bound (Revelation 20:2).[1]

Jesus Christ will be victorious at Armageddon for Israel and His beloved city Jerusalem, and He will destroy every adversary who would defy His right to rule as the world's Messiah. In the aftermath of this battle, His people will recognize Him for who He is:

> And I will pour on the house of David and on the inhabitants of Jerusalem the Spirit of grace and supplication; then they will look on Me whom they pierced. Yes, they will mourn for Him as one mourns for his only son, and grieve for Him as one grieves for a firstborn. In that day there shall be a great mourning in Jerusalem. . . .
>
> . . . And one will say to him, "What are these wounds between your arms?" Then he will answer, "Those with which I was wounded in the house of my friends."
>
> (Zechariah 12:10–11; 13:6)

The "fullness of the Gentiles has come in," and "all Israel will be saved" as Paul predicted (Romans 11:25–26).

Jesus Christ, the true Messiah, Shiloh, the Prince of Peace, the Blessed of Abraham, the Son of David, shall rule and reign forever from the city of Jerusalem, the city of God. Hallelujah to the Holy One of Israel! Of His Kingdom there shall be no end!

CHAPTER NINE

11:58 PM

The Millennium Dawns

This war no longer bears the characteristics of former inter-European conflicts. It is one of those elemental conflicts which usher in a new millennium and which shake the world once in a thousand years.

Adolf Hitler, Speech to Reichstag, April 26, 1942

Hitler clearly had an exaggerated sense of self-importance. World War II, as horrible as it was, was a mere skirmish compared to Armageddon, the war that will usher in the Millennium. Jesus Christ will come again, and He will defeat the Antichrist and the armies of the world in the valley of Megiddo (Isaiah 34:16; 63:1–5; Revelation 19:11–16). After that magnificent victory, and before the Lord of Glory begins His Millennial Reign, there is a pause.

THE SEVENTY-FIVE DAY INTERVAL

Daniel 12:11–12 calculates a period of seventy-five days between Christ's Second Coming and the institution of the Millennial Reign. Dr. S. Franklin Logsdon explained it this way:

> We in the United States have a national analogy. The President is elected in the early part of November, but he is not inaugurated until January 20th. There is an interim of 70-plus days. During this time, he concerns himself with the appointment of Cabinet members, foreign envoys and others who will comprise his government. In the period of 75 days between the termination of the Great Tribulation and the Coronation, the King of glory likewise will attend to certain matters.[1]

We are at two minutes until the End of the Age, a time that will bring great rejoicing for God's people, but before Christ establishes His Millennial Kingdom, several events must occur.

Jesus, the Lion of the tribe of Judah, will cast the Antichrist and his False Prophet into the lake of fire (Revelation 19:20–21). Jesus, the Great High Priest of Israel, will remove the abomination of desecration from the holy temple (Daniel 12:11). Jesus, the Great Shepherd, will regather, regenerate, and restore faithful Israel, for the Word of God declares that "He will send His angels with a great sound of a trumpet, and they will gather together His elect [the Jewish people] from the four winds, from one end of heaven to the other" (Matthew 24:31).

Jesus is met by the 144,000 who remained on earth protected by the seal of the Lord. You will recall this Jewish remnant commissioned to witness during the Great Tribulation. In Matthew 24:14, Jesus said that this select group will preach "this gospel of the kingdom . . . in all the world as a witness to all the nations, and then the end will come." These chosen Jews will be successful in their endeavors, for in Revelation 7:9–17 we see that a great multitude has been protected and redeemed during the dark Tribulation period.

Jehovah Jireh will call the Jews, whom He provided for and sheltered for forty-two months at Petra, back to His Holy City. The righteous Jews, resurrected from the dead according to Daniel 12:2, will follow in this great parade, rejoicing in the arrival of their long-awaited Messiah. What victorious pageantry this will be!

Jesus, the Righteous Judge, will adjudicate the Jews and Gentiles who survived the Tribulation. The Lord will also assign His angel to bind and cast Satan into the abyss as John described in Revelation 20:1–3:

Then I saw an angel coming down from heaven, having the key
to the bottomless pit and a great chain in his hand. He laid hold
of the dragon, that serpent of old, who is the Devil and Satan,
and bound him into the bottomless pit, and shut him up, and
set a seal on him, so that he should deceive the nations no more
till the thousand years were finished.

The Old Testament and Tribulation saints will be resurrected and rewarded for their faithfulness (Isaiah 26:19; Daniel 12:1–3; Revelation 20:4). And now the Architect of the Ages will commence the reconstruction of the holy temple in Jerusalem (Ezekiel 40—48).[2]

We who were taken up in the Rapture will follow King Jesus as He returns to His Promised Land. The barren, devastated lands around Jerusalem will miraculously burst forth with new life as the Messiah passes by, and those with Him will take in the scents of sweet jasmine, the Rose of Sharon, and the lily of the valley. Isaiah foretold of this glorious event:

> *For the* Lord *will comfort Zion,*
> *He will comfort all her waste places;*
> *He will make her wilderness like Eden,*
> *And her desert like the garden of the* Lord;
> *Joy and gladness will be found in it,*
> *Thanksgiving and the voice of melody. . . .*
>
> *For you shall go out with joy,*
> *And be led out with peace;*
> *The mountains and the hills*
> *Shall break forth into singing before you,*
> *And all the trees of the field shall clap their hands.*
>
> (Isaiah 51:3; 55:12)

263

THE JUDGMENT OF THE NATIONS

There is the judgment seat of Christ, which occurs in heaven after the Rapture, where every believer will be rewarded for their deeds. There are then the twenty-one judgments that are poured out on the earth during the Great Tribulation, followed by the judgment of the nations after Christ's Second Coming and before the start of His Millennial Reign. And last, there is the final judgment of the Great White Throne, which occurs at the end of the Millennium.

Shortly after the defeat of the Antichrist and within the seventy-five-day pause, Jesus will execute the judgment of the nations where the earthly Gentile realms are sentenced for the manner in which they treated the Jewish people and Israel (Genesis 12:1–3). Jesus clearly described this event to His followers:

> *When the Son of Man comes in His glory, and all the holy angels with Him, then He will sit on the throne of His glory. All the nations will be gathered before Him, and He will separate them one from another, as a shepherd divides his sheep from the goats. And He will set the sheep on His right hand, but the goats on the left. Then the King will say to those on His right hand, "Come, you blessed of My Father, inherit the kingdom prepared for you from the foundation of the world: for I was hungry and you gave Me food; I was thirsty and you gave Me drink; I was a stranger and you took Me in; I was naked and you clothed Me; I was sick and you visited Me; I was in prison and you came to Me."*
>
> *Then the righteous will answer Him, saying, "Lord, when did we see You hungry and feed You, or thirsty and give You drink?" . . . And the King will answer and say to them,*

"Assuredly, I say to you, inasmuch as you did it to one of the least of these My brethren [the Jewish people], you did it to Me."

Then He will also say to those on the left hand, "Depart from Me, you cursed, into the everlasting fire prepared for the devil and his angels: for I was hungry and you gave Me no food; I was thirsty and you gave Me no drink" . . .

Then they also will answer Him, saying, "Lord, when did we see You hungry or thirsty or a stranger or naked or sick or in prison, and did not minister to You?" Then He will answer them, saying, "Assuredly, I say to you, inasmuch as you did not do it to one of the least of these, you did not do it to Me." And these will go away into everlasting punishment, but the righteous into eternal life.

(Matthew 25:31–46)

You can trust the fact that every Gentile and nation will answer for how they treated the Jews, Jesus' brethren, from Genesis 12 to the End of the Age. God will judge Egypt and the Pharaoh that knew not Joseph for persecuting the Jewish people with cruel and relentless bondage. God will judge the Assyrians, the Babylonians, and the Persians for their conquest, deportation, and enslavement of the Jews. He will judge Antiochus Epiphanes and the Seleucids who desecrated the Lord's temple and who slaughtered and deported tens of thousands of Jews.

The Ruler of the kings of earth will judge Rome for the siege of Jerusalem in 70 CE, which destroyed the city and its temple and killed more than one million Jews. It was the Roman government that later decreed the Jews were "sons of the devil" and prevented them from owning land, voting, or holding public office; denied them the right to practice law or medicine; and made them wear

265

distinctive clothing marking them as "detestable" Jews. Their hatred for the Jews was so intensely evil that it was considered in good form to kill the "Christ-killers" during the Holy Week's celebration of the Lord's resurrection.

The Lion of Judah will judge Spain for the Inquisition, the Crusades, and the expulsion of all the Jews from their nation. The Son of Man will judge Russia, Italy, Poland, and all other nations that, through vicious pogroms, confined Jews to destitute ghetto communities, causing thousands upon thousands to die in the streets from the ravages of starvation and pestilence. Jesus, the Root of David, will most definitely judge Hitler, his goose-stepping Nazis, and all the collaborators who were involved in the systematic annihilation of six million precious Jewish souls.

And yes, God will judge *all* the world's anti-Semites, past and present.

More than eight decades ago, on May 13, 1939, the *St. Louis*, an ocean liner carrying more than nine hundred Jewish refugees, fled Nazi Germany en route to Cuba. The passengers, who had obtained at great personal cost all the legal documents necessary to travel, anxiously waited on the ship in Havana's port for six days hoping to disembark. However, Nazi propagandists convinced the Cuban president to deny their entry. Next, the *St. Louis* carried its unwelcomed cargo to the waters off the coast of Florida.

As the ship floated haplessly in American waters for more than seventy-two hours, Jewish American leaders went to Washington DC and frantically begged President Franklin Delano Roosevelt to let the Jewish exiles disembark in the United States. He, too, denied them entry.

On June 6, the passengers of the ill-fated voyage sailed back into the Atlantic in the hopes that they could find asylum in some world port—but no one wanted them. Tragically, the *St. Louis* was forced to return to Europe, docking in Antwerp on June 17, 1939. After much persuasion and financial inducement by the US Jewish community, the doomed passengers were dispersed to cities in Belgium, France and the Netherlands, thirty-six days after first leaving Hamburg. Tragically, in the end, the majority of the refugees fell victim to the horrors of the Holocaust and Hitler's Final Solution. Every nation and every leader involved in this tragedy will be judged.

The British Empire, which controlled what was referred to as Palestine during World War II, will be called to the judgment bar for their White Paper policies. As Hitler was killing twenty-five thousand Jews a day, multitudes of God's Chosen tried to escape. However, the British White Paper policy only allowed five thousand Jews a year to immigrate to Israel. The British would capture Jews who clandestinely tried to enter the Holy Land, and those who were caught would be briefly detained and then returned to Europe to face their demise at the hands of the demonic Nazis. The British closed the gates of mercy on the Jewish people, but Almighty God will remember their actions on this judgment day. All Gentiles who lived before and during the Tribulation will answer for their treatment of the Jewish people and the nation of Israel.

"I will bless those who bless you, and I will curse him who curses you" *was, is and will always be* the law of God concerning the Jewish people (Genesis 12:3).

Today, America's colleges and universities are flooded with fiercely anti-Semitic professors who are teaching the next generation to hate Israel by blaming the Jewish people for all things evil.

This destructive anti-Semitic spirit is gaining ground. From 2018 to 2019, incidents involving efforts by faculty and students to boycott or impede student participation in educational experiences in Israel increased by 100%. Acts involving the public shaming, vilifying, or defaming of students or staff because of their professed association with Israel increased by 67%. Acts involving the shutting down or impeding of Israel-related speech and the unfair treatment or exclusion of students because of their support of Israel increased by 51%.[3]

The failure to educate people about the evils of anti-Semitism enables its fervent growth. Recent studies show a shocking ignorance about the Holocaust among Americans. One 2020 study revealed that 31% of Americans and 41% of millennials believe that less than two million Jews were killed in the Holocaust. When asked about the Auschwitz death camp, 41% of Americans and two-thirds of millennials did not know what Auschwitz was. Another survey showed that nearly two-thirds of US young adults (ages 18–39) are unaware that six million Jews were killed in the Holocaust, and even more tragic is the fact that one in ten believes Jews caused the Holocaust.[4]

After the Hamas-Israel War in May of 2021, the Anti-Defamation League (ADL) in just eight days tracked more than 17,000 tweets that used variations of the phrase, "Hitler was right"![5] To quote ADL CEO Jason Greenblatt:

> As the violence between Israel and Hamas continues to escalate, we are witnessing a dangerous and drastic surge in anti-Jewish hate right here at home. We are tracking acts of harassment, vandalism and violence as well as a torrent of online abuse. It's happening around the world—from London to Los Angeles, from France to Florida, in big cities like New York and in small towns, and across every social media platform.[6]

Know this, the hand of the Almighty God who chose to bless mankind through the patriarchs, the prophets, Jesus Christ, the twelve disciples, Saint Paul, and through the gift of His eternal Word will judge every nation and individual who has expressed hatred toward the Jewish people.

After the judgment of the sheep and goats (Matthew 25:33), the "goats" will follow the Antichrist and the False Prophet into the "everlasting fire" which is prepared for the devil and his angels (Matthew 25:41). As they followed him in life, they will follow him in eternity. The "sheep" who know the Good Shepherd, Jesus, will follow Him into the glorious Millennial Reign where the lion will lay down with the wolf (Isaiah 11:6) and Earth's Final Empire will be established.

THE THREE WAVES OF
THE RESURRECTION

The ingathering of the resurrection will occur in three waves. The first wave are those who came out of their graves at the crucifixion of Christ:

And Jesus cried out again with a loud voice, and yielded up His spirit. Then, behold, the veil of the temple was torn in two from top to bottom; and the earth quaked, and the rocks were split, and the graves were opened; and many bodies of the saints who had fallen asleep were raised; and coming out of the graves after His resurrection, they went into the holy city and appeared to many.

(Matthew 27: 50–54)

269

The second wave will happen at the Rapture of the Church:

For the Lord Himself will descend from heaven with a shout,
with the voice of an archangel, and with the trumpet of God.
And the dead in Christ will rise first. Then we who are alive
and remain shall be caught up together with them in the clouds
to meet the Lord in the air. And thus we shall always be with
the Lord.

(1 Thessalonians 4:17)

The third wave will consist of the Old Testament saints, the Tribulation believers who are resurrected and rewarded, and also the unrighteous:

Your dead shall live;
Together with my dead body they shall arise.
Awake and sing, you who dwell in dust;
For your dew is like the dew of herbs,
And the earth shall cast out the dead.

(Isaiah 26:19)

"At that time Michael shall stand up,
The great prince who stands watch over the sons of your
 people;
And there shall be a time of trouble,
Such as never was since there was a nation,
Even to that time.
And at that time your people shall be delivered,
Every one who is found written in the book.
And many of those who sleep in the dust of the earth shall
 awake,

Some to everlasting life,
Some to shame and everlasting contempt.
Those who are wise shall shine
Like the brightness of the firmament,
And those who turn many to righteousness
Like the stars forever and ever."

(Daniel 12:1–3)

I have hope in God, which they themselves also accept, that
there will be a resurrection of the dead, both of the just and
the unjust.

(Acts 24:15)

And I saw the dead, small and great, standing before God, and
books were opened. And another book was opened, which is
the Book of Life. And the dead were judged according to their
works, by the things which were written in the books. The sea
gave up the dead who were in it, and Death and Hades deliv-
ered up the dead who were in them. And they were judged,
each one according to his works.

(Revelation 20:12–13)

THE MILLENNIAL KINGDOM

What is the Millennial Kingdom of Christ? The Millennium is the reign of Christ for one thousand years on the earth follow-ing His second coming. Though it is not often preached from Sunday pulpits, the Millennium is mentioned frequently in the Bible. It is known in Scripture as "the world to come" (Hebrews 2:5), "the kingdom of heaven" (Matthew 5:10), "the kingdom of

271

God" (Mark 1:14), "the last day" (John 6:40), and "the regeneration" (Matthew 19:28). Jesus told His disciples, "Assuredly I say to you, that in the regeneration, when the Son of Man sits on the throne of His glory, you who have followed Me will also sit on twelve thrones, judging the twelve tribes of Israel" (Matthew 19:28).

The Millennium was foreshadowed in the Old Testament by the Sabbath, a time of rest. A biblical rest was observed after six workdays, six work weeks, six work months, and six work years. In God's eternal plan, the earth will rest after six thousand years as well, from the time of Creation until the End of the Age, as He ushers in the Millennial Kingdom of the Messiah.

The Millennium will also be a time of rest for the people of God. Hebrews 4:8–10 declares:

> For Joshua had given them rest, then He would not afterward have spoken of another day. There remains therefore a rest for the people of God. For he who has entered His rest has himself also ceased from his works as God did from His.

A rest of grace, comfort, and holiness will be available through the eternal Sabbath of heaven where believers will enjoy the object of all their desires. We will enter into this rest just like God the Father and Christ our Redeemer entered their glorious rest. God, after creating the earth in six days, entered into His rest; and Christ, entered His rest after completing His work of redemption.[7]

The prophet Isaiah echoed this thought:

> And in that day there shall be a Root of Jesse,
> Who shall stand as a banner to the people;

For the Gentiles shall seek Him,
And His resting place shall be glorious.

(Isaiah 11:10)

During the Millennium, the geography of Israel will be dramatically changed. Israel will be greatly enlarged, and for the first time, Israel will possess all the land promised to Abraham in Genesis 15:18–21. The desert will become a fertile plain and a miraculous river will flow east to west from the Mount of Olives into both the Mediterranean and the Dead Sea—but this salted sea will be dead no longer!

Hear how Ezekiel described it:

When I returned, there, along the bank of the river, were very many trees on one side and the other. Then he said to me: "This water flows toward the eastern region, goes down into the valley, and enters the [Dead] sea. When it reaches the sea, its waters are healed. And it shall be that every living thing that moves, wherever the rivers go, will live. There will be a very great multitude of fish, because these waters go there; for they will be healed, and everything will live wherever the river goes. It shall be that fishermen will stand by it from En Gedi to En Eglaim; they will be places for spreading their nets. Their fish will be of the same kinds as the fish of the Great Sea, exceedingly many."

(Ezekiel 47:7–10)

The prophet Ezekiel described fishermen catching the same fish at En Gedi (a city by the Dead Sea) that are found in the Mediterranean Sea. Indeed, the Dead Sea shall live during the Millennial Kingdom when the Giver of Life sits upon the throne of His Father, King David.

273

Ezekiel stated that there will be trees on each side of this river, flowing out of the Temple Mount, and John the Revelator further revealed that these trees will bear twelve kinds of fruit, one for each month of the year. The leaves of these trees will be for the healing of the nations (Revelation 22:2). Isaiah told us that we will enjoy unparalleled health: "In that day the deaf shall hear the words of the book, and the eyes of the blind shall see out of obscurity and out of darkness" (Isaiah 29:18).

Listen to how Zechariah described the land at this time:

> *And in that day it shall be*
> *That living waters shall flow from Jerusalem,*
> *Half of them toward the eastern sea*
> *And half of them toward the western sea;*
> *In both summer and winter it shall occur. . . .*

> *All the land shall be turned into a plain from Geba to Rimmon south of Jerusalem. Jerusalem shall be raised up and inhabited in her place from Benjamin's Gate to the place of the First Gate and the Corner Gate, and from the Tower of Hananel to the king's winepresses.*

> *The people shall dwell in it;*
> *And no longer shall there be utter destruction,*
> *But Jerusalem shall be safely inhabited. . . .*

> *And it shall come to pass that everyone who is left of all the nations which came against Jerusalem shall go up from year to year to worship the King, the LORD of hosts, and to keep the Feast of Tabernacles.*

> (Zechariah 14:8, 10–11, 16)

Jerusalem, the city of God, will become the joy of the world, for Jesus will reign there. The city will become the international worship center, and people from all over the globe will make pilgrimages to worship in the holy temple. Kings, queens, princes, and presidents shall come to the Holy City so that "at the name of Jesus every knee should bow, of those in heaven, and of those on earth . . . and that every tongue should confess that Jesus Christ is Lord, to the glory of God the Father" (Philippians 2:10–11).

The prophet Micah wrote of the Millennial Kingdom, and the poetry of his verse has inspired several inscriptions on public buildings, ironically to include the United Nations headquarters. But Micah wasn't writing about the United Nations, London, or New York; the prophet was writing about God's Millennial capital, Jerusalem:

> Now it shall come to pass in the latter days
> That the mountain of the LORD's house
> Shall be established on the top of the mountains,
> And shall be exalted above the hills;
> And peoples shall flow to it.
> Many nations shall come and say,
> "Come, and let us go up to the mountain of the LORD,
> To the house of the God of Jacob;
> He will teach us His ways,
> And we shall walk in His paths."
> For out of Zion the law shall go forth,
> And the word of the LORD from Jerusalem.
> He shall judge between many peoples,
> And rebuke strong nations afar off;
> They shall beat their swords into plowshares,

And their spears into pruning hooks;
Nation shall not lift up sword against nation,
Neither shall they learn war anymore.

(Micah 4:1–3)

The Holy City, now six miles in circumference, will be referred to as *Jehovah Shammah*, meaning "THE LORD IS THERE" (Ezekiel 48:35) and *Jehovah Tsidkenu*, meaning "THE LORD OUR RIGHTEOUSNESS" (Jeremiah 33:16).

Imagine, if you will, a thousand years of Sabbath-like rest, genuine peace, perfect health, and absolute worship. A place of true harmony where "the wolf also shall dwell with the lamb, the leopard shall lie down with the young goat, the calf and the young lion and the fatling together; and a little child shall lead them" (Isaiah 11:6). These elements will all define the Millennial Reign.

BY WHAT RIGHT WILL JESUS CHRIST RULE THE EARTH?

God promised Abraham, "I will make you exceedingly fruitful; and I will make nations of you, and kings shall come from you" (Genesis 17:6). God revealed to Abraham that he would eventually rule over all the earth—through His appointed King, Jesus Christ.

In Genesis 49, Jacob the patriarch called his twelve sons around his bed to give them a final blessing and to speak a prophetic word over each of them. His word over Judah was especially insightful:

Judah, you are he whom your brothers shall praise;
Your hand shall be on the neck of your enemies;
Your father's children shall bow down before you. . . .
The scepter shall not depart from Judah,
Nor a lawgiver from between his feet,
Until Shiloh comes.

(Genesis 49:8, 10)

The word *Shiloh* may be translated as "He whose right it is to rule." Jacob thus prophesied that a man who had the right to be king would come from Judah's lineage.

In 2 Samuel 7:16, God made this promise to King David: "And your house and your kingdom shall be established forever before you. Your throne shall be established forever." There are three important words in this verse: *house, kingdom,* and *throne.* "Your house" designates the descendants of David who would sit on his throne. "Your kingdom" represents the kingdom of Israel. "Your throne" is David's royal authority, the right to rule as God's representative. The Lord used the word *forever* twice in this one verse to assure David that his dynasty, kingdom, and throne would continuously stand.

The Gospel of Matthew opens with God breaking a silence of more than four hundred years when He proclaimed Jesus' royal lineage to Israel by saying, "The book of the genealogy of Jesus Christ, the Son of David, the Son of Abraham."

If Jesus Christ is the Son of Abraham, He is the *Blesser* promised to Abraham through whom all the families of the earth will be blessed (Genesis 12:3). If Jesus Christ is the Son of David, He is the One who has the right to rule. He is Shiloh!

The angel Gabriel appeared to Mary and said:

277

Do not be afraid, Mary, for you have found favor with God.
And behold, you will conceive in your womb and bring forth
a Son, and shall call His name JESUS. He will be great, and will
be called the Son of the Highest; and the Lord God will give
Him the throne of His father David. And He will reign over
the house of Jacob forever, and of His kingdom there will be
no end.

(Luke 1:30–33)

Jesus Christ was born of a virgin, trained as a recognized rabbi, taught in the synagogue, performed miracles, and did His Father's will by dying on a Roman cross for the redemption of mankind. When He ascended into heaven, God the Father said to Him, "Sit at My right hand, till I make Your enemies Your footstool" (Matthew 22:44).

Jesus Christ rules the Millennium because He alone is worthy. He rules by heritage, by holy decree, and by divine appointment. Blessing, honor, glory, and power be to Him who will sit on the throne of His father, David!

THE KING AND HIS VICE-REGENT

Dr. Harold Willmington pointed out that though Jesus Christ will be supreme ruler during the Millennium, some prophetic passages strongly suggest He will be aided by a second-in-command: David, the man after God's own heart![8]

The Word of God states in Jeremiah 30:9: "But they shall serve the LORD their God, and David their king, whom I will raise up for them." Jeremiah wrote four hundred years after David's death, so he could not have been referring to David's earthly reign.

Ezekiel and Hosea refer to David's Millennial leadership as well:

I will establish one shepherd over them, and he shall feed them—My servant David. He shall feed them and be their shepherd. And I, the LORD, will be their God, and My servant David a prince among them.

(Ezekiel 34:23–24)

David My servant shall be king over them, and they shall all have one shepherd; they shall also walk in My judgments and observe My statutes, and do them. Then they shall dwell in the land that I have given to Jacob My servant, where your fathers dwelt; and they shall dwell there, they, their children, and their children's children, forever; and My servant David shall be their prince forever.

(Ezekiel 37:24–25)

Afterward the children of Israel shall return and seek the LORD their God and David their king. They shall fear the LORD and His goodness in the latter days.

(Hosea 3:5)

But King David won't be the only ruler. He will be aided by many others:

- The Church (1 Corinthians 6:3)
- The apostles (Matthew 19:28)
- Nobles (Jeremiah 30:21)
- Princes (Isaiah 32:1; Ezekiel 45:8–9)
- Judges (Isaiah 1:26; Zechariah 3:7)
- Lesser authorities (Zechariah 3:7)[9]

If there is a lesson to learn for the Church in waiting, it is that those who are faithful now will be given greater responsibility in Earth's Last Empire. "Well done, good and faithful servant," Christ told the man who multiplied the talents he had been given. "You have been faithful over a few things, I will make you ruler over many things. Enter into the joy of your lord" (Matthew 25:23).

THE PURPOSE OF THE MILLENNIUM

Why has God planned a Millennium? God has several reasons for instituting an earthly kingdom over which His Son will reign. First, He has promised to reward His children. Jesus said, "Then the King will say to those on His right hand, 'Come, you blessed of My Father, inherit the kingdom prepared for you from the foundation of the world'" (Matthew 25:34).

Second, God promised Abraham that Israel would become a mighty nation, which has already come to pass, and that his seed would someday own the Promised Land forever (Genesis 12:7; 13:14–17). Israel rightfully owns all the land God gave to Abraham by blood covenant: "from the river of Egypt to the great river, the River Euphrates," and "from the wilderness and Lebanon . . . even to the Western Sea" (Genesis 15:18; Deuteronomy 11:24). Genesis 15:18–21 gives us more detail about the extent of the land God promised to Abraham:

> To your descendants I have given this land, from the river of Egypt to the great river, the River Euphrates—the Kenites, the Kenezzites, the Kadmonites, the Hittites, the Perizzites, the Rephaim, the Amorites, the Canaanites, the Girgashites, and the Jebusites.

Though the identities and locations of some of the tribes listed in this passage are lost to history, it's clear that Israel in the Millennium will occupy an area extending northward from the Nile River in Egypt to the Euphrates River in Syria. Ezekiel 48:1 established the northern boundary of Israel as the city of Hamath; the southern boundary is the city of Kadesh, as established in Ezekiel 48:28.

In modern terms, Israel rightfully owns all of present-day Israel, all of Lebanon, half of Syria, two-thirds of Jordan, all of Iraq, and the northern portion of Saudi Arabia. When Messiah comes, the seed of Abraham will be given that land down to the last square inch.

Some scholars estimate that this means Israel will expand from its present 8,019 square miles to 300,000 square miles or more. Never in its history has Israel possessed this much land. As scholar Harold Stigers has written, this expansion "places future Israel as the most highly prized and immensely important area for trade and commerce and right into the center of international relations, where her message of God was sure to become known to nations both past and future."[10]

Third, God will establish the Millennial Kingdom to fulfill the prayers of His children. When Jesus taught His disciples the model prayer, or the Lord's Prayer, He taught them to pray "Your kingdom come" (Luke 11:1–4). The phrase "Your kingdom come" isn't just a little ditty meant to rhyme with "Your will be done"; it is a plea that God would soon establish His earthly and eternal Kingdom!

Finally, God will establish His Millennial Kingdom to prove a point. In the Millennium, God will redeem creation, resulting in the existence of docile wild animals, plentiful crops, and the purest of water. The world will know one thousand years of peace, joy, holiness, glory, comfort, justice, health, protection, freedom, and prosperity. Satan will be bound and not able to wreak havoc on earth. King Jesus Himself will rule from Jerusalem, and immortal believers with godly wisdom will rule other cities.

But despite all this utopia, man's fallen nature will still pull him into sin and disobedience. The Millennium will be a one-thousand-year lesson of man's ultimate depravity. The secular humanistic idea that man can improve himself to the point of perfection will be proven false once and for all; the concept of pseudo-paradise will vanish like the morning mist. For though Christians will live in their resurrected bodies, the Tribulation believers who go into the Millennium in their mortal bodies will bear children throughout the thousand years. The children, grandchildren, and great-grandchildren of the Millennium will *still* possess a sinful nature and will *still* need a Redeemer; therefore they will *still* have to choose whether or not to accept Christ as Savior and Lord.

The ages will witness one indisputable fact: without God, man has no hope. Harold Willmington illustrated the end of the Seven Dispensations with the following:

- The age of innocence ended with willful disobedience (Genesis 3).
- The age of conscience ended with universal corruption (Genesis 6).
- The age of human government ended with devil-worshiping at the Tower of Babel (Genesis 11).
- The age of promise ended with God's people enslaved in Egypt (Exodus 1).
- The age of the law ended with the creatures killing their Creator (Matthew 27).

- The age of the Church will end with worldwide apostasy (1 Timothy 4).
- The age of the Millennium will end with an attempt to destroy God Himself (Revelation 20).[11]

THE FINAL CONFLICT

If you think our doomsday worries will end with the Tribulation—think again. Millions of babies will be born during this thousand-year period, and they will be babies just like you and I once were, prone to sin and bent toward trouble. Though the Christian parents who enter the Millennium will teach their children right from wrong, some of these children will exercise their free will and choose to do wrong.

Some, Zechariah told us, will "not come up to Jerusalem to worship the King, the LORD of hosts," so on them "there will be no rain" (Zechariah 14:17).

Dr. Rene Pache explains the situation:

As beautiful as the Millennium is, it will not be heaven. . . . Sin will still be possible during the thousand years. Certain families and nations will refuse to go up to Jerusalem to worship the Lord. Such deeds will be all the more inexcusable because the tempter will be absent and because the revelations of the Lord will be greater.[12]

Sin will still have a foothold on creation causing Christ to rule with "a rod of iron" (Revelation 19:15). Sin must be eradicated and for that reason, at the end of Christ's thousand-year reign, the final conflict between God and Satan must take place.

CHAPTER TEN

11:59 PM

The Earth's Final Conflict

Now this is not the end. It is not even the beginning of the end. But it is, perhaps, the end of the beginning.
Winston Churchill, November 10, 1942

Now when the thousand years have expired, Satan will be released from his prison and will go out to deceive the nations which are in the four corners of the earth, Gog and Magog, to gather them together to battle, whose number is as the sand of the sea. They went up on the breadth of the earth and surrounded the camp of the saints and the beloved city. And fire came down from God out of heaven and devoured them.
Revelation 20:7–9

At the end of the Millennium, Satan will be loosed from his prison, and thousands of people from all the nations of the earth will believe his lies and follow him once again. They will gather around Jerusalem, Christ's capital city, and wage a great war.

What will make these people follow Satan? The prophet Jeremiah wrote, "The heart is deceitful above all things, and desperately wicked; who can know it?" (Jeremiah 17:9).

Who can understand what drives men to sin? For those who are living in earthly bodies, even as we are now, the law of sin is like the law of gravity. No matter how much we want to rise above it, it draws us down. It is only through the power of Christ that we can rise above sin at all.

The Millennium will be a time similar to the Garden of Eden. Even within this perfect environment created by God Himself, Adam and Eve chose to sin. Under ideal circumstances—an abundant earth, no sickness, no war—the human heart will prove that it remains unchanged unless regenerated by the power of Christ. When Satan is loosed on the earth, many will turn their backs on God, who has sustained them in a perfect world, and will follow the evil one.

Revelation mentions Gog and Magog in this verse describing the final conflict, but this is not the same Gog-Magog War described in Ezekiel 38–39. J. Vernon McGee believed that "rebellion of the godless forces from the north will have made such an impression on mankind that after one thousand years, that last rebellion of man bears the same label—Gog and Magog. Just as we have called two conflicts World War I and World War II, the people may call this last battle Gog-Magog II."[1]

This army will advance against Jerusalem, where Jesus rules and reigns. There they will learn that rebellion always ends in destruction. To paraphrase Winston Churchill, this will truly be "the end of the beginning." Man will have rebelled against God for the last time.

To purge creation of the evil effects of sin finally and forever, God will destroy the earth with great heat and fire. Peter referred to this massive inferno:

The heavens will pass away with a great noise, and the elements will melt with fervent heat; both the earth and the works that are in it will be burned up. . . . Nevertheless we, according to His promise, look for new heavens and a new earth in which righteousness dwells.

(2 Peter 3:10, 13)

Today, Satan roams the earth, preying on those he can deceive, just like he did with Adam and Eve in the garden. During the Millennium he will be chained in the abyss. After one thousand years, he will be released for a season to continue leading the masses into sin. However, our enemy—the one who has tormented, tempted, and tried Christians from the genesis of time—will be condemned to hell where he will serve his eternal sentence. Satan, the destroyer, will receive God's permanent justice.

Praise and glory be to the Holy One of Israel!

CHAPTER ELEVEN

MIDNIGHT

The Great White Throne

You may juggle human laws, you may fool
with human courts, but there is a judgment
to come, and from it there is no appeal.
Orin Philip Gifford

The Prophetic Clock has reached its apex. Time has run out. The prophet Daniel peered through the periscope of prophecy and saw a terrible, final doomsday for the unrighteous of the world. It is known as the Great White Throne Judgment. Daniel 7:9–10 records this majestic vision:

> I watched till thrones were put in place,
> And the Ancient of Days was seated;
> His garment was white as snow,
> And the hair of His head was like pure wool.
> His throne was a fiery flame,
> Its wheels a burning fire;
> A fiery stream issued
> And came forth from before Him.
> A thousand thousands ministered to Him;
> Ten thousand times ten thousand stood before Him.
> The court was seated,
> And the books were opened.

The Great White Throne Judgment referred to by Daniel is one of seven imminent judgments that will take place at the End of the Age. The other six judgments are as follows:

- The judgment seat of Christ, which will take place after the Rapture. Here, every believer from the Day of Pentecost to the Rapture will stand before Christ and be rewarded in heaven for their deeds done on earth (2 Corinthians 5:10).

- The judgment of the Tribulation believer will occur at the end of the Tribulation. Those believers who were martyred for their faith in Christ during the Tribulation will be rewarded (Revelation 20:4–6).

- The judgment of the Old Testament believers relates to those who will be resurrected and rewarded after the Second Coming (Daniel 12:1–3).

- Another judgment concerns the Jews that survived the Tribulation. They will be judged after the Second Coming (Ezekiel 20:34–38).

- The judgment of the Gentile nations, also known as the judgment of the "sheep and the goats" will be based on how the Gentiles treated Israel and the Jewish people throughout the ages (Matthew 25:31–46).

- The judgment of Satan and his fallen angels, which takes place at the "judgment of the great day," occurs after the Millennial Kingdom (Matthew 25:41; 2 Peter 2:4; Jude 6).[1]

The final judgment is the Great White Throne Judgment of Revelation 20:11–15. This judgment will occur after Satan is thrown into the lake of fire. All the unjust people of the ages who have not been previously judged will come before the Lord and be adjudicated according to their evil works (Acts 24:15). Like Satan and his angels, they will be sentenced to the lake of fire forever.

This court will convene somewhere between heaven and earth. It cannot occur on the earth because the earth will be "burned up" (2 Peter 3:10–11). It will not occur in heaven because sinners would never be permitted in the presence of the one and only Holy God.

Who will be the One sitting on the throne? Christ Himself! In John 5:26–29, Jesus Christ said:

For as the Father has life in Himself, so He has granted the Son to have life in Himself, and has given Him [the Son] authority to execute judgment also, because He is the Son of Man. Do not marvel at this; for the hour is coming in which all who are in the graves will hear His voice and come forth—those who have done good, to the resurrection of life, and those who have done evil, to the resurrection of condemnation.

In Revelation 20:12–13, John continued to describe the Great White Throne Judgment, saying:

And I saw the dead, small and great, standing before God, and books were opened. And another book was opened, which is the Book of Life. And the dead were judged according to their works, by the things which were written in the books. The sea gave up the dead who were in it, and Death and Hades delivered up the dead who were in them. And they were judged, each one according to his works.

Notice that God has two sets of books. The Book of Life contains the name of every person who accepted Jesus Christ as Lord while they were on the earth. When the wicked dead approach the Great White Throne, Jesus will first look for their names in the Book of Life. Obviously, they will not be recorded there. Next, He will open the books that contain His written records of every word, thought, and deed of the wicked. The result? "And anyone not found written in the Book of Life was cast into the lake of fire" (Revelation 20:15).

HELL IS NOT THE LAKE OF FIRE

Hell, sometimes known as Sheol or Hades, is not to be confused with the lake of fire. In this life, the ungodly die and go to hell, where they wait until they are brought to the Great White Throne for the final judgment before Christ and sentenced to the lake of fire (Revelation 19:20; 20:10, 14–15). Satan, his fallen angels, demons, and all ungodly persons will be placed into the lake of fire by the hand of God as judgment for rejecting Jesus Christ as the Son of God (Jude 6–7; Revelation 20:10–15).

According to a 2015 Barna Group survey, only 35 percent of Americans believe there is such a thing as real truth.[2] Naturally, these people also tend to scoff at the biblical assertion that a literal hell awaits those who reject the truth of God and violate His law. Jeopardizing their eternal future, they live by their own rules outside of God's Word.

However, Jesus and the prophets believed in hell. Let's examine the Scriptures about hell, which is the place of waiting for the lost until they face their judgment at the Great White Throne. We can learn many truths about hell from studying the parable Jesus told in Luke 16:19–31:

- Hell is a literal place. Notice that Jesus began this story by saying, "There was." The story is a literal tale of two beggars—Lazarus, who begged in this life, and the rich man, who begged throughout eternity.
- Christ's parable verifies the extreme difference in eternity for the righteous and for the ungodly who reject Jesus Christ.
- This parable confirms that before Calvary, the saved were carried by angels into Paradise. After Calvary, the righteous

go to heaven (see also 2 Corinthians 5:8; Philippians 1:21–24; Revelation 6:9–11).

- Hell is a place where the unsaved go when they die and experience a conscious state of unending torment (see also Deuteronomy 32:22; 2 Samuel 22:6; Isaiah 14:9–11).

- Hell is a place without mercy. The rich man cried out, saying, "Have mercy on me, and send Lazarus that he may dip the tip of his finger in water and cool my tongue; for I am tormented in this flame" (Luke 16:24).

- Hell is a place without escape. Jesus said, "Between us and you there is a great gulf fixed, so that those who want to pass from here to you cannot, nor can those from there pass to us" (Luke 16:26). When you arrive in hell, the prayers of ten thousand saints cannot save you.

- People in hell are aware of people on earth. The rich man begged for someone to warn his family, "for I have five brothers, that he [Lazarus] may testify to them, lest they also come to this place of torment" (Luke 16:28).

- Souls are immortal in hell and heaven (see also Luke 20:38; 2 Corinthians 5:8; 1 Peter 3:4).

- Hell is in "the lower parts of the earth" (see also Psalm 63:9; Matthew 12:40; Ephesians 4:8–10).

NO FUTURE JUDGMENTS

John the Revelator concluded his description of the Great White Throne Judgment by saying, "Then Death and Hades were cast into the lake of fire. . . . And anyone not found written in the Book of Life was cast into the lake of fire" (Revelation 20:14–15).

Paul wrote:

For as in Adam all die, even so in Christ all shall be made alive. . . . Then comes the end, when He delivers the kingdom to God the Father, when He puts an end to all rule and all authority and power. For He must reign till He has put all enemies under His feet. The last enemy that will be destroyed is death. . . .

> *"O Death, where is your sting?*
> *O Hades, where is your victory?"*
>
> (1 Corinthians 15:22, 24–26, 55)

There will be no future judgments after the Great White Throne Judgment. Death and hell will be finished, eternity will commence. We will *all* spend eternity somewhere—where will you be?

CHAPTER TWELVE

ETERNITY

Heaven and Earth Reborn

For behold, I create new heavens and a new earth;

And the former shall not be remembered or come to mind.

But be glad and rejoice forever in what I create;

For behold, I create Jerusalem as a rejoicing,

And her people a joy.

I will rejoice in Jerusalem,

And joy in My people;

The voice of weeping shall no longer be heard in her,

Nor the voice of crying.

Isaiah 65:17–19

Immediately after the clock strikes midnight, a new day dawns. Appropriately, after the dark midnight hour of the Great White Throne Judgment, God will present us with a new heaven and a new earth, to which a New Jerusalem will descend from heaven. John the Revelator described this glorious event:

> Now I saw a new heaven and a new earth, for the first heaven and the first earth had passed away. Also there was no more sea. Then I, John, saw the holy city, New Jerusalem, coming down out of heaven from God, prepared as a bride adorned for her husband. And I heard a loud voice from heaven saying, "Behold, the tabernacle of God is with men, and He will dwell with them, and they shall be His people. God Himself will be with them and be their God."
>
> (Revelation 21:1–3)

Speaking of Jesus Christ, the apostle John told us, "And the Word became flesh and dwelt [tabernacle] among us, and we beheld His glory, the glory as of the only begotten of the Father, full of grace and truth" (John 1:14).

Writing to a primarily Jewish audience, John used the Greek word *sk'enos* (meaning "shelter or covering") and the metaphor of a tabernacle to describe Christ's incarnation. The same word appeared in Revelation 21:3, when the New Jerusalem came down from heaven and God said, "Behold, the tabernacle of God is with men."

We will be able to talk with God in the cool of the day as Adam did. The sinlessness of Eden will be recreated on earth, and in immortal bodies we will enjoy fellowship with God forever.

THE NEW JERUSALEM: GOD'S GOLDEN, GLORIOUS CITY

John offered a panoramic view of the new Jerusalem in the book of Revelation. The city is foursquare: 12,000 furlongs (15,000 miles) in length, width, height, and depth (21:16). To put it in perspective, the city will be as large as western Europe and half the size of Russia, and if you placed the New Jerusalem within the boundaries of the United States, it would extend from the northernmost point of Maine to the southern tip of Florida and from the Atlantic Ocean on the east to the western Rocky Mountains.

The number twelve is represented throughout the city: there are twelve gates, three on each of the four sides, with twelve angels at each gate and the names of the twelve tribes of Israel inscribed on the gates (21:18–20). The city's wall measures twelve times twelve cubits (144 cubits overall), or more than two hundred feet (21:17). Each gate is made of one pearl (21:21), and there are twelve jeweled foundations, and the names of Christ's twelve apostles are written on each one (21:14). The ancient city that has seen so much suffering will exchange streets that have previously flowed with blood for streets of "pure gold like transparent glass" (21:21).

The gates of the New Jerusalem will be open to all whose

names are written in the Lamb's Book of Life—the golden streets will be filled with believers from every kindred, tribe, and nation. The desert sun will bow to the brilliant light of the Lamb, and the hatred of warring nations to the unparalleled peace of God.

The protective walls of Jerusalem, which were built and rebuilt with much toil and struggle, will be replaced by walls designed solely for beauty and glory. The tree of life, not seen or appreciated since Eden, will grow in the center of the city. Nations will no longer look upon Jerusalem with jealousy or resentment but will look to it for the light of God's glory.

The apostle Paul was permitted to see heaven, and words failed him when he tried to describe its beauty. He summed it up by quoting the prophet Isaiah: "Eye has not seen, nor ear heard, nor have entered into the heart of man the things which God has prepared for those who love Him" (1 Corinthians 2:9).

A HOLY CENSUS

Who will live in this Holy City? The holy angels, Gentiles who have placed their faith and trust in Christ, and the redeemed of Israel. Although the New Jerusalem is a wedding present from the Bridegroom to His bride, Israel will be invited to dwell within these beautiful walls.[1]

In the "roll call of faith" of Hebrews 11, the author testifies of Jewish saints who placed their trust in God and obeyed His commands. They will be invited to dwell in His heavenly city: "But now they desire a better, that is, a heavenly country. Therefore God is not ashamed to be called their God, for He has prepared a city for them" (v. 16).

How many people will dwell on the new earth? Nearly forty years ago, Harold Willmington devised a formula for creating an informal "census" of heaven's future residents.[2] However, how can man possibly calculate such a number? John described the incalculable sum thusly:

Then I looked, and I heard the voice of many angels around the throne, the living creatures, and the elders; and the number of them was ten thousand times ten thousand, and thousands of thousands, saying with a loud voice:

"Worthy is the Lamb who was slain
To receive power and riches and wisdom,
And strength and honor and glory and blessing!"

And every creature which is in heaven and on the earth and under the earth and such as are in the sea, and all that are in them, I heard saying:

"Blessing and honor and glory and power
Be to Him who sits on the throne,
And to the Lamb, forever and ever!"

(Revelation 5:11–13)

HEAVEN IS A REAL PLACE

There are some who say heaven is "a state of mind, a fantasy, a dream, or an abstraction." However, Jesus Himself called heaven a real place. He came from heaven to earth and then returned to heaven where He awaits the day when His Church shall join Him in the mansions He has prepared for His own. Jesus called heaven a "house . . . [with] many dwelling places" (John 14:2 NRSV). Heaven is not an illusion. It's just as real as the home in which you live right now.

In Acts 1:11, the angel told the disciples, "Men of Galilee, why do you stand gazing up into heaven? This same Jesus, who was taken up from you into heaven, will so come in like manner as you saw Him go into heaven."

Did Jesus go up into a state of mind? Did He enter an abstraction? No! Jesus went to a real place, an eternal home, a place of perfection God has prepared as a place of reward for those who love Him.

Jesus prayed, "Our Father in heaven." He did not say, "Our Father who art in a state of mind" or "an eternal illusion." His Father and ours was in heaven, a real place.

Our citizenship lies in heaven. Paul wrote, "For our citizenship is in heaven, from which we also eagerly wait for the Savior, the Lord Jesus Christ" (Philippians 3:20).

Our names are written in heaven. Luke said, "Nevertheless do not rejoice in this, that the spirits are subject to you, but rather rejoice because your names are written in heaven" (Luke 10:20).

Our treasures are stored in heaven. Matthew stated, "Do not lay up for yourselves treasure on earth . . . but lay up for yourselves treasures in heaven, where neither moth nor rust destroys and where thieves do not break in and steal" (Matthew 6:19–20).

These words, friend, are faithful and true. They are our guiding light through dark days and troubled times. Though the world shakes and shudders around us, we have placed our trust in Jesus Christ and His revelation. The End of the Age is coming, and those who now believe in Jesus as Savior will be taken up to heaven in the Rapture.

WHAT WILL WE DO IN ETERNITY?

We're not going to sit around heaven plucking harps all day. No, indeed. Scripture tells us that heaven will be a very busy place for very active people:

- Heaven will be a place of praise. We will sing praise to God for all He has done (Isaiah 44:23; Revelation 14:3; 15:3).
- Heaven will be a place of fellowship. Not only will we know one another, but we will also be able to talk to the Old Testament saints, the prophets, Adam and Eve, the apostles, and the Lord Jesus Himself (Hebrews 11).
- Heaven will be a place of serving (Revelation 7:15; 22:3).
- Heaven will be a place of learning (1 Corinthians 13:9–10). If you enjoy learning new things, exploring new worlds, visiting new places, then heaven will be the perfect place for you. Imagine being able to fly to new planets where no man has gone before or exploring a new continent on the new earth. Best of all, we will learn about God, about our Savior and His plan for us. The Holy Scriptures will come together in our minds, and all mysteries will be revealed.
- Heaven will be a place of joy and perfection. "But when that which is perfect has come," Paul wrote, "then that which is in part will be done away" (1 Corinthians 13:10). There will be no sorrow, no pain, no trouble there.
- Heaven is a place of unbelievable real estate. Jesus taught, "In My Father's house are many mansions; if it were not so, I would have told you" (John 14:2).

FACE THE FUTURE WITHOUT FEAR

Today we live in a time when fear, apprehension, and uncertainty seem the order of the day. Our nation has never been more divided. Anger boils over on social media platforms, on the internet, in the news, and in our streets. Distrust of our core institutions is high and pervasive. The future looks grim to many. Pandemics (and our response to them as a society) have taken an enormous toll on our physical, mental, and economic health.

The United States faces growing military threats from Iran, Russia, and China. National and personal debt has never been higher as our government has thrown multiplied trillions of dollars it doesn't have at stimulus programs and entitlements. Financial experts warn that this behavior is unsustainable and a prescription for imminent economic catastrophe.

The technological miracles that so many hoped would save us now seem on the verge of imprisoning and enslaving us, as privacy becomes a quaint thing of the past. We are polarized racially, generationally, economically, and geographically. Inner cities are ticking time bombs. Murder rates in major cities are soaring as order turns to chaos. People trust neither their government nor their neighbors. The world is falling apart, and no one seems to know what to do about it. Consequently, a rising tide of fear, anxiety, and frustration threatens to carry us all away.

Nevertheless, those who know and follow Christ need not fear for their future, no matter how dark things may seem. Chastising His frantic disciples in the midst of a storm, Jesus said to them, "Do not be afraid" (Matthew 14:27; Mark 6:50; John 6:20). From Genesis to Revelation, from Abraham to John the

Revelator on the Isle of Patmos, God tells believers over and over again not to fear.

That same command was given to Jacob, Moses, David, Daniel, the disciples, and Mary the mother of Jesus. Jesus called out those words to Peter when he was sinking in a stormy sea. He whispered those words to Paul as a rolling wave capsized the ship in which he was sailing. The Lord still speaks those words to us today.

You can fear the unknown. You can fear the past. You can fear many things.

Face this fact, friend: Either you will conquer fear, or fear will conquer you. God gave us a wealth of prophecy in Scripture so we could know what the future holds and fear not. God wanted Daniel to look into the future and be assured. When it came time for that mighty prophet to die, I'm sure he laid down on his Babylonian couch, wrapped his cloak about him, and closed his eyes as if yielding to pleasant dreams. Daniel knew he would see the God of Abraham face to face—the One in whom he had placed his trust.

Fear is a product of the Prince of Darkness. If you live in constant fear of a technological implosion, an economic collapse, or a military invasion, worry and anxiety will break your spirit. Regardless of your profession of faith, if you live with the spirit of fear, you are living like an atheist. "For God has not given us a spirit of fear," wrote Paul, "but of power and of love and of a sound mind" (2 Timothy 1:7).

Fear entered the world with sin, when Adam and Eve ate the forbidden fruit. Before that event, God had walked and talked with Adam in the garden. But when Adam sinned, he heard the voice of God and was afraid. Fear comes in by sin, is sustained by sin, and, like a deadly virus, invades the mind and soul.

But the mighty weapon of faith can conquer fear. We are more than conquerors through Christ, and prophecy proves we have nothing to fear. If you are a child of God living before the Rapture, you do not have to fear the Tribulation, the Antichrist, or judgment at the Great White Throne!

However, the spirit of fear would have you cowering before the nightly news, worrying about the stock market, and fretting about your retirement fund, your job, your health, and the future of our nation. Don't be foolish; be prepared for tomorrow, and do not fear.

Fear is contagious. Like a deadly disease, it spreads panic among the population. Riding on the wings of doubt, fear destroys peace like a lethal plague. But faith is the victory that overcomes the world. Faith believes God will take care of His people.

Faith compelled Abraham to look for a city whose Builder and Architect was God. And by faith, we will one day live in that city—the New Jerusalem.

Faith drove Moses into Pharaoh's court and gave him the courage to demand, "Let My people go!" (Exodus 5:1). Faith parted the waters of the Red Sea and crumbled the walls of Jericho.

Faith urged David to face Goliath while forty thousand cowards watched the battle of the ages from the hillside. "You come to me with a sword, with a spear," David shouted, with his faith like a rock of determination inside him. "I come to you in the name of the LORD!" (1 Samuel 17:45).

Faith enabled Paul and Silas to sing in a dank prison at the midnight hour (Acts 16:25). Faith can turn the desert into springs of living water. Faith can calm the troubled sea. Faith is the victory that overcomes the world.

Fear can rob you of your spiritual inheritance. Moses sent twelve spies into the Promised Land, and ten came back shaking their heads in catatonic fear. Only Joshua and Caleb believed the Israelites could take the land (Numbers 13:30), and consequently, only Joshua and Caleb lived to enter the land flowing with milk and honey. A generation of doubters died in the wilderness because they refused to believe God could deliver the giants into their hands.

Perhaps you are afraid of what people will think if you surrender your life to Christ. You may very well be on the verge of allowing fear to rob you of your eternal salvation and happiness.

If you are a believer, maybe you are afraid of what people will think if you actually talk about Christ in the workplace or in secular social gatherings. If so, you are potentially allowing fear to rob your friends and family of heaven. If you renounce Christ, you will not inherit eternal life, for the Lord said, "Whoever denies Me before men, him I will also deny before My Father who is in heaven" (Matthew 10:33).

Fear not!

Fear not because the Holy Spirit is with you. Remember Daniel's prayers in Babylon? The angel Gabriel was dispatched from heaven the moment he began to pray.

Fear not because God will equip you and strengthen you to do the work He has called you to do. He will give you revelation knowledge to accomplish your mission. He is the Mighty Lion of Judah who forces fear to flee.

God gave Samson the strength to kill a thousand enemies with the jawbone of an ass (Judges 15:15). He gave David strength enough to kill a lion with his bare hands (1 Samuel 17:34–37). He gave a donkey the ability to rebuke Balaam (Numbers 22:28). If God can use a donkey, He can certainly use us.

God is looking for men and women who are not afraid to fulfill His purposes on the earth. When God formed the world,

He created Adam and made him guardian of the garden of Eden. When God chose to destroy the world by flood, He found Noah to build an ark for the salvation of his family and the human race. When God wanted to form a new nation, He found Abraham, and Israel was born. When Pharaoh ordered that all Hebrew baby boys be killed, God used Jochebed, Moses' mother, who had faith enough to send her son forth on the Nile in a wicker basket. Because of her trust in God, the destiny of Israel and all of history was floating in that willowed ark, and as a result, the Jewish people were delivered.

When the people of Jericho were about to surround the Hebrew spies, God found Rahab, a woman with courage enough to risk her life and send them over the wall to safety. When the virgin Mary was found to be with child, God found Joseph, whose faith was greater than the skepticism of society, and the Son of God, the Redeemer of mankind, came into their lives. When Jesus Christ left this earth, He found Saul of Tarsus, who became known as Paul, to launch the New Testament Church and write most of the books of the New Testament.

On and on I could continue, listing the names of people like Deborah, the judge of Israel; Gideon, the timid warrior; and Hannah, the praying mother—all overcomers. My point—God is still looking for a few good men and women to accomplish His purposes. He needs men who will be loving fathers and devoted husbands, ending the social chaos of the collapsing American home. He needs women who will not be afraid to stand up against the tide of immorality drowning our nation. He needs people who are not afraid to share the gospel with a world set on the path of certain destruction.

Jesus has a divine destiny for your life but first you must be free from the shackles of sin, fear, and despair. He wants you to live the abundant life of a believer and reign with Him in eternity. The Lord is everything you need in this world and the next. His Word declares that He is the Alpha and Omega—"The Beginning and the End, the First and the Last" (Revelation 22:13).

He is the Almighty God—"The King of the nations" (Jeremiah 10:7).

He is the Righteous One—"For the LORD is righteous, He loves righteousness; His countenance beholds the upright" (Psalm 11:7).

He is the Great Shepherd of the sheep—who oversees and restores your soul (Psalm 23:1; Hebrews 13:20; 1 Peter 2:25).

He is your Father—for "you received the Spirit of adoption" (Romans 8:15).

He is the Lamb of God—the Light of the World who took away your sins (John 1:29; 8:12).

He is your Redeemer—the Great News of your salvation (Psalm 96:2).

He is the Bread of Life and the Living Water—for those who come to Him will never hunger, and those who believe in Him will never thirst (John 6:35).

When you are in a battle—He is your Shield—"Your exceedingly great reward" (Genesis 15:1).

When you are discouraged—He is your Living and Blessed Hope (Titus 2:13; 1 Peter 1:3).

When you are distressed—He is your Prince of Peace (Isaiah 9:6).

When you are depressed—He is your Exceeding Joy (Jude 1:24).

When you are weary—He is your Rest (Exodus 33:14; Matthew 11:28).

When you are grieving—He is your Comforter (Isaiah 61:2; Matthew 5:4).

When you are weak—He is your Strength and Power (Psalm 19:14; 68:35).

When you are sick—He is your Healer (Exodus 15:26; Isaiah 53:5).

When you are confused—He is your Compass (John 16:13).

When you have lack—He is your Provider (Genesis 22:14).

When you feel rejected—He accepts you to the glory of God (Romans 15:7).

When you are bound—He is your Deliverer (Psalm 144:2).

When you are lonely—He is there, "for the LORD your God is with you wherever you go" (Joshua 1:9).

When you have doubts—"Know that the LORD your God, He is God, the faithful God who keeps covenant and mercy for a thousand generations with those who love Him and keep His commandments" (Deuteronomy 7:9).

He is your Tabernacle—for He will dwell with you; you are His, and He is your God (Revelation 21:3).

The Lord is the Great I AM "Who was and is and is to come" (Exodus 3:13–15; Revelation 4:8).

He is everything you need—do not fear.

WHERE DO YOU STAND?

Every person reading this book is either saved or lost, wheat or tares, a sheep or a goat, walking the narrow way that leads to heaven or taking the broad way that leads to hell. You either know Jesus Christ as Savior, or you will encounter the Antichrist. You are either a friend of God or His enemy. James wrote, "Do you not know that friendship with the world is enmity with God? Whoever therefore wants to be a friend of the world makes himself an enemy of God" (James 4:4).

Jesus said, "He who is not with Me is against Me" (Matthew 12:30). Have you become a carnal, compromising, lukewarm Christian whom Revelation describes as "neither cold nor hot, [so Christ] will vomit you out of [His] mouth" (Revelation 3:16)? Are you cursed with a casual Christianity that has a form of godliness but denies the power thereof? You can have ritual without righteousness. Do you profess Christ without possessing Christ?

Again, I ask, where do you stand?

Christ could come today. The End of the Age could begin before you lay down this book. Are you prepared for His coming?

NOTES

Chapter 1: 11:50 PM—The End of the Age

1. John Elflein, "Number of Novel Coronavirus (COVID-19) Deaths Worldwide by Country," Statista.com, https://www .statista.com/statistics/1093256/novel-coronavirus-2019ncov -deaths-worldwide-by-country/. Statistics taken from August 19, 2021 update. Page last updated August 19, 2021.

2. Elizabeth Kolbert, "Hosed: Is There a Quick Fix for the Climate?," *New Yorker*, November 8, 2009, https://www .newyorker.com/magazine/2009/11/16/hosed.

3. Newsweek staff, "1899: The Names Have Changed, but the Worries Remain," *Newsweek*, January 10, 1999, https://www .newsweek.com/1899-names-have-changed-worries-rem-165356.

4. David Nicholson-Lord, "What's Going to Get You First?,"

Independent, October 23, 2011, https://www.independent.co.uk
/arts-entertainment/what-s-going-to-get-you-first-1281705.html.

5. Cover caption, in *Bulletin of the Atomic Scientists* 23, no. 1
(January 1967): 1.

6. "Year 2000 Cultists Arrive Home, Hide," *Tampa Tribune*,
January 10, 1999, 2A.

7. Jack Katzenell, "Israeli Police Fear Christian Suicides on Temple
Mount," Associated Press, November 23, 1998.

8. Robert D. McFadden, "Harold Camping, Dogged Forecaster
of the End of the World, Dies at 92," *New York Times*,
December 17, 2013, https://www.nytimes.com/2013/18/us
/harold-camping-radio-entrepreneur-who-predicted-worlds-end
-dies-at-92.html.

9. From Josephus, *Antiquities of the Jews*, cited in J. Vernon
McGee, *Daniel*, Thru the Bible Commentary Series (Nashville:
Thomas Nelson, 1991), ix.

10. Billy Graham, "My Heart Aches for America," Billy Graham
Evangelistic Association, July 19, 2012, https://billygraham.org
/story/billy-graham-my-heart-aches-for-america/.

11. American Worldview Inventory nationwide survey, conducted
January 2020 by the Cultural Research Center at Arizona
Christian University, cited in "New Barna Poll: The Christian
Church Is Seriously Messed Up," P&P News, August 12, 2020,
https://pulpitandpen.org/2020/08/12/new-barna-poll-the
-christian-church-is-seriously-messed-up/.

12. Dictionary.com, s.v. "syncretic," accessed March 16, 2020,
https://www.dictionary.com/browse/syncretic.

13. George Barna, quoted in "New Barna Poll," P&P News.

14. Paragraph adapted from Pastor Joe Wright (sermon, Central
Christian Church, Wichita, Kansas, January 23, 1996).

15. D. L. Moody, quoted in Josiah H. Gilbert, ed., *Dictionary
of Burning Words of Brilliant Writers* (New York: Wilbur B.
Ketcham, 1895), 622.

16. Henry H. Halley, *Halley's Bible Handbook* (Grand Rapids, MI:
Zondervan, 1965), 336.

17. William Kelly, *Notes on the Book of Daniel* (New York:
Loizeaux Brothers, 1952), 50. For more insights on these matters,

please refer to John Hagee's books *The Three Heavens* (Nashville: Worthy Publishing, 2015) and *From Daniel to Doomsday* (Nashville: Nelson Books, 1999).

Chapter 2: 11:51 PM—Messiah the Prince Enters Jerusalem

1. Bible Hub, s.v. "shabua," https://bibleapps.com/hebrew/7620 .htm.
2. Robert Anderson, *The Coming Prince: The Last Great Monarch of Christendom* (London: Hodder & Stoughton, 1881), 112–13.
3. Vendyl M. Jones, *Will the Real Jesus Please Stand? Seven Riddles of Israel and Messiah* (Tyler, TX: Institute of Judaic-Christian Research, 1983), sec. 7–9.
4. Jones, *Will the Real Jesus Please Stand?*, sec. 7–22, 7–11.
5. Arthur T. Pierson, "Gems and Curiosities from a Literary Cabinet," in Isaac K. Funk and J. M. Sherwood, eds., *Homiletic Review* 13 (1887): 129.
6. Leon J. Wood, *A Commentary on Daniel* (Grand Rapids, MI: Zondervan, 1973), 248.
7. Anderson, *Coming Prince*, 71ff.
8. Thomas Ice, "The Seventy Weeks of Daniel," Pre-Trib Research Center, July 12, 2018, accessed May 21, 2021, https://www .pre-trib.org/articles/dr-thomas-ice/message/the-seventy-weeks -of-daniel.
9. Louis C. Talbot quote adapted from Myer Pearlman, *Daniel Speaks Today* (Springfield, MO: Gospel Publishing House, 1943), 81, in John Hagee, *Earth's Last Empire: The Final Game of Thrones* (Franklin, TN: Worthy, 2018), 334–37. Reprinted by permission of Worthy Books, an imprint of Hachette Book Group.
10. From Hagee, *Earth's Last Empire*.
11. J. Vernon McGee, *The Epistles: Romans (Chapters 9–16)*, Thru the Bible Commentary Series (Nashville: Thomas Nelson, 1991), chap. 9 intro.
12. J. Vernon McGee, "One Hour in Romans: Dispensational, Chapters 9–11," Blue Letter Bible, accessed May 17, 2021, https:// www.blueletterbible.org/Comm/mcgee_j_vernon/eBooks/one -hour-in-romans/dispensational-chapters-9–11.cfm.

13. Michael J. Vlach, "The Church as a Replacement of Israel: An Analysis of Supersessionism" (PhD diss., Southeast Baptist Theological Seminary, Wake Forest, North Carolina, 2004), xv, quoted in Thomas Ice, "What Is Replacement Theology?," Pre-Trib Research Center, July 19, 2018, https://www.pre-trib .org/articles/dr-thomas-ice/message/what-is-replacement -theology/read.

14. Ice, "What Is Replacement Theology?"

15. C. E. B. Cranfield, *A Critical and Exegetical Commentary on the Epistle to the Romans*, vol. 2, *Commentary on Romans IXXVI and Essays* (London: T & T Clark, 1979), 448, 448n2.

16. John F. Walvoord, *Daniel: The Key to Prophetic Revelation* (Chicago: Moody Press, 1971), 237.

Chapter 3: 11:52 PM—And Knowledge Shall Increase

1. Isaac Newton and Voltaire, quoted in H. L. Willmington, *Willmington's Guide to the Bible* (Wheaton, IL: Tyndale, 1984), 242.

2. Willmington, *Guide to the Bible*.

3. Omar N. Bradley, (Armistice Day address, Boston, November 10, 1948), quoted in "Armistice Day Address," What So Proudly We Hail, accessed May 17, 2021, https://www.whatsoproudlywehail .org/curriculum/the-american-calendar/armistice-day-address.

4. William P. Barr (speech, University of Notre Dame, South Bend, Indiana, October 11, 2019), quoted in US Department of Justice, Office of Public Affairs, "Attorney General William P. Barr Delivers Remarks to the Law School and the de Nicola Center for Ethics and Culture at the University of Notre Dame," Justice.gov, updated October 21, 2019, https://www.justice.gov/opa/speech /attorney-general-william-p-barr-delivers-remarks-law-school -and-de-nicola-center-ethics.

5. George Orwell, *1984* (New York: Houghton Mifflin Harcourt, 1977), 4.

6. Yonah Alexander, quoted in Arieh O'Sullivan, "Virtual Terror: Threat of a New World Disorder," *Jerusalem Post*, March 27, 1998, 15.

7. Cat Cronin, "The Growing Threat of Cyberterrorism Facing the

U.S.," American Security Project, June 25, 2019, https://www
.americansecurityproject.org/the-growing-threat-of
-cyberterrorism-facing-the-us/.

8. Cronin, "Growing Threat."

9. Cronin, "Growing Threat."

10. Cronin, "Growing Threat."

11. Selena Larson, "The Hacks That Left Us Exposed in 2017," CNN
Business, updated December 20, 2017, https://money.cnn
.com/2017/12/18/technology/biggest-cyberattacks-of-the-year
/index.html.

12. Scott Neuman, "Woman Charged as Hacker in Capital One Data
Breach Exposing over 100 Million Customers," NPR, July 30,
2019, https://www.npr.org/2019/07/30/746475401/woman
-charged-as-hacker-of-capital-one-data-that-exposes-over-100
-million-custom.

13. Paul Dughi, "Fastest Growing Crime in the United States: Identity
Theft," Digital Vault, Medium.com, July 28, 2018, https://
medium.com/digital-vault/fastest-growing-crime-in-the-united
-states-identity-theft-90ef2243e8b9.

14. Kim Zetter, "LifeLock CEO's Identity Stolen 13 Times," *Wired*,
May 18, 2010, https://www.wired.com/2010/05/lifelock
-identity-theft/.

15. Cronin, "Growing Threat."

16. Mia Jankowica and Charles Davis, "These Big Firms and
US Agencies All Use Software from the Company Breached
in a Massive Hack Being Blamed on Russia," Insider.com,
December 14, 2020, https://www.businessinsider.com
/list-of-companies-agencies-at-risk-after-solarwinds-hack
-2020–12.

17. Larry Elliot, "The three bears that ate the Goldilocks
economy," *South African Mail & Guardian*, accessed May 29,
2021, https://www.pressreader.com/south-africa/mail-guard
ian/20070928/282419869879672.

18. Terrie Walmsley, Adam Rose, and Dan Wei, "The Impacts of
Coronavirus on the Economy of the United States," *Economics
of Disasters and Climate Change* 5 (April 2021), https://
doi.org/10.1007/s41885–020–00080–1, cited in "Impact of

Coronavirus on U.S. Economy Could Be $3–$5 Trillion over 2 Years: USC Study," *Insurance Journal*, December 14, 2020, https://www.insurancejournal.com/news/national/2020/12/14 /593838.htm.

19. "Impact of Coronavirus on U.S. Economy," *Insurance Journal*.

20. "Impact of Coronavirus on U.S. Economy," *Insurance Journal*.

21. "Impact of Coronavirus on U.S. Economy," *Insurance Journal*.

22. "Impact of Coronavirus on U.S. Economy," *Insurance Journal*.

23. Sarah Hansen, "Thanks to Stimulus Spending, U.S. Debt Expected to Exceed the Size of the Entire Economy Next Year," *Forbes*, September 2, 2020, https://www.forbes.com/sites /sarahhansen/2020/09/02/thanks-to-stimulus-spending-us-debt -expected-to-exceed-the-size-of-the-entire-economy-next-year /?sh=5b7bd1d32384.

24. US national debt as of January 28, 2021, Debt Clock Time Machine, USDebtClock.org, https://usdebtclock.org.

25. Simon Black, "Can the US Govt. Pay Off the National Debt?," in "US National Debt: Shocking Facts & How You Can Protect Yourself," Sovereign Man, June 29, 2018, https://www .sovereignman.com/trends/at-21-trillion-the-national-debt-is -growing-36-faster-than-the-us-economy-23157/.

26. Robert J. Samuelson, "The Crash of '99?," *Newsweek*, October 12, 1998, 28.

27. Samuelson, "Crash of '99?"

28. Allan Sloan and Rich Thomas, "Riding for a Fall," *Newsweek*, October 5, 1998, 56.

29. Black, "US National Debt."

30. Michael Snyder, "America's Financial Suicide: The Budget Deficit Rises 26.1% in One Year as Federal Spending Spirals Wildly out of Control," *Economic Collapse* (blog), October 7, 2019, http:// theeconomiccollapseblog.com/americas-financial-suicide-the -budget-deficit-rises-26-in-1-year-as-federal-spending-spirals -wildly-out-of-control/.

31. William P. Barr, in "Attorney General William P. Barr Delivers Remarks."

32. Statistics from various sources, cited in Franklin White, "Pornography Addiction Statistics," *Keylogger Reviews* (blog),

January 5, 2020, https://keyloggers.mobi/pornography-addiction
-statistics/#Pornography-Addiction-Statistics-2019.

33. Gallup poll, "Americans' Views of the Moral Acceptability of
21 Issues," conducted May 1–12, 2019, cited in Megan Brenan,
"Birth Control Still Tops List of Morally Acceptable Issues,"
Gallup, May 29, 2019, https://news.gallup.com/poll/257858
/birth-control-tops-list-morally-acceptable-issues.aspx.

34. 2019 Gallup poll, Brenan, "Birth Control."

35. Statistics cited in Dennis Prager, "America's Accelerating Decay,"
National Review, April 7, 2015, https://www.nationalreview
.com/2015/04/americas-decay-speeding/.

36. Colleen N. Nugent and Jill Daugherty, "A Demographic,
Attitudinal, and Behavioral Profile of Cohabiting Adults in the
United States, 2011–2015," *National Health Statistic Reports* 111
(May 2018), https://www.cdc.gov/nchs/data/nhsr/nhsr111.pdf.

37. Aggregated statistics, cited in "Number of Abortions—Abortion
Counters," NumberofAbortions.com, accessed May 18, 2021,
http://www.numberofabortions.com/.

38. Joe Kovacs, "Virginia Governor Defends Letting Babies Die *After*
Birth," WND.com, January 30, 2019, https://www.wnd
.com/2019/01/virginia-governor-defends-letting-babies-die
-after-birth/.

39. "Calif. Governor Signs State College Campus Abortion Pill into
Law," *Catholic World Report*, October 14, 2019, https://www
.catholicworldreport.com/2019/10/14/calif-governor-signs-state
-college-campus-abortion-pill-mandate-into-law/.

40. Alexandra DeSanctis, "Journalists, Ask Democrats Real
Questions about Abortion," *National Review*, October 16, 2019,
https://www.nationalreview.com/2019/10/democrats-abortion
-journalists-should-ask-real-questions/.

41. "Blessed Mother Teresa on Abortion," catholicnewsagency.com,
accessed May 20, 2021, https://www.catholicnewsagency.com
/resource/55399/blessed-mother-teresa-on-abortion.

Chapter 4: 11:53 PM—The Great Escape

1. Julia Layton, "Scientists Think Humanity Is 100 Seconds from
Doomsday," How Stuff Works, updated January 23, 2020,

https://science.howstuffworks.com/environmental/earth
/geophysics/doomsday-clock.htm.

2. Thomas D. Ice, "The Rapture in History and Prophecy," Scholars Crossing, Liberty University, May 2009, https://digitalcommons .liberty.edu/pretrib_arch/35.

3. Thomas D. Ice, "Why I Believe the Bible Teaches Rapture Before Tribulation," Scholars Crossing, Liberty University, May 2009, https://digitalcommons.liberty.edu/cgi/viewcontent .cgi?article=1117&context=pretrib_arch.

4. Arthur W. Pink, *The Redeemer's Return* (Swengel, PA: Bible Truth Depot, 1918), 252.

5. Ephraem the Syrian, quoted in Grant R. Jeffrey, *Final Warning: Economic Collapse and the Coming World Government* (Toronto: Frontier Research, 1995), 306.

6. Jonas Bendiksen, "Meet Five Men Who All Think They're the Messiah," *National Geographic*, August 2017, https://www .nationalgeographic.com/magazine/2017/08/new-messiahs -jesus-christ-second-coming-photos/.

7. For examples of scriptural references, see 1 Corinthians 8:6, Ephesians 4:6, Matthew 28:19, John 14:26, John 15:26, 2 Corinthians 13:14, and 1 Peter 1:2.

8. J. Vernon McGee, *The Epistles: Second Peter*, Thru the Bible Commentary Series (Nashville: Thomas Nelson, 1991), 746.

9. J. Vernon McGee, *The Prophecy: Revelation (Chapters 14–22)*, Thru the Bible Commentary Series (Nashville: Thomas Nelson, 1991), 128.

Chapter 5: 11:54 PM—Russia Invades Israel

1. J. Vernon McGee, *Thru the Bible with J. Vernon McGee: Proverbs–Malachi* (Nashville: Thomas Nelson, 1982), 511.

2. *Encyclopaedia Britannica*, s.v. "Commonwealth of Independent States," accessed May 18, 2021, https://www.britannica.com /topic/Commonwealth-of-Independent-States.

3. Matthew Bodner, "Vladimir Putin's Power Play Paves the Way for 16 More Years—but Not Without Challenges," NBC News, July 2, 2020, https://www.nbcnews.com/news/world /vladimir-putin-s-power-play-paves-way-16-more-years-n1232783.

4. Alexandra Odynova, "Russian Court Gives Opposition Leader Alexey Navalny a New Prison Sentence," CBS News, February 2, 2021, https://www.cbsnews.com/news/russia-alexei-navalny-putin-critic-sentenced-to-prison/.

5. Zoya Sheftalovich, "Russian Court Bans Alexei Navalny's Organization, *Politico*, June 10, 2021, https://www.politico.eu/article/russian-court-bans-alexei-navalnys-organization/.

6. Pepe Escobar, "Vladimir Putin, Syria's Pacifier-in-Chief," *Asia Times*, October 23, 2019, https://www.asiatimes.com/2019/10/article/vladimir-putin-syrias-pacifier-in-chief/.

7. "Russia's Putin Signs Deals Worth $1.3bn During UAE Visit," youngherald.com, accessed October 25, 2019, Aljazeera, October 15, 2019, https://www.aljazeera.com/economy/2019/10/15/russias-putin-signs-deals-worth-1–3bn-during-uae-visit.

8. Ilan Ben Zion, "Honduras Opens Embassy in Jerusalem, 4th Country To Do So, AP News, June 24, 2021, https://apnews.com/article/donald-trump-jerusalem-honduras-middle-east-religion-49d8f0a908d2a0bf16830071e2c6f5f0.

9. Maayan Lubell, "Israel Says Iran's Raisi Extreme, Committed to Nuclear Programme," Reuters, June 19, 2021, https://www.reuters.com/world/middle-east/israel-says-irans-raisi-extreme-committed-nuclear-programme-2021–06–19/

10. Lubell, "Israel Says Iran's Raisi Extreme."

11. "Russia, Syria, Turkey and Hamas Congratulate Iran's Raisi on Election Win, *The Times of Israel*, June 19, 2021, https://www.timesofisrael.com/russia-syria-turkey-and-hamas-congratulate-irans-raisi-on-election-win/.

12. "Resistance Missiles Exposed the Fragile Security of the Glass of the Occupying Zionist Regime," *Mashregh News*, May 31, 2021, https://www.mashreghnews.ir/news/1220353/. Text translated to English from Persian using Google Translate.

13. Uri Dan and Dennis Eisenberg, "Kremlin's Lust for Oil," *Jerusalem Post*, September 19, 1996, 6.

14. "New Russia-Syria Accord Allows up to 11 Warships in Tartus Port Simultaneously," DW.com, January 20, 2017, https://www

.dw.com/en/new-russia-syria-accord-allows-up-to-11 -warships-in-tartus-port-simultaneously/a-37212976.

15. Susan Fraser and Lefteris Pitarakis, "Russian Forces Deploy at Syrian Border Under New Accord," *Epoch Times*, October 23, 2019, https://www.theepochtimes.com/russian-forces-deploy-at -syrian-border-under-new-accord_3125339.html.

16. April Brady, "Russia Completes S-300 Delivery to Iran," Arms Control Association, December 2016, https://www.armscontrol .org/act/2016–11/news-briefs/russia-completes-s-300-delivery-iran.

17. Alon Ben David, "Iron Dome Blunts 90% of Enemy Rockets," Aviation Week, September 1, 2014, https://aviationweek.com /defense/iron-dome-blunts-90-enemy-rockets.

18. Dov Lieber and Felicia Schwartz, "Israel-Gaza Cease-Fire: What You Need to Know about the Conflict, *The Wall Street Journal*, May 26, 2021, https://www.wsj.com/articles/israel-gaza-ceasefire -what-we-know-11620825247.

19. Dmitry Zaks, "Putin Vows to Boost Arms Sales to Egypt's Sisi," Yahoo News, August 12, 2014, https://news.yahoo.com/egypts -sisi-visits-putin-arms-purchase-talks-150438527.html.

20. Bruce Blair, "Russia's Doomsday Machine," *New York Times*, October 8, 1993, https://www.nytimes.com/1993/10/08/opinion /russias-doomsday-machine.html.

21. Viktor Yesin, quoted in Michael Peck, "Russia's 'Dead Hand' Nuclear Doomsday Weapon Is Back," *National Interest*, December 12, 2018, https://nationalinterest.org/blog/buzz /russias-dead-hand-nuclear-doomsday-weapon-back-38492.

22. Tim LaHaye, *The Beginning of the End* (Wheaton, IL: Tyndale, 1988), 65.

23. D. M. Panton, "The Jew: God's Dial," *Dawn*, August 15, 1924, 197–201.

Chapter 6: 11:55 PM—The Time of the Tribulation Begins

1. LifeWay Research phone survey conducted January 8–22, 2016, cited in Bob Smietana, "End Times, Rapture and Antichrist Focus of New Study," Baptist Press, April 26, 2016, http://bpnews .net/46745/end-times-rapture-and-antichrist-focus-of-new-study.

2. J. Dwight Pentecost, *Things to Come: A Study in Biblical Eschatology* (Grand Rapids, MI: Zondervan, 1964), 235.

3. Deborah Kovach Caldwell, "Apocalypse Soon? As New Millennium Rapidly Approaches, Interest in End of World Is at All-Time High," *Dallas Morning News*, October 24, 1998, 1A.

4. For further information on this subject, please refer to John Hagee's *The Three Heavens* (Nashville, Worthy Publishing, 2015).

5. Pentecost, *Things to Come*, 46.

6. Jim Ulvog, "An Indication of Persian Wealth from the Book of Esther," *Attestation Update* (blog), accessed May 18, 2021, https://attestationupdate.com/2016/06/23/an-indication-of -persian-wealth-from-the-book-of-esther/.

7. Joshua J. Mark, "Alexander the Great," *World History Encyclopedia*, November 14, 2013, https://www.worldhistory .org/Alexander_the_Great/.

8. Robin Waterfield, *Dividing the Spoils: The War for Alexander the Great's Empire* (Oxford: Oxford University Press, 2011), 155–70.

9. Encyclopedia.com, s.v. "Berenice Syra," accessed May 18, 2021, https://www.encyclopedia.com/women/encyclopedias -almanacs-transcripts-and-maps/berenice-syra-c-280–246-bce.

10. Encyclopedia.com, s.v. "Berenice Syra."

11. Edwyn R. Bevan, *The House of Ptolemy* (London: Methuen, 1927), http://penelope.uchicago.edu/Thayer/E/Gazetteer/Places /Africa/Egypt/_Texts/BEVHOP/6*.html.

12. Wikipedia, s.v. "Seleucus II Callinicus," last modified March 2, 2021, https://en.wikipedia.org/wiki/Seleucus_II_Callinicus.

13. *Encyclopaedia Britannica*, s.v. "Antiochus III the Great," by Hans Volkmann, November 13, 2019, https://www.britannica .com/biography/Antiochus-III-the-Great.

14. *Encyclopaedia Britannica*, s.v. "Antiochus III the Great."

15. "Seleucus IV Philopator," Livius.org, accessed May 18, 2021, https://www.livius.org/articles/person/seleucus-iv-philopator/.

16. H. L. Willmington, *Willmington's Guide to the Bible* (Wheaton, IL: Tyndale, 1984), 241.

17. *New World Encyclopedia*, s.v. "Hanukkah," https://www
    .newworldencyclopedia.org/entry/Hanukkah#In_the_Talmud.

18. Edmund Conway, "UN Wants New Global Currency to Replace
    Dollar," *Telegraph*, September 7, 2009, https://www.telegraph.co
    .uk/finance/currency/6152204/UN-wants-new-global-currency
    -to-replace-dollar.html.

19. Lucinda Shen, "The End of the 500 Euro Note Could Lead to a
    Cashless Economy," *Fortune*, May 4, 2016, https://fortune.com
    /2016/05/04/cashless-economy-500-euro/.

20. Christopher A. McNally, "The DCEP: Developing the Globe's
    First Major Central Bank Digital Currency," China-US Focus,
    accessed May 19, 2021, https://www.chinausfocus.com/finance
    -economy/the-dcep-developing-the-globes-first-major-central
    -bank-digital-currency.

21. Brock Chisholm, quoted in Christopher Story, *The New
    Underworld Order: Triumph of Criminalism* (London: Edward
    Harle, 2006), 441.

22. Moses Maimonides, quoted in Peter S. Knobel, ed., *Gates of the
    Seasons: A Guide to the Jewish New Year* (New York: Central
    Conference of American Rabbis, 1983), 90.

23. John F. Walvoord, *The Revelation of Jesus Christ* (Chicago:
    Moody Press, 1966), 126.

24. Robert Kaplan, *The Ends of the Earth: A Journey to the
    Frontiers of Anarchy* (New York: Random House, 1996), 45.

25. Food and Agriculture Organization of the United Nations, *The State
    of Food Security and Nutrition in the World: Building Climate
    Resilience for Food Security and Nutrition* (Rome: FAO, 2018).

26. Brad Plumer, "This Terrifying Chart Shows We're Not Growing
    Enough Food to Feed the World," *Washington Post*, July 1, 2013,
    https://www.washingtonpost.com/news/wonk/wp/2013/07/01
    /this-unsettling-chart-shows-were-not-growing-enough-food-to
    -feed-the-world/.

27. Plumer, "This Terrifying Chart."

28. Plumer, "This Terrifying Chart."

29. J. Vernon McGee, *The Prophecy: Revelation (Chapters 6–13)*,
    Thru the Bible Commentary Series, (Nashville: Thomas Nelson,
    1991), 45.

30. Frank Holtman, quoted in McGee, *Revelation*, 45.

31. David Nicholson-Lord, "What's Going to Get You First?," *Independent*, October 23, 2011, https://www.independent.co.uk /arts-entertainment/what-s-going-to-get-you-first-1281705.html.

32. NASA Jet Propulsion Laboratory, "Largest Asteroid to Pass This Close to Earth in a Century," Center for Near Earth Object Studies, August 6, 2019, https://cneos.jpl.nasa.gov/news/news203 .html.

33. Jim Heintz, "Meteor Explodes over Russia, 1,100 Injured," AP News, February 15, 2013, https://apnews.com/article /6ca527bc2e604c64b494aaf832af5015.

34. Walvoord, *Revelation of Jesus Christ*, 151.

Chapter 7: 11:56 PM—For Then Shall Come Great Tribulation

1. Prophetic descriptions of the Antichrist in Scripture adapted from Arthur W. Pink, *The Antichrist* (Swengel, PA: Bible Truth Depot, 1923), 3–4.

2. John F. Walvoord, *The Revelation of Jesus Christ* (Chicago: Moody Press, 1966), 210.

3. J. Vernon McGee, *The Prophecy: Revelation (Chapters 6–13)*, Thru the Bible Commentary Series (Nashville: Thomas Nelson, 1991), 86.

4. McGee, *Revelation*, 86.

5. Nicholas St. Fleur, "Two-Thirds of the World Faces Severe Water Shortages," *New York Times*, February 12, 2016, https://www .nytimes.com/2016/02/13/science/two-thirds-of-the-world-faces -severe-water-shortages.html.

6. Worldwatch Institute, cited in David Nicholson-Lord, "What's Going to Get You First?," *Independent*, October 23, 2011, https://www.independent.co.uk/arts-entertainment/what-s-going -to-get-you-first-1281705.html.

7. McGee, *Revelation*, 106.

8. H. L. Willmington, *Willmington's Guide to the Bible* (Wheaton, IL: Tyndale, 1981), 503.

9. Willmington, *Willmington's Guide to the Bible*, 42.

10. Willmington, *Willmington's Guide to the Bible*, 80.

11. Willmington, *Willmington's Guide to the Bible*, 568.

12. John F. Walvoord, *The Revelation of Jesus Christ* (Chicago: Moody Press, 1966), chap. 17, https://walvoord.com/article/275.

Chapter 8: 11:57 PM—Inching Toward Armageddon

1. Adapted from J. Dwight Pentecost, *Things to Come: A Study in Biblical Eschatology* (Grand Rapids, MI: Zondervan, 1964), 358.

Chapter 9: 11:58 PM—The Millennium Dawns

1. S. Franklin Logsdon, *Profiles of Prophecy* (Grand Rapids, MI: Zondervan, 1964), 81.

2. Adapted from Mark Hitchcock, *The End: A Complete Overview of Bible Prophecy and the End of Days* (Carol Stream, IL: Tyndale, 2012), 467.

3. "Statement from ADL CEO Jonathan Greenblatt on Current Surge of Antisemitism Amidst Crisis in Israel," ADL.org, May 20, 2021, https://www.adl.org/news/press-releases/statement-from -adl-ceo-jonathan-greenblatt-on-current-surge-of-antisemitism.

4. Ben Sales, "Study: More than One in 10 Americans Under 40 Thinks Jews Caused the Holocaust," *The Times of Israel*, September 16, 2020, https://www.timesofisrael.com/study-more -than-one-in-10-americans-under-40-thinks-jews-caused-the -holocaust/.

5. "Preliminary ADL Data Reveals Uptick in Antisemitic Incidents Linked to Recent Mideast Violence," ADL.org, May 20, 2021, https://www.adl.org/news/press-releases/preliminary-adl-data -reveals-uptick-in-antisemitic-incidents-linked-to-recent.

6. "Preliminary ADL Data Reveals Uptick," ADL.org.

7. This paragraph is inspired by Matthew Henry's examination of the book of Hebrews found in his six-volume commentary from 1710. It still rings true today, more than three hundred years later. See *Matthew Henry's Concise Commentary on the Whole Bible* (Nashville: Thomas Nelson. 1997), 1205.

8. H. L. Willmington, *The King Is Coming* (Wheaton, IL: Tyndale, 1988), 250.

9. Adapted from Willmington, *King Is Coming*, 250.

10. Harold G. Stigers, *A Commentary on Genesis* (Grand Rapids, MI: Zondervan, 1976), 159.

11. Adapted from Willmington, *King Is Coming*, 250.

12. Rene Pache, *The Return of Jesus Christ* (Chicago: Moody Press, 1955), 428.

Chapter 10: 11:59 PM—The Earth's Final Conflict

1. J. Vernon McGee, *The Prophecy: Revelation (Chapters 14–22)*, Thru the Bible Commentary Series (Nashville: Thomas Nelson, 1991), 152.

Chapter 11: Midnight—The Great White Throne

1. Adapted from Mark Hitchcock, *The End: A Complete Overview of Bible Prophecy and the End of Days* (Carol Stream, IL: Tyndale, 2012), 205–6.

2. Barna OmniPoll conducted July 3–9, 2015, in Barna Group, "The End of Absolutes: America's New Moral Code," May 25, 2016, https://www.barna.com/research/the-end-of-absolutes-americas-new-moral-code/, cited in Michael F. Haverluck, "US Barna Survey: Goodbye Absolutes, Hello New Morality," One News Now, May 29, 2016, https://onenewsnow.com/culture/2016/05/29/us-barna-survey-goodbye-absolutes-hello-new-morality.

Chapter 12: Eternity—Heaven and Earth Reborn

1. H. L. Willmington, *The King Is Coming* (Wheaton, IL: Tyndale, 1988), 300.

2. H. L. Willmington, *Willmington's Guide to the Bible* (Wheaton, IL: Tyndale, 1984), 686.

ABOUT THE AUTHOR

John Hagee is the founder and senior pastor of Cornerstone Church in San Antonio, Texas, a nondenominational evangelical church with more than 22,000 active members. He is the author of more than forty books including several *New York Times* bestsellers, his latest being *Earth's Last Empire: The Final Game of Thrones*. Pastor Hagee is the founder and chairman of Christians United for Israel (CUFI) with more than ten million members. Hagee Ministries's television and radio outreach spans America and the nations of the world.